Sparks

Gr

Published by Wayfinder Press
Post Office Box 1877
Ouray, CO 81427

Typesetting - The Typeshop
            Montrose, Colorado

Printing - Walsworth Press, Inc.
           Marceline, Missouri

Map - Steve Johannsen

Cover Design - Clarke Cohu
              (Barn - Aimee Dixon;
              Map - S. T. King)

ISBN 0-9608764-8-0

Acknowledgments

To Wallace Eubanks of the Paonia Historical Society and to Mrs. Shirley Lund, Head Librarian of the Paonia Library for their help in assembling photographs and other materials; to George (Shorty) Hunten for permission to use photographs from his extensive collection.

To all those who reviewed the book—Carter George, Jerry McDonald, Bill Barton, Garber Davidson and others; to Doris Swanson, who spent tedious hours editing it; and to my wife, who guided me around the computer pitfalls in putting it into final shape.

Table of Contents

III. DOWN IN THE TOWN

IV. EPILOG

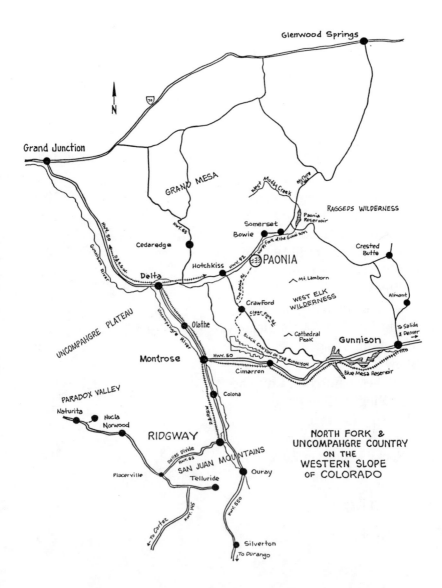

Glenwood Springs

N

70

Grand Junction

GRAND MESA

West Muddy Creek

McClure Pass

RAGGEDS WILDERNESS

Paonia Reservoir

Somerset

Bowie

North Fork of the Gunnison

PAONIA

Crested Butte

HWY. 65

HWY. 50 D.& R.G.W.

Cedaredge

Hotchkiss

HWY. 92

Gunnison River

Delta

Mt. Lamborn

WEST ELK WILDERNESS

Almont

The Dobe Rd.

UNCOMPAHGRE PLATEAU

Crawford

Uncompahgre River

Clear Fork Rd.

Olathe

Cathedral Peak

BLACK CANYON OF THE GUNNISON

Gunnison

To Salida & Denver

Montrose

HWY. 50

Cimarron

Blue Mesa Reservoir

PARADOX VALLEY

Colona

Naturita

Nucla

Norwood

D.&R.G.W.

RIDGWAY

NORTH FORK &
UNCOMPAHGRE COUNTRY
ON THE
WESTERN SLOPE
OF COLORADO

Dallas Divide

HWY. 62

SAN JUAN MOUNTAINS

Placerville

Telluride

Ouray

To Cortez

HWY. 145

HWY. 550

Silverton

To Durango

6

Foreword

I grew up on Colorado's Western Slope, spending a few of my early years at Ridgway in the foothills of the San Juans, but most of them in Paonia, a town on the North Fork of the Gunnison River below the West Elks, so it is Paonia that to me is my "long home."

In the account that follows, some names have been changed, to protect the guilty and exasperate the innocent. And there are errors, of course; my memory has played me false here and there, but the stories I have told are in the main true as I remember them, which is to say they are the purest kind of fiction.

I toyed with the notion of changing some of the place names, (like that of Paonia, which I have never liked anyway, to North Fork) but gave it up as pointless. One of the problems with the name, Paonia, is that no one knows exactly what it means. There is a province in old Macedonia called Paeonia, but I never heard that anyone was attempting to adapt that name to our town. The best theory seems to be that when it was officially named, the intention was to honor the flower, the peony, that flourishes in the town, and it somehow was misspelled.

In my days in high school the cheerleaders found it hard to deal with; the vowels roll out pleasantly enough when shouted, but it's hard to imbue them with any fierceness. It is an essentially feminine, romantic sort of word. And meaningless. When someone asks you the name of the town in which you were born and raised, a Paonian is apt to feel a little reluctant and foolish in giving it. A cousin of mine responded to such a query once and the lout who had asked promptly came back with a vulgar and far-fetched pun:

"Well 'pee-on-you', too."

My wife and I no longer live in Paonia, but we go back often to see her relatives and a few friends surviving there. Economically, the area has had its ups and downs; rather more downs than ups since I lived there in the thirties. Still, it is a beautiful little town, and anyone who stays there long is apt to leave reluctantly.

I dedicate this book to my dear brother, who never read it and wouldn't have thought much of it if he had; and to the good people of Paonia, who, chances are, won't think much of it either.

I. RIDGWAY

Riding Around the Range

Funny about a little kid and an old man like Old Man Kelly. You knew he was out to give you a hard time—you could tell by the glint in his eye. He'd say things you didn't understand, ask you foolish questions, and the other men in the barbershop—if there were any around, and there usually were—would laugh at your answers. And that was the least of the embarrassing things that could happen to you. But, you were like a pup around a skunk or a porcupine. Overcome with curiosity and full of bravado.

He had all kinds of cute tricks. You learned pretty quick not to shake hands with him—that always turned out to be painful—and when he'd offer you a nickel, you'd reach for it, he'd palm it, and you'd end up with your finger in his fist. Or if you were walking by his chair—chances are he'd be sitting there with his eyes closed and his hands folded over his paunch—his foot would shoot out and trip you. And, of course, he'd always apologize afterward and help you up and then maybe actually give you a nickel. You got so you were pretty careful about how you moved and what you did around Old Man Kelly.

This was in my father's second shop. Earlier he had barbered in Paonia up the narrow valley of the North Fork of the Gunnison, and he must have been doing well in those days when fruit from the North Fork was the sensation of Eastern markets and the coal mines in the upper valley were already active, but he did have competitors. And then he acquired a family, a wife and two young sons—my brother Harold, born a year and a half before me, and myself—to look after. So when he heard about an opportunity in the town of Ridgway, south and west on the Uncompahgre, he was interested. The Rio Grande roundhouse was there, the town was small but lively. It was the gateway to the beautiful and wild San Juans, to the great gold camps around Ouray, Telluride, and Silverton. And, besides, he was by nature a discontented, restless man.

The little shop he opened there—deserted and neglected now— faces on Ridgway's main street, that points like an arrow toward the Dallas Divide. Across from it slumps the once proud Mentone Hotel, now a ruin.

At first we lived in the back of the barbershop in an apartment consisting of two bedrooms and a kitchen. The front of the building was divided to accommodate both the shop and the real estate office of Mr. Huffnagle.

During working hours all sorts of interesting noises filtered back from the shop to our kitchen. The slamming of the front door, boisterous greetings, the scuffing of shoes and boots in wet or snowy weather, deep-toned laughter, our father's laughter the quickest and loudest of all. These sounds were magnets to the ears of small boys, but if either of us made for the door opening into the shop, Mother warned us away. The trick was to go out into the backyard to play, wait until she was immersed in household chores, and then scoot around the back of the grocery store and come in the shop from the front entrance.

I think our parents were in agreement that there were certain rowdy influences in the shop. Sometimes when one or both of us would put in an appearance up front, Dad would hearken to his parental responsibilities and send us back, but at other times he was apt to relax the rules. This was especially true on dull afternoons when Old Man Kelly was in the shop.

Old Man Kelly had been a famous road-builder in his day, constructing "Kelly's Trail" north of town, leading over the rimrock towards the Black Canyon and Montrose. Now he was retired, and he liked to pass the time in the barbershop on a dull afternoon. And when my brother and I would show up, we were Old Man Kelly's meat.

One afternoon when my brother was napping in the second chair—there was a second chair in the shop, though only on rare occasions was there ever a second barber—Old Man Kelly took a cork and charred it with a match and carefully went over my brother's face with it so it was good and black, and then he shook my brother awake and gave him a nickel to go down to the drugstore and buy a sack of candy. This caused no end of merriment in the shop and along the street.

Then there were the jokes, none of which I understood. The jokes were where I sometimes came in. My father, no respecter of my tender years, enjoyed coaching me to tell some racy joke, the point of which entirely escaped me, but which was usually uproariously received by his customers, probably for that reason. In fact, most of what went on in the barbershop went over my head. One time when a prankster came in carrying a little white cardboard pail with a bail on it, the kind obtained in butcher shops, he asked me if I would like to see some limburger cheese. I said I would, so he opened up the carton and there was a material coiled inside, the shape, color, and smell of which even I could recognize. But, since I had no idea what Limburger cheese was supposed to be like, I was merely confused.

Our apartment in the back of the shop was far from commodious. There were three rooms in all, two bedrooms and a kitchen; the bedrooms were cramped and dark, but the kitchen was of a good size. I remember this particularly because at Christmas when I was four I received a tricycle and my first trial runs were around the kitchen stove, which sat well out in the room. I was mad to learn to ride but I had a hard time getting the hang of it. Then, one night after supper when my parents were sitting with their stockinged feet in the cookstove oven—the fire had been banked for the night—I suddenly put it all together, and began riding around and around the linoleum track. Great. But soon I found I was in orbit, my shoulders flaring out on the curves, the tricycle well over on two wheels. I begged my dad to help me to stop but he only laughed, and every revolution I was coming closer and closer to the coal scuttle. I think my parents were fed up with my long training period and wanted to see that I got my fill of tricycling for a while. After what seemed a very long time Dad took pity on me and helped me off. I had saddle burns.

The apartment did have the advantage as far as my brother and I were concerned of being near both entertainment centers in the town: the barbershop, and the motion picture theatre next door. The entire family enjoyed the movies, particularly in the summer, for whenever a film was showing the management sooner or later was obliged to open the big window on the barbershop side to provide ventilation and our whole family could sit out on the back porch of our apartment in luxurious ease, taking in the film for free.

When "Birth of a Nation" came, we saw President Lincoln sway forward in his box at Ford's Theatre, shot by the dastardly Booth, and watched the Klan riding out after the war in the ravaged South, and all we missed was the musical accompaniment on the automatic piano. On Saturday afternoons, though, dad shelled out the twenty cents or so which entitled my brother and me to go to the theatre in style with our noisy peers and see the current serial, playing along with a two-reel comedy and an occasional newsreel. The serial that sticks in my mind was "The Masked Rider" who every week came riding down the pass with the piano bravely hammering out "Whispering," to wreak destruction on the poor settlers in the valley below. He turned out to be a sneak of a banker, played by Warner Oland, later better known as the original Charlie Chan.

And there were occasional stage shows. One coasts just on the margin of my memory's range. This was a travelling minstrel show, perhaps the last of its kind to play in western Colorado. It must have been an unusual occasion, one that would justify the outlay of what at

11

that time must have been a considerable sum of money, because we, all four of us, were seated in the audience that night. I faintly recall dark-faced figures clothed in colored suits with flowing ties and glaring white shirts, seated in a wide arc on the stage, the end men snapping tambourines against their knees. And when one of them opened wide his vivid mouth, I set up quite a howl, I'm told.

There was a dream I had about this time, perhaps a mesh of my minstrel-show trauma and images from an African newsreel. I am standing beside the shop, looking down through a grating. Below the grating, glaring up at me, is a black man in a grass skirt with a wooden plug in his nose and ivory rings in his ears, a spear in one hand and a shield in the other. I called, and people came, among them my father, leaving a customer in the chair.

My father was a big man for those times, when 225-pound, six-foot-four high-school athletes were absolutely unheard of. He was six-one, well set up, with red hair (I never realized how red it was until later, when I saw him in his coffin), and with a rather florid complexion. He came out in the dream with a thin barber's comb tucked behind his left ear and open scissors in his right hand, and bent down, one long leg out, to look at the warrior. He was wearing the pants to his gray suit, suspendered and belted, a white shirt with a

Father in barbershop, feeling low

stiff, detachable collar, and a narrow, washable, blue-striped white tie. On his feet were tan button oxfords, sporty in those days, with blucher toes.

Strangely, his appearance in that dream is the most vivid image that remains to me of my father. And the dream itself was so real that when I finally recalled it to my family years later, I could hardly be convinced that the incident had not really taken place.

My father was a good barber, a good host to his customers, but he was not always as happy as he appeared to be. He looked at me ominously one gray day when he and I were alone in the shop.

"Being a barber is like being in jail," he said. "If you ever even look like you want to be a barber, I'll tan your hide so you can't sit down for a week."

But he liked the good fellowship of the shop when he was in a decent humor. When a man was invited into his chair, my father treated him with deference, drew him out, listened to his brags and complaints, and propelled him smoothly out again, feeling better, I think, both mentally and physically.

There was a cowboy who clumped in early on a quiet afternoon looking pretty used up, probably after a fling in the Ouray fleshpots. He dozed through a shave and a haircut, the last "store-bought" ones he would get in quite a while, he said. Then he went out to the hitchrack, checked the bedroll behind his saddle, the ties on his bulging saddlebags, and climbed aboard. I went to the window and watched him out of sight as he loped out across the wooden bridge north of town, headed over the Dallas Divide for a job in the Paradox Valley.

Little Men

My father, in that second year in the Ridgway shop, was doing well enough so that he bought a house on the southern outskirts of town. An old house, facing east, on a pleasant street, with a line of great cottonwoods across the road bordering a big field. Further south, across a footbridge spanning a gully where the creek ran high in the spring, was the yellow-brick grade school, an imposing structure at least in my eyes, sitting on a little rise in the midst of a wide playground.

My mother must have been relieved to have my brother and me further removed from the temptation of the shop; I have no doubt that we now and then ripped out a word or an expression that made her wince, conversation in a barbershop being what it was. Though just moving didn't solve the problem altogether. It wasn't easy riding herd on the two of us, keeping us at or near our new home. For my brother and me it was heady stuff to be able to amble in to the barbershop to be greeted jovially by Old Man Kelly and anyone else who happened in. It was true that a tyke ran certain risks to his dignity and even, now and then, to his well-being, but the game was worth the candle.

Once when I had a disagreement with my mother, probably over my plans for the day, I ran away from home. I loaded the little red wagon with some necessary supplies, and I arrived at the barbershop with a bucket of honey, a pound of butter, a loaf of bread, and a bar of laundry soap.

My father agreed with my mother in general about the advisability of having his small sons lead a better and more restricted life. Except for an addiction to vulgar stories, which might be considered a tool of his trade, he was a clean-living man. He neither drank nor smoked, and both he and my mother were determined that neither should his sons—though they might have disagreed on the methods used in discouraging us. For my father's approach where smoking was concerned was direct and spartan. One day when Old Man Kelly lay stretched out in the chair napping after a shave, my father saw me eyeing the old gentleman's cigar, which reposed on a nearby smoke-stand, with the fragrant smoke curling lazily up from it.

My father said, "Think you'd like to try that?"

I was interested, all right, so he said, "Go on. Take a puff."

I did. I coughed a little at the beginning, but it really wasn't half bad—really rich and smooth, like the coffee appears to be in today's television commercials. My dad smiled wolfishly.

"Go on," he said, "try a few more."

I had a really good time there for a while, puffing away and swaggering over to the spittoon occasionally, but eventually a little wave of nausea stole over me, followed by stronger and stronger waves until I lost my lunch and all interest for some time in smoking cigars. I was pulled home that evening by my father, sprawled in the little red wagon, and every jounce added to my misery and humiliation. I can just hear my mother saying "Oh, Bob," as he carried me into the house and explained my predicament.

It would be pleasant to report that after this experience I was permanently cured of the smoking habit. And it's true that it was a long time before I could "stomach" cigars. As late as half way through high school, though, I was still trying—on a Between the Acts, an unassuming mini-cigar that came in a neat tin box—and it knocked me as firmly on my popo as a cigar three times its size might have.

But cigarettes were a different story. Over the years, in alleys in Ridgway and in Paonia, behind barns and sheds and outdoor toilets, my friends and I tried everything—from 111's and Wings which only cost ten cents then (though I don't think the price made all that difference; we were never directly sold cigarettes by merchants and how we got them I've conveniently forgotten) through Camels, Lucky Strikes, Chesterfields, roll-your-owns with Bull Durham in the sack, or with Prince Albert in the red can or Tuxedo in the green.

There was at least one box of exquisite Murads, with Egyptian insignia outlined in gold on the cover of the box. I even tried a weird cigarette called Twenty Grand, which consisted of a package of four foot-long cigarettes, packed that way to beat the tax, and the customer was supposed to scissor them into manageable lengths after purchase. What I could have done with my life if only I had shown half as much fortitude and determination in worthwhile pursuits as I did in trying to learn to smoke!

Today I no longer smoke cigarettes, but I enjoy an occasional cigar. And perhaps my father's lesson bore some fruit; I never learned to inhale.

My brother and I, to my mother's relief I am sure, did begin to depart the barbershop orbit soon after we moved to the house. We both made friendships in the neighborhood, and the men downtown had to find other kids to play their tricks on, or even resort to playing them on each other.

But there was one game, perhaps the last into which my brother and I were inveigled by the barbershop jokers. It could be called "Little Men."

This game began as most such games did, by a man coming over to you in the shop and leaning over and putting a friendly hand on your shoulder and talking to you in a gentle, confidential half-whisper, his eyes holding yours, and you were naturally flattered by all that attention from an adult. Actually it happened that way to my brother first. The man said:

"You know, if you was to go up to the sidewalk in front of the church and go down to where there's a loose board, about the third or fourth one from the end, near the alley, and you was to move that board around a bit, why, a little man will come out and talk to you … "

My brother did try it, and sure enough, the "Little Man," an angry bumblebee, came out and saluted him on the forehead.

I didn't put two and two together very well in those days, because I fell for the same scam a little later on, when some jokester told me that I could become acquainted with some little men that lived out on the ditch bank across the field beyond the schoolhouse. I thought about it for quite a while, and of how pleasant it would be to meet a troop of slender, smiling, friendly little men, and one bright spring afternoon I took the red wagon and my toy shovel and I struggled out there, and dug and dug where I'd been told to, but I was luckier than my brother. Not a single little man did I see.

A tasteless joke, and even cruel, perhaps, but actually I did enjoy that afternoon, digging in the warm sunlight, expecting any moment to be greeted by my little friends. We all come to realize that there's more pleasure in anticipation than fulfillment, and that was certainly the case here. For a long time afterward I was convinced that those little men were living out there, thriving, maybe settling new colonies roundabout. Perhaps they knew that I was looking for them, and perhaps they really preferred not being disturbed by strange giants.

So I never encountered those little men, but a year later when I went to school the charming vision was recreated for me in a poem in our primer which began:

> Up the airy mountain,
> Down the rushy glen,
> We daren't go a'hunting
> For fear of little men …

Disillusionment

Disillusionment starts early in life, when a baby first finds it can't always have what it reaches for. My wife's baby sister once cried for an entire evening because nobody would give her the moon. And then there are all those other disappointments that come along until that big, final one, when you are apt to discover that you are not going to live forever.

My first memorable disillusionment came at the age of four. We were just getting settled, through late fall and early winter, in our new Ridgway home (an old house, but new to us) and I had been hearing much about Santa Claus, and how he came down the fireplace chimney on Christmas Eve to fill the stockings of good little girls and boys. I was prepared to accept the idea, but I worried about it. Our house was comfortable enough, but it had no fireplace. What would Santa do?

It was plain that he couldn't make it through the freshly blacked tin stovepipe that descended to our Royal Oak heater in the dining room. Still, I was pretty certain something could be worked out. If nothing else, and if he was in all that hurry—and with all the stops he had to make he must be—he might just dump everything in the snow behind the dining-room window that looked out on our backyard. I just couldn't see him strolling in through one of the doors. But, that's what he must have done, or it was made to appear that that was what he must have done, because I was up even before my brother on that memorable Christmas, and there, stacked on a plain old dining-room chair, were the Tinkertoys, the Tiddly-winks, the sacks of hard candy and nuts, the oranges, the Buster Brown comic book, and the handkerchiefs from out-of-town relatives. It wasn't that I wasn't grateful, but on a dining-room chair? It seemed to me that if there was a Santa Claus, he was certainly lacking in imagination. The seeds of a lifelong cynicism were planted within me from that very hour.

And of course this was only the beginning. The next substantial disillusionment had to do with religion. That first year in our new home my mother was evidently determined that my brother and I should have a proper start, so she arose early on Sunday mornings and dressed us in our best, and saw us off to Sunday School at the white-steepled church which is still a Ridgway landmark. I remember the opening hymns and the prayer, the bewildering custom of dropping good spending money in the collection plate, and then the bustle and confusion while students were shepherded to their various Sunday School classes behind the monks'-cloth curtains. It was all rather exciting, what with the buzz and clatter from the other classes, and the greetings from the lady teacher in her high-pitched, over-friendly voice.

Then there were the Bible stories. Some were a little difficult to comprehend. It seemed to me that Cain got the short end of the stick just because he thought vegetables and fruit were a better offering than the meat which Abel brought. And later, when Cain found a wife in the land of Nod, and there were all those other people there, when he was the surviving son of the first and only other man on earth. Where did they all come from? Still, the lady was telling the stories and they were interesting enough so it didn't seem polite to question.

And later on, when the teacher did ask questions, they were obviously loaded:

"Is it better to be a good little boy or girl, or a bad little boy or girl?" or

"If your little playmate has a toy or a doll that you like, should you ask if you may please play with it too, or should you not ask anything and just take it?"

Any kid with a lick of sense would know that you should just take it if the playmate is that little, and figure some other way to rip it off if the playmate is too large to argue with, but at Sunday School I learned that there is (1) a correct answer and (2) a desired answer, and that in dealing with grownups you are wasting your time giving correct answers. That was disillusioning enough, but of course there was more. One Sunday after a session at Sunday School during which we were informed that in heaven the lion would lie down with the lamb (instead of the more usual arrangement where the lamb lies down *inside* the lion) I asked my mother, who was busy getting dinner, what it would be like in heaven.

"What do you do in heaven?"

"You just rest," she told me.

"Can't you even play?"

"Oh yes, you can play."

"Do you get dirty?"

"No, you don't get dirty."

"Do you get tired?"

"No, I don't think so."

"Do you sleep?"

"You don't need to."

"Do you eat?"

"Yes, you can, but you don't get hungry."

"Well, what happens, then?"

"What do you mean, what happens?"

"Well, does it rain, or get muddy, or cold?"

"No, it's always pleasant and sunny."

"Well, what happens, then?"

"Nothing happens. Everybody is happy, and children play and old people rest."

I thought and thought about it, but I couldn't make any sense out of it.

Then there was prayer. My mother assured me that if you prayed for something, sincerely, to God, that He would give it to you. I was interested in acquiring a camera at the time, so I put in several sessions on my knees just before bed, asking God for the camera. I never specified what kind, I didn't really know that much about it, and besides I didn't want to appear choosy. Any old camera would do. But, after almost a month of earnest prayer, without any result whatever that I could see, I decided to give it up.

I suppose you could say my whole early religious experience was disillusioning. Even the attitude of my parents. I can't remember that my father ever attended church—the only time I definitely remember seeing him there was years later at his own funeral. And as for my mother, she must have gone with us occasionally in the beginning, but problems arose. There was always dinner to be prepared, the most important noonday meal of the week, and now and then there was an excursion, planned for later in the day, that required extensive preparations. She attended more and more irregularly, and my brother and I found our own ways to keep from going, and finally Sunday School was given up altogether.

My mother was not a truly religious woman, but she wanted to be. I remember little quotations she treasured and liked to repeat during religious discussions that sometimes took place, perhaps during a long evening when visiting with relatives or friends in those days before radio or television. One of her favorites she commonly used to refute the notion that any gifted individual or religious sect knew the time of the world's end:

"The Bible says that not even the angels in heaven know."

And another, which had a variety of uses, including as a rejoinder to a smart-alecky son bringing home from school or from his reading some notion of which she did not approve:

"The Bible says that the wisdom of your wise men will fail you."

Both still considered reliable in some quarters.

So her efforts to provide us with early religious instruction were not entirely fruitless. And disillusionment, one comes to realize, is after all the common lot in life. It has its uses. With it, sometimes, comes understanding.

Heavy, Heavy Hangs Over Thy Head

Our neighbors to the south of us on the street where we lived in Ridgway were a family whose name may have been Payne. Mr. Payne was a railroad man. I remember nothing of him, but there was a son, Marion, then perhaps 12 or 13, and Mrs. Payne. I was especially taken with Mrs. Payne. She was a handsome woman with long dark hair which she did up in the current fashion, and she had a warm, creamy complexion and large, expressive, dark blue eyes.

The Paynes' home was a pleasant one with a piano in the front room; both Mrs. Payne and Marion could play and the family often sang together on weekends. But I loved going over there on weekday midafternoons when the rest of the family was away and Mrs. Payne was busy in her kitchen. I would make myself at home in the living room, examining and touching everything. I could sit in each of the easy chairs in turn, look at the photograph album and study the pictures on the walls and displayed on top of the piano. And then, the best part of all, I would go into the kitchen, have a satisfying conversation with Mrs. Payne, and receive a cookie.

I remember only one occasion involving Mrs. Payne that was tinged with embarrassment and regret for me, although under the circumstances I do not feel I was at all to blame. The Paynes had a spacious back yard, bisected by a narrow boardwalk leading down to the outdoor toilet at the rear of the lot, and the builder had violated one of the cardinal principles of good construction for this sort of edifice. It was years later, of course, when that eminent rural sage, Chick Sales, codified the rules for outdoor privies; as so often in human affairs, important problems are never adequately examined until the need for such examinations has peaked and declined.

The principle violated by the builder of the Paynes' sanctum sanctorum was that of the hanging of the door. Instead of swinging inward as it should have, so that the occupant could maintain adequate control at all times, it swung outward. And I innocently ran down there one day and tugged the door open to discover Mrs. Payne enthroned within.

My first impression was of the look of startled alarm and dismay in those large blue eyes. And then she screamed and I was absolutely stunned and helpless, not only because she was there, but also because up until that time it had never occurred to me that there was any occasion for her being there. I just hadn't thought about it, really, and my immediate impulse was to get away as soon as possible, and this I proceeded to do, but then Mrs. Payne screamed again, and I froze in my tracks.

"You come here." She was smiling, but the smile was strained. "Come back," she demanded, in a low, urgent voice, "and close the door."

I made myself scarce at the Payne's for a time, telling no one what had occurred. But when, on a day I smelled cookies baking, I decided to chance another appearance, I found to my great relief that we were apparently as good friends as we had ever been.

There were other families on the block, pleasant families of course, since all neighbors were pleasant in the eyes and mind of a small boy growing up in a western town then. Directly to the north was the house of a family containing one and I think several girls, all of them considerably older than my brother and I and therefore impenetrable beings. Small boys have trouble relating to girls of any age. They can be treacherous playmates, because in a sticky situation they are apt to turn on you and side with the grownups.

But my brother and I were always on good terms with those girls. Someone snapped a picture of one of them and my brother and I and our dog Cricket, standing at the side of our house. It was on a chilly Sunday afternoon I think. Chilly because the girl's cloche is well down over her ears, and her dark cloth coat is pulled snugly about her, and Sunday because my brother and I are wearing light shirts and neckties.

In the long evenings of summer, all we neighborhood children played together, and in all these activities, Marion Payne, slender and dark, was the acknowledged leader. He chose the game, expounded the rules, and defined the method for choosing sides. I am sure that the older children never looked on my brother and me as team assets in these games, considering our youth and inexperience, but I was never aware that they accepted us grudgingly.

We played run-sheep-run, and kick-the-can and pump-pump-pullaway and a game that includes a ritual in which a child is seated blindfolded and another player stands behind him and holds an object over his head and drones,

"Heavy, heavy hangs over thy head."

The seated one responds, "Fine or superfine?"

The catechism goes on until the blindfolded player suggests a way in which the owner of the object can "redeem it," but the further details of the game have sifted down into the swamp of memory.

22

With a neighbor girl

When we tired of the usual games, Marion would think of others, and he was quite capable, I'm certain, of creating a game when necessary, making up the rules on the spot. All our parents trusted him, and we were even permitted, under his guidance, to hike through the darkening town, down past the railroad roundhouse and the old flour mill, and as far as the railroad right-of-way where the main line ran north from Ouray to Montrose.

Marion made up a game for us to play as we walked along— partly, I suspect, to keep us out of harm's way when automobiles were passing. If a car approached, we were all to group at the side of the road, and close our eyes tightly. He assured us that if we stared into a car's headlights it was very dangerous and one could even lose one's eyesight. It was even more dangerous, he said, to look into the searchlight of a locomotive. We would arrive at the tracks sometimes when a train was about to go by, and we were told to stand well back and keep our eyes shut; but once in a moment of madness I opened my eyes and stared directly into the great, goggling, bobbing orb and was stunned, but relieved, not to have suffered any immediately disastrous effects.

There must always, it seems, be elements of danger and suspense in games of childhood if they are to be truly enjoyable. I learned, for instance, a little jingle somewhere to while away the monotony of trips to Yeoman's grocery store:

> If you step on a crack
> You'll break your mother's back—

On summer evenings after it grew too dark for games, and just before our mothers called us in, Marion or one of the older children would tell ghost stories. To the very young, ghosts and the dead are different species, as they are to many savages, and one of the most effective stories was the sort where a ghost is described as approaching nearer and nearer, and suddenly the narrator reaches out and clutches a younger, engrossed listener with a scalp-tingling

"I've got you!"

Very satisfactory to both parties, and with the sort of audience participation you don't achieve from sitting before the tube.

Yes, those were pleasant times, and all contrived out of our own resources—particularly the resources of Marion Payne.

But life goes on like that quaint old game, with something fine or superfine suspended over each of our heads. And heavy, heavy it often is, and bitter in the redeeming. As it must have been for Marion Payne. For I have heard that not too many years after we all played there together, amiable and carefree, that beguiling boy, so confident and talented in our eyes, took his own life.

Don't You Know Them Taters Got Eyes?

The life of a housewife in present-day Ridgway may not be all beer and skittles, but in the Ridgway of World War I, before convenience foods, paper towels and permanent press, it was considerably more difficult. My mother had two small sons and a barber husband to do for—all the sewing and mending, cooking, cleaning, and washing. She was also the family disciplinarian—at least in a deputized capacity ("You just wait till your father gets home!")

She was responsible for the shopping too. My father with his 60-hour workweek wasn't too much help, though he did a little impulse buying. For instance, he liked to stop at the butcher shop at noon and bring home a piece of meat for lunch; he did it so consistently that my mother formed the habit of preparing the rest of the meal and keeping a skillet ready at the back of the stove for whatever he arrived with.

Except on Mondays. Monday was wash day, and all bets were off. Mother might take the time to fry the noon steak, but at supper we were apt to sit down to soup or sandwiches. Or hash. As I remember, my father didn't complain. He needed a clean light-colored shirt every day, a wash tie and a detachable white starched collar, handkerchief, socks, underwear—not to mention a weekly supply of towels for the shop, both small linen and large and small turkish, and I suspect he didn't feel like making any waves over the quality of the wash-day meals.

But my brother and I suffered. We liked three hearty meals a day. In fact, one Sunday evening as the twilight was fading, my mother observed wonderingly that she had somehow got through the day having prepared only two meals, and this revelation so aggrieved and shocked my brother and me that we both began crying, though we were not hungry at all.

So I don't remember Monday in our Ridgway home with any pleasure. The house was in complete disarray with washable clothing pulled out of closets and off beds, the doilies and antimacassars off parlor furniture. By the time my brother and I arose, even the kitchen and dining tables were occupied with mounds of clothing in various stages of the washing process. My mother would clear a place for us and bring the oatmeal from the warming oven, all tepid and glutinous, and we would be encouraged not to waste time over it.

It didn't take much encouragement. The whole house steamed, and stank of the brown soap which my mother brewed in the back yard every few months, and besides, if we lingered, she might think of some errand or chore we could help her with. She early conceived the notion that laundry and cleaning were operations important to the family as a whole, and we should do our part, and if we were within reach we might be sent to the store for bluing or clothespins, put to carrying water or even, heaven forbid, to sorting dirty clothing or turning wet socks. We recognized all such tasks as woman's work, not fit for a man, so although we weren't about to defy her if she asked us to do something, we made ourselves scarce as soon as possible on Monday morning—"hiked out," as my mother put it. It was "provoking" the way we could disappear, she often said.

Wash day for my mother began with the boiling of the clothes, which she stirred and pummeled in the steaming tubs with a club the size of a baseball bat, and then, in the backyard in warm dry weather and in the kitchen in cold or wet, she took the garments full of the most stubborn soil to the washboard. After everything was rinsed and the white things "blued," the entire washing was wrung out by hand or ground through the hand wringer and hung out to dry. I can see my mother at the backyard clothesline, an apron clothespin bag of cotton ticking about her waist, her left hand full of wooden pins, a few more in her mouth, while she wrestled a rag, towel, or sheet into position. Her brow was furrowed, her abundant brown hair tied up more loosely than usual, unbraided, and if the weather was on the cool side she might be wearing one of my father's old suit coats.

In winter the wash might hang out overnight and be woman-handled into the house the next morning after breakfast, where the ghostly long johns, frozen solid, expired on the kitchen table. Everything that had to be ironed—and most things were—had to be sprinkled. Towards evening Tuesday my mother would be at the ironing board—petticoats, playclothes, underwear, socks, shirts, towels—all had to go under the iron. I have gone asleep, lulled by the muffled sigh and bump of the flatiron or "sadiron" as it was sometimes called, moving over the board, punctuated every so often by the creaking of the kitchen floor as my mother moved to the stove to release a cold iron from the wooden handle and raise a hot one, and if I was still awake enough I could hear the faint lisp of burning saliva as she tested the fresh one with her moistened forefinger.

My father had his own chores. He had bought a pair of neat little heifers, a Jersey and a Holstein ("One for quality and one for quantity," he said) and they had to be milked and cared for. Then there was the wood and coal to keep in supply for the fires, and the ashes to be disposed of—all matters that he saw to it that his two small sons began to be involved with. Besides these, there was the clearing of the walks in the winter, the mowing of the lawn in summer, and, in the spring, a favorite family task—planting the vegetable garden.

All of us helped. There was a carnival aspect to it. The soft airs of spring would suddenly come, and my father would get a man in to plough up the back yard. Out would come the tools then—the slender hoe and rake, the shovel and the grubbing hoe, heavy enough to take a small boy over backward if he tried to shoulder it. My father, after conversations and debates with customers at the shop and with the neighbors to the right and left of us, would bring home packets of seeds blazoned with bright promise, but the seeds themselves looking singularly unprepossessing, drab and lifeless. The yellow line would be staked out and the furrows drawn. Laying lettuce seed was almost ghostly—who could believe that these tiny objects smaller than insect wings or the parings of a baby's fingernail could go whispering down into the dark soil and come up in such a short time all leafy green.

Potatoes were different. You put a piece of potato in the ground and from it came other potatoes. And when my brother and I helped cut up the seed potatoes, my mother cautioned us to be sure there were two or three "eyes" in each piece. Why were they called eyes? My mother didn't know. This was the time for my father, out of his repertoire of rough jokes from the barbershop, to trot out the one about the lady who looked out into her garden one afternoon to discover her half-grown daughter squatting there.

"Liza," the mother bawled, "get outa that. Don't you know them taters got eyes?"

My mother would always say "Oh, Bob," disapprovingly when my father would tell such a joke, and then she would laugh but in a sort of disgusted way.

My father laughed at my mother, too, over the potato planting. My mother always took her time about it.

"There's a right time and a wrong time to plant potatoes," she would explain, when pressed.

But my father said that my mother's people came from the Blue Ridge Mountains of Virginia, where people believed that potatoes had to be planted in the dark of the moon to do well (his people were from Missouri). He said that it was all superstition, and she agreed that it likely was, she could even laugh about it in a restrained way, but she always managed to put off the potato planting for one reason or another—not being able to get around to it on this or that day—and year after year planted in the dark of the moon they were.

One of those years in Ridgway my father had a real gardening triumph. Neighbors and friends always had pet varieties of peas or beans or corn they swore by and planted consistently, and a general favorite in corn was "Country Gentleman," a white-kerneled, long-eared variety, sweet and good. But this particular year the seed growers introduced a variety of yellow corn, called "Golden Bantam." The fact that it was yellow was an argument against it from the start. Field corn was yellow, the new variety was yellow; "Country

Wedding picture

Gentleman" was white and known to be good; why change? But my father planted four of our six rows of corn in the new variety and endured the scorn and jibes of customers at the shop until the crop tasseled out.

"Golden Bantam" proved a resounding success. My father told everyone how flavorsome it was and how robustly it grew; he gave batches of the new corn to skeptics and Golden Bantam won converts right and left. My father never picked up an ear of that corn at the dinner table that summer without congratulating himself all over again.

This boost to my father's ego was very welcome to him. He wanted at all costs to have the very best of everything. He even bragged once about the length of the firebox in the cookstove. I heard him telling my mother in the kitchen one evening.

"A fella come down the alley while I was splitting the kindling and he watched me a while and he said, 'You cuttin' that kindling to go in your cookstove?' and I said yes. And he said 'Well you're going to have to cut it again, because that kindling's too long.' No it ain't I told him. It's the right length. And he said, 'Well, if that kindling fits in your cookstove, you've got the longest firebox in your cookstove I ever heard of.'"

My mother's lips would push down a little when he would tell a story like that, and she would go right on with her work and not say anything. In this particular instance I had watched my father split the kindling and I hadn't seen any "fella come down the alley," but even at that tender age I knew better than to say so.

Sometimes when my father felt my mother was ignoring him, he would take umbrage and storm about, saying that his words weren't worth anything in his own house. And my mother would chuckle and say, "Oh, Bob, don't be such a fool," and he would calm down after he had let off a little steam, and everything would be all right again. Other than for such very occasional outbursts, my parents' marriage was not a tempestuous one. They loved and respected each other, I felt, and really seemed to get along quite well.

My Brother the Gunslinger

When my brother and I were approaching school age, our mother seemed chiefly interested in our spiritual welfare, while our father was more concerned in seeing that we got off to a good start as "men." He was especially concerned, I think, that I did not become a "sissie."

He had some cause. I was small for my age, my interests were bookish, and my mother had encouraged my hair, which was blond in my early years, to grow into curls all around my head with bangs across the front. (In fact there is a picture taken of me at the old Tyler Studio in Paonia when I was sporting that hairdo. There I stand in my white Buster Brown suit, a building block in one dimpled hand, about as fetching a little tyke as one was apt to come across.)

My father itched to do it, I am sure, and one Sunday morning in the Ridgway shop he did. He lured me into his barber chair and off came the curls. I remember the novel coolness of the clippers on my naked neck and saw, out of the corners of my eyes, the golden locks slipping floorward. It was sad for my mother—no doubt she murmured an "Oh, Bob," when she first saw what he had done—but she accepted it as inevitable, although I think she kept some of my golden tresses among her souvenirs. As for me, perhaps it is to my credit that so far as I can remember I didn't think about it one way or the other.

My father didn't have all that much to worry about where my brother was concerned. Harold was only a year and a half my senior, but he outgrew me amazingly—a family joke, promulgated by the grown sons of my mother's sister, had it that in our infancy he had crowded me away from the milk bar—and he was soon busy at so many vigorous outdoor pursuits that he didn't have time to pull up his stockings, button his knickers at the knee, keep his shoes tied when he wore shoes, or even, often, to wipe his nose.

We acquired a dog—the truth was, I think, that he acquired us—a little fox terrier named Cricket, and he followed my brother everywhere, sharing his triumphs and tragedies. Now and again my brother got sufficiently out of line to merit an interview in the kitchen with my father and the razor strop—sometimes I quakingly awaited my own turn—and Cricket stood loyally by, making little barking sorties of protest from under the kitchen table. Once Cricket made the tactical error of actually nipping my father, who laid out a blow in his direction, sending him yipping under the table again. My father was annoyed, and mumbled something of having to "get rid of that blamed dog," but he couldn't help smiling a bit. We had Cricket for several years after that, we all loved him, but one Fourth of July—fireworks drove him mad—he disappeared and we never saw him again.

My brother and I often played together and got into mischief together, but as with many brothers we soon began to go our separate ways. One incident which indicated a divergence in life styles had to do with a BB gun or air rifle which he had acquired. My father had bought it for him and like most articles my father bought, it had to be of the best quality—a fabled Daisy. My brother was from the first chronically out of BBs, using up any supply he acquired as rapidly as he could, but he still carried the gun everywhere, pumped it, and pretended it was loaded, squinting down the barrel in utter concen-

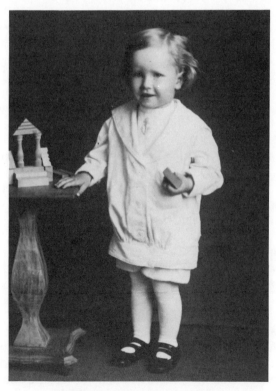

At the old Tyler Studio

tration, with his lip lifted to bare his left canine.

On one occasion he had enlisted a companion other than myself—perhaps Buster Davies, or Albert Albertson, who became special friends of his—and had organized a game of Scouts-and-Indians in the dry gulch below the bridge leading to the schoolhouse. I was the lone, reluctant Indian, and I crept out at one point from behind a clump of sagebrush and looked down into the gully to find my brother and his companion staring up at me. My brother, alert scout that he was, promptly drew a bead on me with his "empty" gun and fired. Fortunately the air chamber hadn't been pumped sufficiently full, but his aim was good, and he caught me squarely in the middle of the forehead with the half-spent BB.

It didn't hurt in the least, but as we continued to stare into each other's eyes, I saw a dawning amazement and concern in my brother's face. His mouth fell open, and his expression, together with a warm little trickle of blood that moved down between my eyebrows, alerted me that something unusual had occurred. I hadn't thought much of the game anyway, having been lured into it against my will, and now I saw a chance to get my brother in hot water, so I set off for the house, bawling hysterically. My mother was considerably agitated, and Harold was in solitary until my father arrived home for lunch, but he looked upon the episode, after examining the wound and finding it superficial, as less than a capital crime, and my brother got off with a scolding and a warning, and the loss of his weapon for a week.

Another time my brother, armed with a loaded beanie or slingshot made by attaching two strips of inner-tube rubber to a crotched stick, was stalking for likely game in a backyard, and he happened to kneel down and look through a knothole opening into an adjoining yard. A strange and intriguing sight was presented to his view—another eye, that of the neighbor's rooster. My brother acted instinctively, as usual, and the eye disappeared. The rooster did not survive.

My brother and I usually got along well enough, going our separate ways as we increasingly did, with arguments surfacing only over important problems, such as who was entitled to the next hot pancake at Sunday breakfast, or whose turn it was to bring in the wood. I read and he played outdoor games that usually concerned hunting, and eventually hunted for small game with my father after it was concluded he was responsible enough not to do anything foolish.

My father enjoyed hunting but was not all that active because of his long hours in the shop. He went when he could. He owned at least two guns, a 22-caliber Winchester rifle, and a 12-gauge shotgun. He may have also owned a 30-30, or at least borrowed one on occasion.

On a Sunday evening after my father had been out hunting he

liked to sit in the kitchen beside the oilcloth-covered table and clean the gun. He would run the ramrod lovingly down through the barrel and pull it out with a slow flourish, and slowly caress the stock with an oiled rag. Afterward, once he made certain everything was safe, he would sometimes help me to squint down the barrel and admire the spiral grooves gleaming in the lamplight.

He didn't go after larger game often—although there was one time that we had bear steaks, heavy with the wild taste. But he brought home rabbits, and sage hens, and ducks—I remember the feel of the soft, plump bodies as they were skinned or plucked and eviscerated.

None of this aroused in me an appetite for hunting, but it was different with my brother. And, like his father, after the hunt he took pleasure in cleaning the gun. Years later in our home in Paonia, Harold was sitting beside the kitchen table, cleaning another "empty" gun, this time a 22-caliber rifle. When he finished cleaning it, instinctive hunter that he was, he felt the need of a live target in his sights. I was out of bounds as such ever since the BB incident, so it was the turn of the family cat, dozing in the corner. My brother lifted his lip, squinted, and pulled the trigger. There was a loud report, and a fearsome squall from the cat, as it crashed out through the door screen and leaped over the backyard fence in a flash. We were all desolated over it, and I helped Harold search for the poor creature for hours without success. Days later it returned to us. It had been shot through the head, but it survived and was a cherished member of our household for years after.

Once established in our home in Ridgway so that we could comfortably entertain visitors, relatives of both our parents came for short stays in the summer months. There was my father's widowed sister and her daughter Mary, and on my mother's side her sister Ina, and husband Henry Elmendorf, from their cattle ranch on Clear Fork outside Crawford. They came with their two daughters, Marva and Cena, several years older than my brother and I, but welcome all the same. They drove a Chevrolet, and the trip from Clear Fork, some sixty miles distant, easily took up a day—a day that included long, punishing stops to repair tires.

But as pleasant as it was to have them visit us, it was even more pleasant from the viewpoint of Harold and me, to visit the ranch, where we enjoyed the attentions of our older cousins. The Elmendorf family consisted of five boys and two daughters, and with the exception of Sid, who had club feet and wandered away early to take up gambling as a living, the other boys each served an apprenticeship on the ranch before he reached his majority, became restless, and moved away. These defections saddened the parents, who had hoped

Baby Harold on the ranch

to have their boys settled around them, as was the case with another family on the Clear Fork, the Carters, whose sons were cut from a different bolt of cloth, boys of a more quiet sort, lacking the streak of deviltry that most of the Elmendorf boys possessed. But in the days when my brother and I were very young, Boyd, the youngest of the sons of Ina and Henry, seemed to be more inclined to stay on; he had a girl in the neighborhood, he was strong and steady, and his parents pinned their hopes on him.

Both Harold and I loved the ranch, but I think that Harold was even happier there than I was. I liked it all, wandering around in the wake of Boyd or Uncle Henry as they did chores, or riding the gentle old mare, Nellie, in the pasture below the corral. But more and more often I preferred to spend my time checking out the "library" ranged along the top of Uncle Henry's roll-top desk in a corner of the dining room, and which consisted of a number of dog-eared western novels by Zane Grey and Max Brand, the Flying U novels by E.M. Bowers (a name that effectively hid the author's feminine identity) and those novels by Clarence E. Mulford which featured a happy-go-lucky red-headed character named Hopalong Cassidy, who somehow was metamorphosed into that rather grim, black-shirted paladin of the range as played on the screen by William Boyd.

Harold, however, could always be found out-of-doors; the boys, who showed up from wherever they had drifted during haying and wheat harvesting, enjoyed looking after this fun-loving, vigorous boy, whom for whatever ridiculous reason they nicknamed "dough-belly." And he felt more in his element with them, riding with them on the rake or hay wagon to and from the fields. A photograph discovers Harold at a tender age—perhaps on his very first visit to the ranch—under a lilac in front of the old ranch home. A storm appears to be coming up, and my mother, hair flying in the freshening wind, has come out to see to him. Predictably, he is quite happy there.

I think, though it did not occur to me at the time, and he and I never discussed it, that he felt a little annoyed that I, because of my smaller size and lively ways, usually received more attention than he from the general run of adults.

On the ranch this was not so. The boys, particularly Boyd, took him under their wings, and showed him the guns that hung on the washroom wall, and the traps which Boyd set for beaver, or for coyote, with a horrid-smelling bait derived from rotting cattle carcasses.

Both my brother and I formed a deep affection for Boyd, although we were aware that one characteristic of his was best not imitated. For some reason, perhaps because his older brothers had teased him so much, he had a certain insecurity, and made up tall stories about his exploits as a hunter and trapper, and was inclined to embellish almost any event in which he had played a part. And, no matter how often he was ridiculed or proven wrong, he persisted in these tales. Once, on a morning hunting expedition across the road in a patch of wild pasture with my brother Harold, he misplaced his hat; the two of them combed the sagebrush clumps in every direction but never found it.

When the two hunters passed through the kitchen on the way to the washroom to clean the gun, Aunt Ina's sharp eyes took in the situation.

"Boyd, what have you done with your hat?" she asked.

"Momma," Boyd replied, wide-eyed as usual, "the darnedest thing happened. A hawk, a sparrow hawk, come by and jerked it right off of my head." My brother stood solemnly by; Aunt Ina, busy preparing for the noon meal, smiled a small weary smile, and did not question either boy further.

Unlike his brothers, Boyd did remain on the ranch, although when his wife died and times were lean he took his orphaned family into town and worked at whatever he could for a time. We saw him occasionally, and he had lost his habit of telling fantastic tales.

We always felt, my brother and I, about all the Elmendorf boys as if they were older brothers, and they reciprocated. They were rough boys, and except for Boyd, had a taste for gambling and drink. To some extent they proved role models for Harold and me; we both developed a taste for gambling. It may be unfair to ascribe any undue influence in this regard to the Elmendorf boys, but in Harold's case, there is some justification; when he was still in his mid-teens and looked to be older—we were back living in Paonia by then—Sid, the gambler, without our mother's knowledge, took Harold to a nearby town and encouraged him to sit in on a poker game.

It is a tribute to the force of Harold's personality that he could pass himself off even at that early age as a grown man. He was always a leader during his developing years, clever at games and a good athlete. In those years he and I had our differences, occasionally descending to an exchange of blows, even, but all such altercations were brief. I was no match for him, so our fights were not the violent affairs that took place between Uncle Doc's two sons, who were physically closer to a match. One winter day when he and I were alternating turns on the slope with the Flexible Flyer, he decided to usurp my turn, and I put up a bit of a struggle, which ended predictably. And truthfully, he was usually fair enough; he only transgressed as a means of demonstrating to our peers that we were after all brothers and natural enemies, as brothers, among the boys we knew, were supposed to be.

There were two events that did demonstrate that we had come to a parting of the ways. One day when Harold had disobeyed one of Mother's injunctions, she proceeded to "strap" him, and he bore it without a move or a whimper. He was into his early teens by then, and both of us, or all three of us, were aware that from that time on, the course of punishment would have to be conducted for him, at least, on a different plane. My mother put away the strap as far as he was concerned, and never used it on him again, though I was to feel its sting for another year.

This was about the time that we entered junior high school, and there had been indications of a disquieting change in Harold's behavior. He became suspiciously more interested in his appearance. Sometimes on a day or an evening at home he would walk around with his "pomp" smoothed down by a cap made out of one of my mother's stocking ends. He began to spend a considerable amount of time before the mirror in the dining room, combing it back. I was annoyed by this and one Sunday morning when he was so engaged, I sneered.

"Don't you look pretty!"

He was enraged, and came for me, hitting me somewhere around the chest, and the blow together with the strategic retreat I was making, landed me in the coal scuttle. As with the incident years before with the BB gun, I was not hurt physically, but I was injured in spirit. I went out for a long, self-pitying walk along the railroad tracks, and when I came home he was gone somewhere. Mama told me that he was sorry for what he had done, and he evidently was, for he treated me with consideration in the next few days—as near as he could come to an apology.

And about this time another important event took place. It all began with students being bused in from outlying grade schools. The ones from mesa schools were of a familiar sort, but among those arriving from the mining camps upriver were a number of girls who piqued the interest of their new classmates, and one in particular was distractingly different.

Myrtle Hibbard was petite and pretty in a flamboyant way. Her blouses bloomed outward emphatically, and where other girls who were showing delightful indications of feminine endowments carried themselves modestly or even self-consciously, Myrtle frankly shared in the pleasure that her charms inspired among the boys. Her father, once a miner, had moved down into town and opened a filling station, but by all accounts he was no better able to provide for his family than any others in the same circle, but there was no doubt that Myrtle dressed more lavishly than her classmates. And where other girls used makeup sparingly if at all, she used it plentifully, giving herself a doll-like appearance; her blonde locks were always marcelled, some said by beauty operators, and she walked in beauty, as the poet said, in her silk stockings and high-heeled pumps, radiating exotic scent.

At the high school dances that winter, held in the Masonic Hall upstairs in the Kennedy Building, junior high students came to watch. Most boys of that age didn't dance at all; they stood around in groups, pushing and shoving or goosing or tickling one another, and trying to look cool and sophisticated, although some of the girls would dance decorously together. But this didn't bother Myrtle; she danced with other girls of her acquaintance, and she danced with upperclass boys whenever she was asked, as she was with more and more frequency. On weekend evenings she could be seen now and then escorted by a boy to the movies; and one Friday I learned through the grapevine— Myrtle was not one to hide such social items from the world—that my brother, Harold, was taking her to the movies the following evening.

Word got around like wildfire among the circle of boys my brother and I spent most of our time with, and when my brother left the house the following evening, the clan was gathering. Those of us who could afford it attended the movie, and the rest of us hung around and waited. When Myrtle, escorted by my brother, emerged from the theatre, we four or five fell in behind the couple and saw them up to the Hibbard residence on north Third, catcalling and hooting. Mrs. Hibbard was evidently up, and invited the pair inside, and the escort broke up then, and went home.

We, any one of us, would have been hard put to say why we had done what we had. But I suppose it was in our eyes an act of treachery; you could tell jokes about girls, even admire them privately, but you didn't break over and actually go places with them.

I must say I awaited Harold's return home that night with some trepidation. He and I were sharing the back bedroom upstairs, and I kept to my side with my face to the wall. When he came in he switched on the light, and I kept my breathing even to indicate I was asleep, expecting any minute to feel a hand on my shoulder. He took off his clothes and hung up his good pants and his shirt and tie and dress sweater. I stole a quick glance to see what sort of a mood he was in, but his expression told me nothing. When he turned out the light and came to bed I still was a little tense. But nothing happened. He didn't even choose to make an issue about the covers, a usual ploy, but moved in quietly beside me and his breathing soon grew rhythmical. He was asleep. It was plain that a change had taken place; he had crossed a divide that I had yet to reach.

Harold didn't go with Myrtle long, but that didn't bother her. She had other fish to fry. And his interests, formerly in the great out-of-doors, inevitably funnelled down in high school to athletics and girls—girls more decorous in their ways and dress than Myrtle was. Harold's hunting days were not ended, but the game he sought was from then on of quite a different character.

Passersby

The main street of Ridgway on a weekday morning during the first World War was often alive with salesmen and tradesmen. All the big mercantile firms and many of the smaller ones had salesmen out "on the road" covering "territories;" first by train, and for years afterward by car. They served every business house in every city, village and hamlet, arriving with a joke or a jibe and an order book, catalogs, and a sample case, each selling his line of shoes, clothing, groceries, hardware, drugs, jewelry, or barber supplies.

Among the number of barbershop "drummers" that besieged my father in his Ridgway shop from time to time was an amiable older gentleman named Mr. Burger. All salesmen dressed well, but Mr. Burger dressed with quiet richness, wearing a fine tan fedora, an expensively tailored woolen suit, usually brown, and tan shoes of kid leather. My father always received him pleasantly—as indeed he did everyone, salesman and customer alike—but with Mr. Burger there was a special deference, for he travelled for his own firm, Burger Brothers Supply of Denver. He was one of the founding brothers. He carried neither sample case nor catalog; he knew my father had a catalog. And he only travelled in a business way because he enjoyed it.

Burger Brothers provided everything needed by the barber, from the sublime to the ridiculous; from the barbershop chair, sculpted in stainless steel and upholstered in the finest cowhide, down through clippers, shears, and scissors, to linens, soaps, tonics, pomades, massage preparations, and tapers for singeing beards.

As a small boy I was fascinated by singes. The customer sat upright, swathed in towels. My father would light the wax taper and bend his tall frame down and touch each hair in mustache or hairline with elaborate care. All conversation in the shop ceased until the operation was over. There was something primitive and pagan about it. The odor, certainly, was primitive. And I could never discover why that occasional customer requested a singe. Did the hair grow back more slowly once it was singed? Was it supposed to improve the customer's appearance? I couldn't see that it did. My father was no help. When I asked him about it, he merely shrugged.

"If they want a singe I give it to 'em," he said.

In most barbershops of that day there were two prominent sets of shelves. One for mugs and one for tonics. The mug shelves in my father's shop were on the long wall opposite the big mirror and just to the rear of the row of captain's chairs provided for waiting customers. The shelves were divided into niches and each housed the shaving mug of a regular customer. Each mug was resplendent with enameled decorations such as Victorian still lifes or scenes from the hunt, and often with the name of the owner in gold leaf, done in a fine Spencerian hand.

The tonics were arranged on shelves and commodes on the opposite wall within easy reach of the two barber chairs. They consisted of supplies of the cosmetic sort, in colorfully labeled bottles and jars, giving the customer something to ponder while the barber pulled up the rosy skin around the neckline hunting for stray whiskers to razor, or snipped the last few rebellious spears of the haircut.

My father's collection of such barber supplies was a considerable one, including tonics, shampoos, lotions, pomades, and massage preparations. It attested not only to his professional zeal but also to the fact that he was a fairly easy touch for a salesman, so that a man new to the territory need only to glance at the collection to confirm that he was in the presence of a pigeon.

I was never able to get my hands on these fascinating bottles and jars during business hours, but sometimes when my father went down to the shop on Sunday to clean up, he would let me gingerly go over the collection. There was always a bottle of bay rum, the standard aftershave of the day, and Eau de Cologne, Wildroot Shampoo and Boncilla massage. When I was learning to read I pored over the labels, whispering the names of the faraway places from which those exotic preparations came: Pueblo, St. Louis, Sheboygan, Chicago.

The Boncilla massage, like the singe, was another arcane barbershop ritual. It was supposed to clear the skin of blemishes. A grayish mud was plastered over the face and allowed to harden. A customer swathed to the neck in cloths and towels, and stretched full-length in the chair waiting for the stuff to dry out, looked like the honored inhabitant of an Egyptian tomb. One Sunday while we were still living in back of the shop my mother even tried the massage. Once the mud was applied, my brother and I looked so lost and so shocked that it very nearly caused her to smile, thus wrecking the treatment, and we were warned away.

When my father ran a shop later in Paonia, there was a barber named Roebuck who worked for him, and he had a wife vain and shameless enough to come down to the shop every week during working hours and have her husband give her a Boncilla massage. This annoyed my father. Women just didn't invade barbershops in those days. Of course, a lady could step to the doorway in search of her husband, and if he happened to be hidden beneath a hot towel in one of the chairs she would be invited in to wait. But any woman with an eye to her reputation would gently refuse the offer. On a Saturday evening when the shop was apt to be crowded, a lady would even hesitate to come to the door, but would send a small son instead.

The old order changeth. The small towns in the West, especially mining towns—and railroad towns as Ridgway was—are apt to be ghost towns; the few barbershops remaining are no longer important centers for noisy male camaraderie and gossip. Supplies arrive by mail or in panel trucks; the jaunty, jesting salesmen are gone to other territories.

On that quiet street where our house sat in Ridgway, there were certainly more passersby than nowadays. We saw fewer salesmen, occasionally a book salesman or even, rarely, a saleswoman, but there were tradesmen in the late spring and throughout the summer: the butchers' carts, the scissors grinder in his untidy little van, peddlers of vegetables and fruit like Mr. Davis, the watermelon man, from his farm in Austin, Colorado, with a Missouri twang to his voice like the song of a red-winged blackbird—a sound particularly pleasant in the ears of my father—and, that annual event, the arrival of the gypsies.

They came trailing through the streets in late summer, driving the dogs frantic and setting the children agog. The men drove creaking carts pulled by donkeys and discouraged old horses—sometimes teamed together. The women wore blouses, dusty wide ruffled skirts, and scarves over their heads, all in hard, bright colors, blue and green and red and yellow. Brass bracelets jangled on their dark arms and bold earrings swung from their ears as they strode along, arms folded. They were barefoot—an astounding thing, that, to see a barefooted woman in those post-Victorian days, or a barefooted man, for that matter.

The women told fortunes. They would also buy anything—at the right price. Generally, they were able to acquire old clothing and worn-out household objects and garden vegetables for a little of nothing and receive small to middling coins of the realm for reading a palm.

There was a rumor at the time among the younger set of Ridgway citizens that the gypsies stole children. My mother didn't altogether deny this canard. But she amended it, with a suspicious little quirk of her mouth, by saying that gypsies stole *bad* children only. Good children had nothing to worry about.

This reassured me to a degree. Not because I felt that I could unqualifiedly place myself in the elect company of good children, but I had learned, even by the age of five, that when parents laid out a behavior standard, as for Christmas, when only good little children were supposed to receive presents, there was some margin for error.

Still, it was just as well not to tempt providence. So when my cousin Mary, daughter of my father's widowed sister, Addie, who was visiting us when the gypsies arrived one year, and my brother—both of them a couple of years older than I—yelled,

"The gypsies are coming! The gypsies are coming!" and ran inside the house and held the door against me, I did rather lose my head. I looked all about for a place to hide and finally wedged myself through the cat's crawlway under the front porch.

And the gypsies didn't take me. In fact, they showed a rather disillusioning lack of interest in me altogether.

The most noted gypsy of the time was Gypsy Joe. He may have been the leader of the band, but he didn't walk the streets with them. He stopped in stores and other places of business along the main streets of the towns visited and renewed old acquaintances. He came to my father's shop early one afternoon when we were still living in rooms at the rear, and my father brought him back to share a watermelon he had just bought from a peddler.

We all sat down, and in spite of the distraction of the watermelon, I spent a good deal of time studying Gypsy Joe. He wore a suit coat over bib overalls, a gray, unblocked fedora, a gray shirt buttoned at the neck, but without a tie. There was a diamond stud on the shirt, and copper bracelets on his wrists. He was a dignified man with a heavy head that hung forward.

After we finished the watermelon, he told my father's fortune by the position of the watermelon seeds that swam in the rind. He talked in a deep monotone, and my father listened carefully and nodded as Gypsy Joe made each statement, but he was grinning most of the time, and I had the feeling he didn't take it all that seriously. Perhaps Gypsy Joe told my father that he was going to get rich off the few shares of gold mining stock he held in a mine up in Yankee Boy Basin, but if he did tell him that, he was eventually proved wrong.

Gypsies are much maligned, though of course where there's smoke there's apt to be some fire, and there's no doubt that given the proper opportunity, an alert gypsy has been known to try for a score. Even now a band of gypsies called the Williams Family occasionally run a roof repair racket around the West.

Instances of chicanery I have heard of often involved a gypsy woman fortuneteller and a lonely old man. One of these victims inventoried his ailments for his exotic visitor. She sympathized and assured him that she could help, and coyly began poking him in various locations of his anatomy, murmuring,

"You're going to get well here, and you're going to get well there, and you're going to get well here—" until she came to a bulge on his right hip, which she reduced on the spot.

I have never had my fortune told by a bona fide gypsy, but there was a lady who lived just outside Ridgway, a dairyman's wife, and although I doubt she was a gypsy, she resembled one in appearance, and told fortunes purely as a recreation.

After we left Ridgway for Paonia she was widowed, and came down to visit us. She wore dark purple and brown dresses, her dark hair was worn pulled back smooth and straight with bangs across the forehead. She had gold rings on her fingers and wore an elaborately carved gold watch as a lavaliere.

My fortune as she read it to me out of my palm was pleasant, but not memorable. What I do remember is that I was troubled with warts at the time, a total of eleven on my hands, and she instructed me how to get rid of them. I was to tie a piece of yarn around each wart in turn, place the yarn between the halves of a bean, wrap the bean in a washcloth and bury it in the ground. When the bean sprouted, or the washcloth rotted, or both, the warts were supposed to disappear. I did as she told me and in good time the warts were gone.

A welcome peddler along those small town streets then was the iceman; he evoked visions of homemade ice cream. I don't remember any iceman in Ridgway but in Paonia where we lived in the 1920's the iceman was Jay Blake, a big and muscular man with a bowed back and a jutting chin. He had a large family of bright children, and he was a man of pronounced views and lively wit. Once a rather corpulent customer took the rude liberty of chaffing Jay about his back. Jay wiped the sweat from his forehead and looked pointedly at his customer's protruding stomach:

"Well," he said, "if I have to have a bulge somewhere, I'd rather have it in the back than in the front."

The peddlers of provender and ice were not noted for the neatness of their equipages, with a big scale swinging from the right rear of the wagon, and the tailgate down and leaking liquids, but there were other vans that were trim and well maintained, with representations of their many wares stenciled on their brightly varnished sides.

These were the Watkins and Raleigh vans. They were rolling drugstores that also carried complete lines of spices and herbs. The Raleigh man I knew was Mr. Roth, a merry, round little man who roamed far and wide in his horse-driven van, making stops at even remote ranches. On my Uncle Henry's ranch up on Clear Fork outside Crawford, it was always an occasion when his van came into view down the lane. Mr. Roth always had a joke or so, a free lemon drop all around, a wink for Uncle Henry's two daughters, and a hard pinch on the arm for a small boy like me, if I happened to be visiting there.

The trash pile on the ranch of my Uncle Henry Elmendorf was an indirect tribute to the sales prowess of the Raleigh and Watkins men. I became pretty well acquainted with that trash pile. It was across the ditch next to the chip pile, which I was required to visit once or twice a day with an old fruit basket to pick up chips for cookstove fires. Naturally I sought out any means to postpone the task, so I always managed to kill a little time at the trash pile.

The trash pile was burned periodically, but there were many objects that burned poorly or not at all. These included old corset stays, discarded high-top shoes, broken jugs and crocks, the scorched tin frame of a baby buggy, a slop jar with a hole in the bottom, and a bald female doll with a severely cracked cranium. But the bulk of the agglomeration consisted of tins, bottles and jars that had once held cooking extracts, cake colorings, spices, canned smoke for curing meats, mange cures for cattle, salves, elixirs, balms and tonics. Raleigh and Watkins were well represented, though Raleigh predominated, except for liniment bottles where Watkins was the clear winner; I think it was pretty generally agreed around the countryside then that the Watkins liniment had more zing.

Of course, no ranch family depended exclusively on Raleigh or Watkins for supplies, particularly medical supplies. There were a number of old favorites no one could do without, like Vapo-Rub and Mentholatum, obtainable only in town. And on the trash pile were bottles that had contained "Pain-Killer," that sovereign remedy with a taste so nauseous that it literally drove Aunt Polly's cat up the wall when Tom Sawyer provided her with a spoonful of it. There were tins once harboring Carter's Little Liver Pills—which, it has turned out since, could have as accurately been labeled Carter's Little Pancreas Pills or Carter's Little Spleen Pills, because there was no conclusive proof that they helped one organ more than another. Then for the females in the family, there were bottles with the stern visage of Lydia E. Pinkham on the label, which had contained that precious vegetable compound so mysteriously important to the health of womankind.

The proliferation of trash did not indicate that my Uncle's family were hypochondriacal. It was just that in those days home remedies were in very wide use, particularly in homes on the frontier as that country so recently had been. For a long time doctors and veterinarians were very few and any family had to doctor ranch humans and animals alike. Nearly every ranch had at least one and perhaps several books dealing with remedies and cures for all the common diseases of both man and beast.

And, there is no doubt many of the old-fashioned cures were more effective in their way than the modern ones. Paregoric, for example, widely given to calm fretful babies, did work extraordinarily well—as it should have, with its potent opium base. Many medicines of half a century and more ago were liberally laced with morphine and opium, and Tiger's Milk, that standby of the medicine show (and many a more reputable tonic, too) contained far more alcohol than wines do today. Even Coca Cola, as we all know now, once contained cocaine, and its devotees—today they would be called addicts—gathered festively every workday afternoon at the small town soda fountains for the daily "fix."

We know a lot more now than we did then—unfortunately, one might almost say. There were all those sterling old remedies then that one absolutely depended on. Today dependability is a mirage that fades the more closely it is approached. It seems that there isn't any preparation that won't raise a rash at least on a rat in the laboratory if it is rubbed into his skin—or kill him, if it is fed to him in sufficient quantity. And the miracle drugs that come along now grow less attractive if not downright evil as the years pass and the side effects emerge to assault the coming generations.

And the ranch trash piles of today, I think, cannot be as interesting as they once were. Containers are apt to be plastic, not collectibles like many of those old glass bottles were, and with all the means of disposal today, you're not apt to encounter so exotic a collection of trash as I combed on my uncle's ranch when I was supposed to be collecting chips. And, although varieties of medicines and particularly of cosmetic preparations and hygienic products have proliferated wildly, I don't think the buying of them in the drugstore supermarket as we commonly do now is as pleasant a chore as it was when the Raleigh and Watkins vans bumped along the country roads from customer to customer.

No free lemon drops, either.

The Katzenjammer Kids
and the Kaiser

My interest in learning to read developed gradually. At first it seemed enough to look at pictures, and there were in our house enough resources of that kind to keep me occupied. Mail-order catalogs had become common, and they were looked through by the whole family. Examined indoors and out, if you get my meaning. But I was baffled by the photographs of models in the lingerie and underwear sections. I couldn't understand why a gaggle of clean-cut, grown men, or a bevy of what appeared to be respectable, presentable females could stand around half-dressed like that, casually engaging in conversation. What in the world was going on there? And all the men's underwear so clean and smoothly fitted—no gaps, front or back. Marvelous. And unbelievable.

Of the more formal volumes of printed matter available to me, the most prestigious was a 30-volume set of world histories, bound in solemn black, which reposed on shelves behind a glass door in the secretary desk in our parlor. My father, who acquired all sorts of things he didn't have that much use for, had bought them from a particularly persuasive travelling salesman.

Those books may have been opened by someone when they first arrived, but no one looked into them afterward, I am convinced, except me. And I didn't waste much time on them. The illustrations consisted only of frontispieces—one to a volume—and were of two types. In one, generals and their aides stood around on a hill above a battle, right legs advanced, right hands tucked into blouses, with maybe some soldiers in the distance waving weapons or flags; or, in the second type, men in formal dress stood around in over-decorated halls, right legs advanced, right hands tucked inside vests.

Then there there was the family Bible, bound in black leather, but unillustrated, and two small leather-bound volumes of poetry which reposed on the bottom shelf of the stand positioned in front of the main parlor window—also unillustrated. They were never disturbed except to be dusted once a week.

But two other books my father had acquired were real rousers. One was a book about lodges. Mostly about lodge initiations, and with cartoons and illustrations on practically every page. They showed grown men—fat, skinny, tall, short, bald, bearded—suffering all sorts of indignities. They were nearly always blindfolded, and about to step into an open trap door, or down a set of stairs, or through a doorway with a bucket of water poised above it. But the favorite theme of all was that of a dignified fat man of fairly advanced years, rather richly dressed, with a billy goat in full charge at his unprotected rear.

The other book was a copy of Dante's Inferno, with the grim, overpowering illustrations by Gustave Dore, showing the damned undergoing innumerable tortures in the smoky caverns and fiery lakes of hell. I certainly learned, from those two books, about man's inhumanity to man, and God's abandonment of the damned to the fiends. A short hell on earth for the lodge initiate, and an eternal hell for the sinner thereafter. I think I early acquired from these books a distrust of fraternal societies and organized religion, feeling, as do most sinners and social outsiders I suppose, that if you don't join you won't be subject to the rules and penalties.

But of course all else paled in my eyes before the funnies in glorious color which arrived every Sunday in the *Denver Post*. I think the parents and critics of today who do not find the violence dished out nightly on the tube to be particularly edifying, would have a similar reaction to the funny papers of those years.

The tricks the Kids played on the Captain were invariably destructive and usually violent. Mutt customarily laid out little Jeff, and not a week passed when Maggie didn't crown Jiggs with a rolling pin. Then there was fearless Harry and his villainous rival, Rudolph, of the black formal clothes and skinny mustache, who perpetrated outrageously violent schemes to destroy Harry and claim the charms of Harry's beautiful blonde fiancée. And Buster Brown, who was my favorite, although he always dressed neatly, and was accompanied by his dog Tige, a proper enough canine, regularly became involved in violent escapades—even though at the end a comforting moral was always provided.

And on the screen the short comedies of the great age were flickering, replete with as much vigorous and mad violence as could be conjured up. Still, there was this to be said about it all; it was good, clean fun. There were no schizos or neurotics involved. Villains did what they did just for the pure enjoyable hell of it.

Following the action at the movies did not present any difficulty for me: there was always someone conveniently near in the audience who (probably compulsively) read the subtitles aloud. But with the funnies, to keep abreast of all the happenings without being able to read was a problem. In the beginning our mother was dragooned into reading them to my brother and me. She had her problems with the dialects in many of the strips, based on the vaudeville turns of an earlier day. The mouth-filling oaths, for instance, that floated over the heads of the tortured Captain and his diminutive friend the Inspector in the Katzenjammer Kids ("Donnerwetter, Mama! Vot in himmel is dot in der bathtub?"); the Irish brogue of Happy Hooligan, who wore, for reasons never made clear, a tin can tied to his head; and the French gabblings of those over-polite loons, Alphonse and Gaston.

She read them all to the best of her ability, and even seemed to enjoy it in some measure, but she proved balky and unreasonable when implored to read the same page over two and then three times, so there was nothing for it but for me to pick up a smattering of Katzenjammer English on my own.

But the importance of learning to read was brought home to me most vividly when I started school at the callow age of five. There I met Velma Ruth Bates, daughter of the local doctor. She was in my grade and she had long, golden curls, and she liked me well enough to invite me to her house to play. We hid in the garage from the gypsies.

I was very flattered by her attention, and unwisely bragged of our friendship to some of the neighborhood children gathered in our yard one evening. They scoffed at it, and declared that Velma Ruth Bates didn't really like me particularly, and I said that she did, and had in fact sent me a postcard. Marion Payne said that was crazy and dared me to show the postcard; so, hoist on my own petard, I rushed in the house, went through a number of postcards stored in a pigeonhole of the secretary in the living room, and brought one out.

This created more merriment among my tormentors because it turned out that there was a message on the back of the card from my aunt and uncle in Denver. Up until then I hadn't realized that postcards bore messages—I only knew that they showed up in the mail. Now it was plain that learning to read was absolutely necessary.

The serious business of my education was taken up by Miss Cusick, teacher of the first grade, a small, formidable lady, erect, and slow to smile. The one time I remember her smiling was during a class exercise for which each student was provided with a number of small colored sticks and told to construct an outline of a house on the desk top. Then Miss Cusick passed among us with a ruler, and if she thought the finished house outline did not represent a best effort, she whacked the failed architect across the knuckles with the ruler.

I did my level house-building best, aware of the penalty for shoddy construction, but in the end my house turned out a bit on the ramshackle side. When the specter of Miss Cusick loomed over me with the ready ruler, I murmured desperately,

"This house doesn't look so good because the people just moved out."

She paused, and my knuckles tingled in anticipation. But then she smiled thinly and passed on.

But I didn't escape the ruler on other occasions. I had the misfortune to be left-handed, and Miss Cusick, the acknowledged authority on education in the community at that time, convinced my mother that I must by all means be broken of writing with the left hand; otherwise I would become a pariah, an outcast from polite society, possibly an idiot. So, broken of writing with my left hand I was.

How gauche my writing would have been if I had been able to continue writing with my left hand there is no way of knowing. Certainly my writing is very bad as it is—and, justly or not, I have always blamed Miss Cusick for it. And, bolstered by deductions I have freely made based on psychological theories advanced since that time, I have laid the blame for a number of other of my failures and shortcomings at the grim lady's door; from an inability to think quickly in crises, to poor performance in teenage seduction activities. Two shortcomings fairly closely related, come to think of it. But I learned to write, and I learned to read.

Meanwhile World War I was grinding wearily across the face of Europe, generating big black headlines in the *Post,* and providing wonderful material for lurid cartoons. The headlines meant little to me, though the French and Belgian words—Ypres, Louvain, the Somme, Verdun—even mispronounced by adults as they commonly were, rang with melancholy music; but the cartoons were another matter. Not that the *Post* wasn't doing fine without the big war; it was in its greedy and loud adolescence and was carrying on its own small wars right and left. So, interspersed between reports from far-off battlefields, the *Post* would pillory state and national politicians, and promote causes on both levels with what it considered high-minded zeal. I learned to recognize in its cartoons the spirit of Prohibition, a rail-thin figure in funereal black with a stovepipe hat and mourning band. His opposite number, representing the liquor interests, was blowsy old John Barleycorn, sometimes shown as a whisky bottle with legs and arms.

On the war scene, I became familiar through the cartoons with the figure of Uncle Sam, and his feminine counterpart, Columbia, a calm-faced matron in a Greek himation and cockaded French bonnet, carrying the torch of freedom. England was fat John Bull—but not as big of belly as he had been when American sympathies were not so fully with Britain. John's feminine alter ego was Britannia, in martial gown, helmeted, and carrying a spear in one hand and a shield in the other, emblazoned with the Union Jack.

These figures dimmed beside such personifications as War, a gorilla in Grecian armor and helmet, carrying a short sword and wading through seas of corpses; Famine, an emaciated woman in tattered dress, followed by starving hollow-eye children clutching begging bowls; and Death, the shrouded skeleton bearing a scythe.

But the cartoonists' best licks were reserved for the figure representing the Enemy, the Central Powers—Kaiser Wilhelm II, emperor of Germany. He was depicted as wild-eyed and demented, a Prussian officer in spiked helmet and with glistening monocle, his mustache curved upward in stiletto points. His black jackboots and white-gloved hands dripped with blood. He was a figure reviled and detested but at the same time there was a gross, primally humorous spirit in the public attitude—as there is nowadays in the way we have regarded the Ayatollah Khomeini or Colonel Kaddafi.

There was that bit of doggerel widely recited and applauded as the German armies began to suffer reverses on the Western Front:

> Kaiser Bill went up the hill
> To have a look at France;
> Kaiser Bill came down the hill
> With bullets in his pants.

The motion picture early reflected the growing public conviction that the nation should enter the war. In one film a foppish German lieutenant, skin-headed, monocled, had been wounded and captured by the Allies. How polite he was, as he clicked the heels of his glistening boots and bent low over the hand of the apple-cheeked heroine, a Red Cross nurse. She was invariably courteous to him, gentle, trusting soul that she was, but it was plain that she didn't trust him, and neither did the audience. And, sure enough, he at last revealed himself for the treacherous, insensate brute we all knew him to be, eaten up with lust, and by the time our heroine was rescued by Allied soldiers in reel seven, he had lured her into a locked room and stripped her down to her camisole.

In the spring of 1917, the year that I started school, the United States declared war on Germany. When the Germans desperately began all-out submarine attacks on Allied and American shipping, the handwriting was on the wall. Once in, the nation was overwhelmed with patriotism and such songs as "Over There," and "When Johnny Comes Marching Home," were recorded on cylinders to be played on the new Edison phonograph and printed as sheet music to appear on the piano of our next-door neighbors, the Paynes, and on the pianos in living rooms all over the country.

We children played war games and because of the emergency, the usual proscription against boys playing with girls was suspended, and diminutive female Red Cross nurses were enlisted to treat casualties in a neighbor's cellar during the daily bombardments and assaults that were taking place. One evening as I was going reluctantly into the house to bed I remember hearing faintly from across the town where a bloody engagement was evidently still in progress, a small boy piping,

"Hold yer fahr, men; Ar leader's ben injured!"

During the following year a catastrophe apparently quite unrelated to the war occurred: the great influenza epidemic. Everywhere people were dying of it, and the authorities became so desperate that we all, men, women, and children, were fitted with white gauze masks which we were enjoined to wear whenever we were out of doors. Our two cows were dry at the time and we were buying milk from a family across town. My brother and I had been going after it of an evening, fetching it home in a small pail; but when the masks were issued, either my mother or my father would go along with us, holding us by the hand, fulfilling a pathetic need to feel that we were further protected by their presence.

It was a ghostly little journey, with friends and neighbors going about like errands, each in a carefully isolated group, speaking in subdued voices, moving in and out of the shadows cast by the street lamps.

More American soldiers died in the training camps of influenza than in the trenches of France; but the "flu" epidemic and the war too, finally ended.

All of it was only a dark, fantastic episode in the lives of my brother and me. The shadow of the draft floated briefly over my father's head, but that was all. Eventually our only souvenir of that time was a five-volume set of bulky books bound in blue cloth and replete with photographs, which my father had received on a promotional deal from *Collier's* magazine.

It was called, simply, *The Great War*. No one then could conceive of a greater war being possible.

The Great Adventure

Life in Ridgway revolved around the railroad. The roundhouse of the D&RGW—Denver and Rio Grande Western—represented the town's only significant payroll, and everything in the way of provisioning and supplies that came any distance arrived in a railroad freight or baggage car. There were no houses in the town that weren't within hearing of the reassuring chuffing and whistling of the steam locomotives, the bumping of the cars, and the squealing of the air brakes as freight and passengers were moved up and down the narrow, rugged valley of the fierce Uncompahgre, to and from the outside world.

In the summer of 1917 my father's sister, my Aunt Hettie, came to visit us from Denver, arriving, naturally, by rail. Her husband, Uncle Ed Poole, was a glamorous figure in those days—a locomotive engineer. He had not been able to accompany my aunt on this trip, and perhaps partly because of this she conceived the notion of availing herself of the company of my brother or me on her return trip to Denver. My brother Harold was looking forward to visiting on the ranch of our Uncle Henry, so the choice fell on me.

I was five at the time and my parents were reluctant to let me go—after all, I would have to come back, clear across the state, by myself. But everyone had faith in the railroads then, and the railroads reciprocated by being very solicitous of passenger welfare. My Uncle Ed was enthusiastic in the letters he wrote. He welcomed any opportunity to prove the efficiency and safety of railroad travel.

So, my parents consented, and one day, dressed in my best Buster Brown outfit, and carrying a shoe box full of fried chicken that my mother insisted on sending, my aunt and I were seen off at the Ridgway station by my mother and brother. A crisis arose when my mother insisted that my brother kiss me good-bye. I was going on six and my brother was going on eight, and the idea revolted both of us. It was a high price to pay for a trip, even such a trip as this promised to be, but she was determined and so he and I moved toward each other finally like a couple of mechanical dolls and brushed each other's cheek for a nauseous moment.

Now I was free to be lifted up by the conductor to the rear

platform of the passenger car, and my aunt and I were ushered into our seats, we waved our good-byes, and the journey to wonderland began.

It was at the time when one era of railroading was ending and another had begun. The narrow-gauge lines that webbed the Rockies during the great gold and silver strikes were phasing out and the standard gauge lines were taking over. But the Moffat Tunnel and the Dotsero Cutoff were still only newspaper pipe dreams, and so we had to make that marvelous journey over the Continental Divide by way of Marshall Pass. The passage up was a thrilling one. One engine after another was added, until a total of four puffing, grunting giants tugged us to the heights. Cliffs and pine-shrouded slopes lay far below us while we watched from the red-plush comfort of our car. Once the conductor let me open the window for a minute or so, and I leaned out and listened to the roar of the locomotives and breathed deeply of the outside air, so fiercely pure and cold. I also got a cinder in my eye.

At last we arrived at the snowsheds, great man-made caverns at the summit, and as the day waned started our journey down the eastern slope of the pass. The carbon-arc lights came on, making everything more luxurious and cozy than ever. The train swayed on and on; sometimes a wall of rock outside our window would mirror the interior of our car briefly, with everyone sitting motionless, like people in a photograph or a dream.

In Salida we changed trains and then there was the delight of the Pullman sleeper. I had a whole upper berth to myself, and it seemed such a luxurious idea to lie there and sleep in a bed that moved swiftly through the night. But I did little sleeping at first—it was more fun to lie snugly there and watch the little baggage hammock above my feet swing and shudder on the curves, and listen to the clack of the rails, with each clack moving us one step nearer to the city.

Denver was a blur of pleasure. My cousin, Aunt Hettie's son Floyd, was a young man just entering employment. At that time he was working as a trolley conductor and he took charge of me, and I rode the entire day with him on his street car, and on another day he took me down town and we visited many shops. In one he bought me a candy-striped shirt. On one street there was a store with talking parrots for sale, though in my fevered memory it seems to me that there were talking birds, green and glittering, the whole length of that enchanted street.

Later, in company with another young man who drifted into our company, we went to the zoo, and after we said good-bye to our friend of the day, we rode the street car up Broadway to alight before the majestic capitol building. There we bought hot tamales wrapped in newspaper from the vendor on the corner. Then the scramble for the homeward-bound trolley. I loved to hear the conductor sing out the street stops after the double-pulling of the bell. It was all an untranslatable litany until you came to your own stop, when the name emerged from the resonant gibberish as if an inspired lunatic were suddenly to start making sense.

But it was all over soon enough and it was time for me to return to my Ridgway home. I think the adults involved, my parents and Aunt Hettie, were rather worried. Not my Uncle Ed. He thought the workings of the railroad were under direct license from God Almighty, and he was absolutely certain that everything would be all right. He and Aunt Hettie accompanied me to the train, and Uncle Ed strutted around, making arrangements, and fell into earnest conversation with a brakeman, after which he assured Aunt Hettie and me that the brakeman was taking me into his care and would see to it that I made the change in Salida to the train that would then take me home. Aunt Hettie saw me to my seat, kissed me, dispensed a wavering smile and walked to the doorway of the car. The locomotive emitted a departing hoot. Aunt Hettie gave me a last, aborted wave. She had a handkerchief to her mouth, and her eyes were red.

Whatever instructions Uncle Ed gave to the brakeman, I saw him only once again, when he helped me off the train at Salida and directed me into the waiting room of the depot. He did not seem particularly friendly and didn't impress me as a dependable sort no matter how much trust my Uncle Ed reposed in fellow employees of the D&RG. People were coming and going, but for most of the time I was quite alone. I passed the time staring at the big clock over the shuttered ticket window or at the maps along the walls, and napped on the wooden bench. In the cold gray of morning I got up, sore, cold, and sleepy, and wandered out to the platform. A train was just leaving.

"Where is that train going?" I asked a man on the platform.

"To Ridgway," he said, and I ran to the train and clambered up the steps of the last car just as the train was getting under way.

Of course, we went over my odyssey many times afterward, and it was agreed by all that it was very fortunate indeed that the Ridgway roundhouse was the final destination of that train, for if the man I had asked had told me the train was going to Ouray, for instance, I would not have boarded it, because I would never have made the deduction that a Ouray-bound train would have to pass through Ridgway.

I don't recall hearing whether Uncle Ed ever talked to that brakeman about his oversight, but if he did, I am sure that the brakeman remembered it for some time after, because Uncle Ed was never slow in pointing out lapses of duty or defects in character to anyone with whom he came in contact. Years later, for instance, on another trip to Denver, I was riding with Uncle Ed in his big Buick sedan enroute to a grocery store, and he was just the same sort of automobile driver as he was a locomotive engineer. He drove at a brisk pace, down the exact center of the street, wheels straddling the center line. On this occasion, a car approached us from the opposite direction and the driver, a small, meek-looking, dark-complexioned man, seemed under the impression that Uncle Ed was wool-gathering and would come to his senses and move over sufficiently to permit safe passage on the inner lane. But Uncle Ed drove straight on, and the result was a grinding sideswipe of the cars. The approaching car swerved and parked at the curb, and Uncle Ed, on the opposite side of the street, did likewise.

The other driver continued to sit behind the wheel of his car, probably a little dazed, but Uncle Ed got promptly out, settled his gray fedora on his head, straightened his black overcoat with the velvet-trimmed collar, pushed his black leather gloves more snugly down on his fingers, and strode briskly to the little man's car. The other driver had rolled down his window and I feel certain anticipated an apology of some sort, but in that he was certainly mistaken. I don't know what was said, but judging by the way Uncle Ed's head was bobbing, it was an expression of definite opinion. Then he straightened up, with a "That'll take care of you, Buster," jut to his heavy chin, strode back, got in, and drove away. The last I saw of the little man he was still sitting there, his mouth open, and his eyes fixed on his rear-view mirror. So I have every reason to think that the brakeman who neglected to put me on the Ridgway train got an earful from my Uncle Ed.

I was tired on the rest of the journey over the pass and on to Ridgway. A couple in a nearby seat gave me a piece of chicken at noon, and I napped and watched as the locomotives huffed and strained to bring us once again up the pass. It was well into the day, a Sunday, when we came down into Montrose, a warm day in midsummer—probably the Fourth of July—and I, who was not all that sensitive in matters of personal cleanliness, was nevertheless beginning to feel grimy and in need of a bath. Up the Uncompahgre valley we chuffed, toward Ridgway. As we approached the station it seemed deserted, there was no one there to greet me (I found out later that my parents had not expected me on that day) and the conductor said,

"Well, that's all right. It's the day of the barbecue and everybody's up at the park. We'll just let you out up there and you'll find your folks, all right."

And that is what he did. The train rolled up the track to where the park lay, a grassy meadow beneath a grove of trees, and several other passengers and I alighted. Under the old cottonwoods long picnic

Ridgway depot

tables had been set up, there was much laughter and talk, and women wearing hats full of flowers and bright feathers, and dresses full and pinched in at the waist were setting out plates and silverware and crocks of potato salad. From the barbecue pit, where a whole steer was gently roasting in the coals, came a pervasive, delicious smell. Someone called my name, and I ran to my mother and father.

I was home.

Diversions and Excursions

My mother grew up on a homestead outside Crawford and she had learned to be careful with money. She never did any impulse buying. It was my father who bought the books he never got around to reading, and it was he who had a fling at learning the Hawaiian guitar by mail, and it was he who bought the stereoscope and the phonograph.

Both the stereoscope and the phonograph gave my brother and me a great deal of pleasure. The stereoscope, a viewing device on a little handle, permitted you to see double-mounted photographs as a single three-dimensional one. There were views of Niagara Falls, of Virginia's Natural Bridge, of the Statue of Liberty, and the buildings at the St. Louis World's Fair. They looked so real that they made you hold your breath in awe.

The Edison phonograph played cylindrical records. These records were stored in cardboard containers and it was a thrill to simply read the title on the top and to pull off the lid and inhale the dried rubber smell together with the faint scent of oil from the machine. Then you held the cylinder—shiny black, iridescent blue or coral—up to the light. All those gleaming tiny grooves, carrying the music from far-off voices and instruments! I could listen for hours, and on rainy or snowy days I often did, to records such as "Where the River Shannon Flows," as sung by the "silver-voiced tenor", Henry Burr.

My father would stop now and then at Boyer's drugstore after work and buy another hit of the day. I was with him one halcyon evening in midsummer when he picked up "Just a Song at Twilight" sung by a famous soprano.

But of all the records the favorite of my brother and me was a gut-buster called "Uncle Billy's Dog-fight." It was recorded by an old vaudevillian who imitated all the individual voices of half a dozen dogs engaged in a brawl—as well as the voices of the dogs' owners and a couple of cats besides. I think my mother and my father may have found this record amusing for a time, but through repeated playings it lost its appeal, and when his requests and finally demands proved unavailing in preventing us from playing it endlessly, a mysterious accident occurred. I pulled the treasure from its case one day to discover it shattered beyond all hope of mending.

There was another noteworthy cylinder, a recording from a musical comedy sung by a soprano in an arch and roguish way. It was called "If the Wind Had Only Blown the Other Way." The refrain went:

> If the wind had only blown the other way,
> I'd have been a single girl today.
> Instead of nursing twins and triplets,
> I'd be taking ocean diplets,
> If the wind had only blown the other way.

I was rather taken with the rhyming of "triplets" and "diplets," and my mother explained that the song was about a young lady whose hat was blown off by a vagrant breeze at the seashore, and it was recovered by a strange man. She and the man fell in love and married, and between them they got her into the fix with all those triplets.

And then my mother did an unusual thing, for her; she went on to tell me how she and my father had met—as accidental and unpremeditated a meeting as the one told of on the phonograph record. It was on the train when they were returning to their respective homes in western Colorado; she from a visit to her childhood home in the Blue Ridge, and he from a trip to the St. Louis World's Fair with some other young bucks from Paonia, where he was barbering at the time.

It was all, apparently, a matter of chance—even as it was with the lady who acquired the triplets. This presented to me the paradox of love, its delights and concomitant burdens. As to those exotic delights which seemed to arrive earlier in the course of a courtship, there was a living, breathing example of that, very near to hand at the time. A teenage girl came to stay for a while to help with the housework when my mother was incapacitated with an attack of blood poisoning in her left arm. The girl was jolly and pretty and answered to the euphonious name of Guinevere Stump. And she had a boyfriend. I was bewildered by the way they behaved. Her young man and she would sit for hours on the couch in the living room, as close to each other as they could get, holding hands, and with set, foolish smiles on their faces. If you suddenly left the room and as suddenly returned, you would catch them hugging and kissing. It struck me as more of an affliction than anything else—a sort of baffling, comic disease.

We didn't have a car then, or even a buggy, but my father had friends, and while Guinevere was available to look after the house and feed the cows, he determined that we should make a weekend excursion—my mother's arm was healing well—and a friend and customer of my father's, a man named Collins, lived on a ranch in the high country and had invited us all to visit with his family there.

One problem concerned me; I had rescued a robin nestling which had fallen from a cottonwood in the yard. But I asked Guinevere if she would look after it for me, and she said she would, and I took her out to the storage shed and showed her the little box in which I had arranged a nest for the orphan.

The Collinses had two cars. My brother and I rode in the back of the Collins pickup with the younger Collins children, chauffeured by an older scion of the family, while his folks and ours rode on ahead in the touring car.

We were going along at a pretty good clip, and I was on my knees at the back, leaning over the tailgate and watching the road flow by underneath, when the car struck a good-sized rock, and over I went into the road, striking my head on that selfsame rock. I was unhurt—not having been struck in a sensitive spot—but when I struggled to my feet it was to see the pickup disappearing up the road with no one aware, apparently, that I was missing. I struck up a wail and started off in pursuit. Once the pickup arrived in the ranch yard a tally revealed the loss of a passenger and the pickup returned to rescue me. But in all my life up to that time I never felt more lonely than when I first scrambled up and saw the pickup disappearing down the road.

We had a pleasant couple of days and nights with the Collinses, but when we returned, I went out to the storage shed and discovered that the nestling robin had shrunk to a mummy; I doubt if Guinevere ever gave it a second thought once we had departed. It was cruel and inhuman, I reflected bitterly with the tiny corpse in my hand; I should have known better than to give over the care of a pet to a person with the sort of affliction that Guinevere was evidently suffering from—an affliction that has bewildered and troubled far better brains than mine.

My father hungered to buy a car, but was not yet in a position financially to do so. But he had other friends with cars, among them Johnny McKnight. Johnny had a yellow roadster that he was very proud of, and he came around on a Sunday in late spring to take us all out for a ride. It was a very dashing vehicle—an Oldsmobile, I think.

My parents were helped into the front seat, my brother and I were wedged into the rumble seat along with Johnny's sons, both somewhat older than Harold and I, and away we went.

"Whoooooo," my mother exclaimed decorously as Johnny shifted gears, and everybody was shouting or laughing, and my brother and I were sitting well forward in the seat, partly because there wasn't too much room back there, and partly, perhaps, because we were afraid to put our weight down. Through town we rolled, with dogs barking, and out into the countryside. It was exhilarating to see the fence posts whizzing back, and pleasant to gulp the cold mountain air. Horses shied and bucked as we went by. Cows stared in wild disbelief.

Johnny took us many different places on various such Sundays that year in his handsome machine. On each occasion my mother packed a picnic lunch, which we would eat just about anywhere it occurred to us to stop. It wasn't important to go anywhere in particular. Just the sensation of riding was enough. Of course, there were the flats. Invariably one and sometimes more on every excursion. If there were only one, Johnny would replace it with the spare; if there were more, he would get out his patching kit while Dad would work the jack and later the pump, spelled by one of Johnny's sons.

Johnny seemed always happy. He ran sheep with the help of his sons and appeared to be doing very well at it. Always on these outings he wore a well-tailored light tan suit, a white shirt and red or blue tie, and a light tan fedora. His sons were clean and neat in Levi's, work shirts, Stetsons and laced boots—they pretended to make fun of their father's sartorial elegance, but actually I think they were proud of him. He was a man of more than fifty, single, and his two sons were adopted. They all played together and worked together; on several of our excursions, though, the older of the boys was unable to come because he was busy with the sheep, as my father pointed out admiringly. Today, I don't suppose it would be possible for a middle-aged single man to adopt a pair of boys. Too bad. I never knew a happier family than Johnny McKnight's.

There was one other modest little excursion I remember; this time a local customer and friend of my father's took the four of us for a drive up the pass leading over the divide, on a quiet evening in the fall of the year. All the aspen and live oak had turned and the mountains were glowing in the blue mists of Indian summer. Now and again you could hear the impudent call of a magpie, the challenge of a prairie dog, or the faint bawling of cattle. We were picking chokecherries, which my mother would can and make into pies, and we were on the lookout for bears, who appreciated the berries too, but even my mother was not all that concerned. It was one of those moments when all was right with the world. And a splendid world it was.

II. UP ON THE MESA

Breakout

In the spring of 1919, my father broke out of jail, which is to say that he disposed of the Ridgway barbershop. He had a failing common to his family, of sinking now and then into a deep depression, digging himself ever deeper, like Shakespeare's Melancholy Jacques, feeding on the mood as a weasel sucks eggs. In such a mood, he felt trapped and desperate in the shop, resentful of his fate.

The event that really precipitated his decision to leave the shop was the death of his father on the family fruit ranch on Lamborn Mesa outside Paonia. He went down to the funeral and came back with his head full of dreams of fruit ranching. Not that the home place would be immediately available. It was the home of his mother, at least for the time being, and as things go with families, it was a complicated situation, since there were other heirs involved—four sons and two daughters to be exact, and one daughter, his widowed sister Addie, and Addie's young daughter Mary, were living with Grandmother Haley on the old home place.

But the ranch across the road from the family homestead was for sale. I suppose he talked it over with my mother, the two of them sitting at the kitchen table of an evening in the Ridgway house they had worked so hard to make livable. I don't know whether she approved, but certainly the handwriting was on the wall as far as barbering in Ridgway was concerned, ever since the railroad round-house had been moved down to Montrose. And both of my parents had some notion of what the change would mean; both of their parents were farm people. If she had misgivings he overrode them, and they bought the ranch, and my father, certainly, for the time being was a happy man.

We left Ridgway in style once the arrangements were concluded, riding on the red plush seats of a D&RGW passenger car, with my father in high good spirits. The last memory I have of the place where I had spent most of my young life was of looking out a train window to where white sheep grazed in a green meadow below red, cedar-covered bluffs, along the rim of which ran Old Man Kelly's famous trail.

Children do not take well to moving, giving up familiar settings and playmates, and I don't know how it was with my brother, but I was not happy, particularly when we drove up the Lamborn Mesa road in a buggy one twilight, and as we turned in the lane leading up to the mountains my father pointed to the right, at a building with low, wide eaves, crouching in a barren fenced yard.

"There's where you boys will go to school," he said.

I was affronted and appalled, and I assured him with bitter resolution, "I'm never going to *that* little old school."

But that was a bridge I wouldn't be obliged to cross, and a gauntlet I wouldn't be obliged to run, for several months, and meanwhile we were getting settled in our new home. The "new" home—new to us, at any rate—sat at the head of the road which most closely approaches Mount Lamborn, where it curves north to return through Dry Gulch to Paonia.

It was a big, roomy old white house—white at least when my father and mother finished painting it—still standing across the road from a venerable, unpainted clapboard barn. West and north of the house were orchards and hay fields, and from the front windows of the house one could look across the creek and past Grandfather's barn to the old, lank, leaning gray house in which both my brother and I had been born.

With my grandfather dead, there was no man to run the place. Two of the sons were far away—Ed, the eldest, a barber in Missouri, and Ben, an osteopath in Puerto Rico. Waldo was practicing medicine in Paonia. But that first summer there was a festive gathering of the clan. My Aunt Hettie came over from Denver with her half-grown son, Floyd; my father pitched in; and Dr. Waldo Haley came up from town as his practice permitted, bringing with him his wife, Connie, and their two small sons. My Aunt Addie and her daughter Mary were already living on the place, so the old house echoed in the warm months of that year with talking and laughter and the tramping of many feet.

I have a recollection of Floyd, a boy of perhaps seventeen, working with the men shocking hay, a wide-brimmed straw hat on his head, and a red bandanna tied around his neck. He had a fair skin, city-pale ordinarily, but now nearly as red as the bandanna. Under the high-country summer sun he radiated little waves of heat as he stopped to take a drink from the dipper in the bucket of cool water we children were passing. He was an adolescent, one of those strange creatures too old to talk to children and too young to be understood by adults. I was aware that all those older relatives there that summer laughed at the things he said and did—asked him questions and then grinned and winked at each other when he answered. I didn't understand it—his answers sounded all right to me.

But it was pleasant to be among them all. There were splendid big meals three times a day in the dining room of the old gray house, with the women and little Mary serving and then, while the men ate, standing behind the chairs waving folded newspapers to keep the flies from settling on the food. And the conversations among these people who had spent their childhoods together were happy and enjoyable to listen to, jokes and stories of old pranks, and accounts of strange quirks of character.

At the noon meal there would be big platters of crusty fried chicken, with steaming bowls of gravy and mashed potatoes. Not the sort of fried chicken so common nowadays, when fryers are apt to be those tired hens who have flunked a laying test, but meat from real fryers, meat that almost melted in the mouth. And at such a meal someone was apt to recall the story of brother Ben, the Puerto Rico osteopath, who as a youth developed a system of commandeering all the best pieces. He would carefully select a piece every time the platter

Old barn on the mesa

was passed, take a bite from it and set it aside; then, when all the other children had finished their chicken and all the best pieces would be gone, Ben would still be calmly eating away at his horde of chicken goodies.

And this recalled still another story of how Ben had once hidden in the icehouse down near the woodpile on the old Missouri farm while my father, Bob, and sister Addie were fetching firewood. Ben had slipped a sheet over his head and made ghostly sounds at the upper window of the icehouse, and Bob had picked up a chunk of firewood and nearly brained the specter.

Then at night, with the men in from chores, there would be another big meal, ending with strawberry shortcake with real cream, or fresh cherry pie and homemade ice cream. And other stories and jokes would crop up, punctuated by Aunt Hettie's wry chuckle, and the hearty laughter of my father and my "Uncle Doc." Afterward, with the dishes done and the kerosene lamp set out to give off its serene and calming light in the center of the dining table, the stories might turn somber; perhaps the story of Charlie, eldest of the sons, the one who had disappeared, would be related.

There is a photograph of Charlie as a young man, taken on that bright spring day when he left the old ranch in Missouri for the last time. He is seated in a smart little cart with a fringed top, the horse in the harness and ready. Charlie's carpetbags are stored under the seat, the long tasseled whip is in the socket. He is wearing a stiff collar with the tips turned down, a resplendent tie, a suit with stripes an inch wide, button shoes, and on his full head of curly red hair a Panama boater. He is going out into the world to seek his fortune.

Letters came back after he left, and in them Charlie appeared to be doing well. The letters dwindled as the letters of a young man will, but about two years after he left, word was received by the family that something was wrong, and Grandfather Haley left for St. Louis. In a week or so he returned. Charlie had been killed on the streets of St. Louis by a madman, or so Grandfather told his family. He was of course shocked and saddened, but he was also strangely reticent. He refused afterward to talk about it, or to give any details at all.

So the talk would go on in the dining room, cool after the abatement of the day's heat; perhaps it would descend to more mundane topics, such as the price of hay or fruit, and the women of the family would go upstairs to prepare for bed. There was a door at the base of the narrow stairway which opened into the dining room and the front door opened in so that when both doors were fully open they nearly touched and formed a little passage, permitting the women in their night clothes to trail down in modest and stately dignity for a nocturnal visit to the sanitary facility behind the house without having to suffer the profaning glances of the men.

We younger children played together, but Doc Haley's two sons were already in to sports, and Ralph, the younger of the two, was an avid fisherman, and must have found our childish games less than engrossing. Not that he didn't enjoy himself, as we all did, during the pleasant summer, and particularly he enjoyed eating cherries. One day he partook too freely of cherries and ice cream and became rather indisposed. That night we four small boys slept upstairs in one of the big, unfinished bedrooms in my parents' house. Toward morning, Ralph leaped up and capered about on the bed in his sleep, shouting,

"Fishing's no good here; let's go on up the river—let's go up to Coyote Eyes—that's where the big ones are!"

But all good things end and the company returned to their homes—Uncle Doc and his family to his practice in Paonia, and Aunt Hettie with her son Floyd to their home in Denver. A man was hired part time to help out on the home place and now my father could concentrate more upon his own affairs. There was his own fruit thinning to be done, his own mowing, and in the fall, the picking of the fruit. The peach orchard was too small to bear and it was a slack year for the apple crop. But the cycle was supposed to swing in our favor the following year. A big crop was predicted, and on that our future on the farm depended.

And at least my father was not staring glumly around his barbershop on slow afternoons; now, there were no slow afternoons. If there was no mowing, or thinning, or irrigating or fence-mending to be done, then he was on call to help my mother as she cleaned and painted and papered the walls of the new old house. And at night he could relax after supper not having to "relax his face," as he said, from being pleasant to customers all day.

We all went to bed tired, and as the weather turned colder, we were serenaded each night by coyotes in the wild hills below Mount Lamborn. I had heard coyotes in Ridgway but they were at least a little distant then. Now they were neighbors, near neighbors at that, and there were many more of them. Here they gave regular concerts, or operas, with first one and then another performing a solo while his mates provided the chorus. I was always glad, after walking out before bed to have a last look at the stars, to dash up the kitchen steps, clutch at the knob and step inside and hear the door shut solidly behind me.

A Ranch is not a Barbershop

After our years in Ridgway, the whole family faced changes in our way of life on Lamborn Mesa. For one thing, my brother and I learned that once you left school at the end of the day, you weren't going to see your schoolmates again until the next morning; you wouldn't be playing with them after supper, or studying with them, or going to a movie. You had chores to do, you ate supper and then after dark the entire family would all be in the house, where each found some way to occupy himself until bedtime.

My father had brought along from Ridgway his two little milk cows, and he had purchased a neat team of mares which he stabled on his father's place—his own barn being only large enough to accommodate the cows. My brother and I—he was nine, I was seven—were indoctrinated into chores: bringing in the cows from pasture, helping to feed them, carrying milk from the barn to the separator in the kitchen, keeping the woodbox and the coal scuttle full and taking out the ashes. I suppose much of the time we were underfoot and as much of a nuisance as a help, but at least my mother knew where we were, which wasn't always the case in Ridgway.

And, my brother and I learned. There are opportunities on a ranch for a child to acquire certain types of information that are not that easy to come by in the town. Country children are not so mystified by the miracle of birth as their town cousins; they know, through the testimony of their own eyes, that the stork theory doesn't hold water where calves and foals are concerned. Of course all that mystery has pretty well disappeared now anyway, with the advent of television. But a country kid learns too that you have to do certain things for animals that they can't do for themselves, and you have to protect them from certain dangers.

If you bring a calf a bucket of milk, you can't just set it down in front of him and say,

"There's your supper."

If you do, the little fool will butt it over and the milk will flow out on the ground.

We acquired a dog, of a variety that was called "shepherd," although Border Collie is a more accurate description, and you learned that "Tip" could not be allowed to race around the hay field sniffing out snakes or field mice during mowing, because he was apt to have his legs sliced off by the mower's sharp blades. And when the mares foaled, one mare refused to allow her foal to suckle. She ducked her head at the unsteady little thing, nudged it away, and galloped off to the pasture, as unwilling as some human mothers are to give up girlish freedoms.

And as we children learned, so did our father. Once we went up to the Farmer's Mine after coal—my father, my brother and I—and on our way back the wagon became stuck in the river at the ford below the old Allison ranch. For an hour or more, as the early winter dark came on, my father urged and whipped and begged and threatened his little team, availing himself finally of the considerable vocabulary of expletives held over from his barbershop days, but the wagon with its load of coal could not be stirred. A man named Billy Underhill came along, though, and he unhitched his shaggy-looking team (Billy himself was rather shaggy-looking too) and my father's team was led away and Billy's harnessed to the load.

He spoke to them. They did not lunge frantically nor tug spasmodically. They seemed to know exactly what was expected of them. Their bellies moved down into the water of the ford and with a sudden but sustained lunge forward the load wavered a bit, and a bit more and came forward, and they pulled it swiftly and steadily up on to the gravel on the other side.

I often begged to be allowed to drive the team. Once when we came to a closed gate before my grandfather's barn, my father was driving his team in to hitch them to some instrument or other, I begged to be allowed to drive them through. He gave me the reins then, and went to open the gate, and I yelled "Giddup!" and strutted along behind the team, my shoulders back, feeling proud. My father didn't want it to go to my head.

"You're lettin' the reins drag in the mud," he said, but he smiled a little.

There was a problem that first fall with one of the cows. It was a rainy evening, and Dotty, the Holstein, always the greedy one, got into a patch of wet clover and gorged herself. During milking Father noticed that she was very quiet, and he finally concluded that she was bloated.

The first the rest of us knew of it was when he came rushing through the back door into the kitchen, not even removing his oiled slicker or his dripping hat, and reached down a book from the shelf behind the kitchen stove where the "doctoring" books were kept. He told my mother his fears, and he found the right page at last, and spelled out the instructions with his finger and his lips. Then he fumbled through the knife drawer in the work table and came up with a large butcher knife. He tested the edge of the blade, and bent prayerfully over the page in the book again.

"Oh Bob," my mother wailed, "are you sure you know what you are doing?"

"I'm sure she's a goner if I don't do something," he said, and spread out his hand in the air in front of him, as if he were measuring the space on the flank of a phantom cow. We all tramped along behind him down to the barn, my mother huddled in one of his discarded suit coats. The lantern he carried in his left hand made great shadowy arcs through the dark and the steel-colored rain. We crowded into the barn, and looked at Dotty. She was standing absolutely still in her stanchion, her ears back and her eyes rolling. But her head was about all I recognised of the Dotty I knew. No ribs were showing in her sides, and her hip bones were dimples.

"Come over here and hold up the lantern," my father called to my mother. "Hold it high. And hold it steady."

He laid his hand on Dotty's flank, measured a hand's breadth from where her hip usually was, took a deep, quiet breath, raised the knife up before his chin in both fists and drove it in.

Dotty sagged down. "Oh Bob, you've killed her!" my mother cried.

There was a wet whistling and a green cloud of vapor rising from where the knife had gone in. My father backed Dotty out of the stall and tugged her out and led her around the corral. She walked very slowly at first, but then faster, and her head came up and my father grinned at us.

"What do you think now?" he asked.

Another incident involving one of our animals that year didn't turn out as well. Tip, our dog, still little more than a pup, got out into the road when a horseman was driving some cattle by and was run over. My father took up in both hands the furry gray mass of what had been our pet and brought it tenderly into the yard. It was one of the few times I ever saw my father angry with another man but this time he was, because he thought the act was done deliberately.

And on a ranch, too, I was to learn, along with the tasks of bringing animals into the world and looking after their needs and protecting them from danger, there is another sort of task of an even less pleasant nature. For there comes a time when some of the stock are intentionally made to suffer death.

Some men, courageous enough otherwise perhaps, have trouble killing animals in this way. In some families it is the wife who is obliged to take up the axe or hatchet and face the moment of truth with the family rooster or pet hen at the woodpile. One relatively painless killing of a chicken took place in our orchard on a Sunday when my Uncle Doc and his two boys came up for dinner, and volunteered to dispatch the fryers. One bird, after being shot cleanly through the head, ran swiftly out through the orchard an astonishing 50 yards or more.

The slaughter of the pigs on my grandmother's place that fall was especially harrowing for my cousin Mary, who had become increasingly attached to the young pigs from the time of their birth. I was not that close to them, myself, and although I didn't actually look forward to their execution, I would have been able to handle it well enough, but she insisted that we go into a state of mourning, and she led the way upstairs, persuaded me to kneel with her beside the bed, and wailed and covered her ears at every report of the gun.

The only other encounter with the grim reaper that year was the natural death of a canary—it may have belonged to the Shoemaker children who lived nearby—but no matter; Mary supervised a formal interment for the departed bird. It was laid to rest in a match box decorated in pink tissue paper and surrounded with wildflowers down in the old woods pasture, after suitable ceremony.

One other incident involving the stock added to my fund of experience. In the winter thaw the cows were out in the orchard, where they ate some of the "shiners"—apples missed in the fall picking. These apples, some on the ground, a few still on the trees, were mushy and a wrinkled brown but the cows didn't seem to mind. They ate them greedily and when my mother looked out of the kitchen window where she was doing the noon dishes, she couldn't believe her eyes. Our two cows, usually rather dignified, were staggering blowsily around, belching, and leaning in an unladylike manner against the trees. They were drunk from the fermented fruit, and even my mother, who at once labeled the spectacle degrading, couldn't help laughing.

And we found ways to amuse ourselves in the evening without television or radio. Sometimes my cousin Mary and her mother, Aunt Addie, who lived with my grandmother, would come over after supper and we would pop corn. When winter came, on such an evening my mother would make ice cream by mixing thick cream and sugar and vanilla flavoring with a bowlful of fresh snow. On one such night, though, she decided to achieve a little variety by using lemon flavoring rather than vanilla, and my brother, first to get to the bowl, took a spoonful and held his mouth, howling "Limament! Limament!" alerting the rest of us to the fact that my mother had poured "flavoring" from the wrong bottle.

On those nights we three children under Cousin Mary's direction would present "shows" in which I would recite a Christmas poem I had learned for a holiday entertainment at the Ridgway school and

Mary and my brother would present an improvisation based on the rustic old song we had sung at school, "Reuben and Rachel." These entertainments were hardly professional in quality, but the audience, and particularly my father, seemed to find them amusing.

There was never any trouble finding something interesting to do. One day a winter blizzard came up; out of the windows, from morning light until dark, there was nothing to see but a white blankness, the steady swift fall of the snow. But my father made his way to the corrals and looked after the stock, my mother was busy hemming curtains, and my brother and I spent the day constructing little "tanks" out of empty wooden thread spools. The graduated ends of the spool were notched to make the treads, and power was provided by sticking a rubber band through the center hole, anchoring it on one side with a short length of match stick and on the other side with a match of ordinary length to act as a balance, and then twisting the rubber band to provide motive power. These little engines would crawl up and over small obstacles and rattle along at a good clip on a level linoleum floor—an early version of "The Little Engine that Could."

So life on the ranch that year was full of interesting happenings, some sad, some lively, some comical. On the whole, my brother and I must have found it a pretty satisfying experience. And so, I suppose, did our parents. And my father must surely have reflected now and again that winter, as he sat with his feet stretched to the heater, that it was certainly different on a fruit ranch than it was in the barbershop.

In the shop, his customers stepped out of the chair and deposited a quarter or a half dollar in his hand, and these went toward the keep for his shop and home and family. But now he was on a ranch, and half dollars were scarce and far away—in the pockets of customers who would pay only for good fruit. And out in the orchards the dormant apple and peach trees stood, bearing within them the secret of success or failure for the entire year for all of us—a secret not to be revealed until the fall rolled around again.

Don't Kill the Teacher, Jake!

My first reaction when I saw the little schoolhouse on Lamborn Mesa that I was fated to attend was indignation. Compared with it, the brick schoolhouse in Ridgway seemed palatial. But fall finally arrived and I was obliged to swallow my pride and trail off to school.

I had plenty of company. Not only was there my brother, a year and a half older, but my cousin Mary, a couple of years older, who promptly assumed the role of guardian and mentor. And then there were the Shoemakers, children of a family who lived just around the curve in the road that ran past my grandfather's old place and on down Dry Gulch to Paonia.

Now we took lunches to school, and it was pleasant, at first, to own a neat tin lunch box with a pair of hinged handles, its sides bearing brightly painted portraits of the Father of Our Country, though I never heard that he favored the plug tobacco the box had originally contained. The shiny interior of the box was lined daily with a clean dishcloth and it would contain sandwiches, an apple, and, around Christmas, more exotic surprises, such as an orange, hard candy, or dates. Then there was that new confection to which I was introduced by my cousin Mary, a bread sandwich with a filling of cream and sugar. Sometimes I would find a little jar of canned fruit— peaches, plums, cherries or pears—tucked in, along with a spoon. On the way home the empty jar and the used spoon would bump and rattle around in the box as we played tag with the Shoemaker children.

There were children of all ages in the school that year, as a photograph I still own attests, a few of us in every one of the eight grades. We are posed on the wooden front steps. My brother is standing in the front row, his knickers mussed, his stockings twisted, his shoes untied. His head lolls over on his shoulder; his features are idiotically distorted.

I look much more presentable. One of the reasons for that is that I am standing a row in front of a pretty little blonde-headed girl with whom I don't remember ever holding a conversation, but who was nevertheless "my girl." The older boys and girls are in the back row with our teacher, a plump-faced pretty young woman of Scandinavian ancestry with warm brown eyes. A decided improvement I had to admit over grim Miss Cusick of the punishing ruler who patrolled the aisles of the Ridgway school.

My brother got into the bad graces of the larger boys early in that first term. At noon we all sat in the schoolhouse to eat our lunches during inclement weather, and on this day the boys had gathered in the primary section and sat on the little children's chairs. As one of the boys started to seat himself, Harold pulled the chair back, and the victim's rump bumped to the floor from a height of perhaps ten inches. I think it did him no harm, but it was a blow to his dignity, and moreover it was delivered by the new boy, who was still not fully accepted, so the victim, looking into the solemn faces of his companions and assessing the situation correctly, began to cry. He was eating canned Royal Anne cherries with the seeds in at the time, and as he cried, he spit cherry pits out of the corner of his mouth; a truly forlorn spectacle. So that night after school the other boys conspired to teach my brother a lesson. And I, instead of staying at his side and doing my best to help out, ran in to enlist the support of the teacher, who couldn't make up her mind to act in time to do Harold any good. As a result, my brother tramped home that night looking a little more used-up than normal, and I received a well-deserved lecture from my father on family loyalties.

But over the days and weeks that followed, differences were composed, and we all became, as most country school student bodies do, a family unit. The school day began with a song or two, and ended, if there was time, with the teacher reading to us from a general favorite, such as one of the Oz books. In between there was little time to be bored. Classes usually lasted 30 minutes and sometimes less. Eighth-graders could nudge each other over the amusing recitations that went forward in the lower grades, and members of the lower grades, when the upperclassmen clumped to the front in their turn, could listen and wonder at revelations in history, geography, science, and current events.

When the snows came, getting to and from school down the three-quarter-mile lane from our home proved a bit more difficult. On one morning my brother and I were out on the road considerably later than the other children, and the snow was coming down steadily as we thrashed and stumbled along. I deeply dreaded arriving late, picturing all those scornful eyes focused on us, and continually sought encouragement from my brother. And on one of the occasions when he impatiently waited for me to catch up, he said,

"You see the way all the snowflakes slant to the right?"

"Yes."

"Well it's not nine o'clock then, because after nine o'clock they all start falling crossways."

I never questioned this. It sounded reasonable enough, and I was encouraged to flounder on, but although the snowflakes were still definitely slanting to the right when we arrived at the front steps of the school, singing was going on inside and it was somewhat after nine. (My brother went on to do well enough in a financial way eventually, but I have often thought that if he could have gone early into sales, and had the same success with convincing customers as he had in convincing me of various "facts" all through our earlier years, he would indeed have been a rich man.)

The snow had its uses, though, for the children at least. It proved a marvelous aid to entertainment. At recess we younger children tramped out wide circles in which to play games of tag, and we built snowmen, and the older boys built forts and pelted each other and the girls with snowballs. By the time the holidays were coming along I was quite reconciled to our new school. The room had been decorated for Halloween, and again for Thanksgiving, and at Christmas there were not only decorations, but a Christmas program and party, attended by all the parents. My brother provided a few moments of excitement after refreshments, by racing down the aisle during a game of tag and falling against a desk, chipping a tooth.

After the February thaw came the cold, shrill winds of March, with the ruts in the road stone hard in the morning, and ankle deep in mud by midafternoon. Meanwhile we classmates were all learning more about each other, and beginning to piece out the fabrics of each other's lives.

There was Jake. He was in the upper grades, perhaps the seventh, and he claimed to be half Indian. He was tall and slender for his age, rather light in complexion, with a sharply defined nose, and eyes rather close together and slightly crossed over which he wore thick glasses. He was remarkably good at drawing pictures and cartoons, and was actually taking a course by mail in the subject. One of these cartoons was of a knight of the road tramping down a railroad track, and the drawing gave me my first conception of perspective as I saw how those tracks in Jake's drawing seemed to merge in the remote distance.

Jake was a good son to his middle-aged parents, both of whom looked much more Indian than he. He never had time to dally on the school grounds to play after school, and in the mornings he never came into the school yard until shortly before the final bell, although their farm was quite near, because he was doing chores. If he did arrive early, those boys who had made our first days at school more difficult also loved to think up ways of bedeviling and testing Jake. One morning they began a game of seeing who could hold a pocket watch out at arm's length without moving for the longest period of time. They naturally timed this game to coincide with Jake's arrival at school and challenged him to compete, knowing how proud he was of his Indian blood.

Jake was bare-headed, in his usual cold-weather costume of denim shirt open at the throat and bib overalls tucked into laced boots. He took the watch, extended his arm stiffly from the shoulder, and held it there for five minutes—much longer than any other boy was able to. Then without any sign of fatigue he stalked into the school.

Another contest which Jake himself initiated—and which no one else cared to attempt—was to hold himself erect, arms at sides, and fall over backwards on the frost-hardened ground. Again, of course, without any display of emotion.

But there was a game one day which did arouse Jake's emotions, and he was known to have a fierce temper when aroused. The game was "Cops and Robbers," which the big boys often played at noon. On this particular noon the other players contrived to capture Jake and lock him in the coal shed where robbers were customarily incarcerated for ten-minute intervals—after which they were released with a full pardon and became "cops" in their own turn. But as we all know sometimes the machinery of the law works very slowly, and in this case the 10 minutes elapsed, then 15, then 25, and not until the bell rang for the return to classes was Jake released.

He came out with his Indian blood at a war-path boil, like a Spanish fighting bull into the ring, and with his hands full of pebble-sized pieces of coal. Disregarding the teacher's commands and pleadings—or probably not even aware of them—he chased his tormentors around and around the school. Into the back door they went and out through the front; he shied a piece of coal at the head of one of them which fortunately missed, but made a deep dent in the door frame. Then out the door he loped, and away to his home, to return at once with a corn knife in his hand. The teacher had seen him coming and had gone out in the road to forestall him, but one look into those glasses and the blue eyes behind them, smoking with wrath, convinced her that Jake was in no mood to be reasoned with, and she turned, in her fragile shoes and narrow skirt, and hobbled up the road in front of him, crying out the name of a school board member who lived nearby. When she arrived at the gate leading into the school yard, she turned in, and Jake neatly and securely planted the tip of the corn knife in the top of the cedar post nearest her head.

He turned back then, toward his home. There was a furor over the incident, and there were those excitable adults in the community who said that Jake had attempted to murder the teacher. But good sense prevailed in the end. The school board decided that Jake had not really intended to murder the teacher; a board member pointed out that he had more respect for Jake's accuracy with a weapon than that—if he had intended to harm the teacher he would have done so.

Our teacher, too, evidently concluded that he bore her no animosity and was only out for revenge against the other boys. He was shortly back in school, and there were no more problems. Jake kept his distance from the other boys, and they, awed by his rage, left him strictly alone.

Jake went on up through the grades in the town schools, making good records, and years later I met him face to face on a narrow mountain road near Lake City. His pickup was headed downhill, and my sedan was headed up. The rule of the road in such circumstances is that the vehicle headed downhill should give way, but I didn't want any trouble. There wasn't any. Jake, by then an engineer with the U.S. Bureau of Reclamation, cheerfully and courteously backed up around the curve in the road to a pullout and waved as I passed by.

Old Folks at Home

I had the usual number of grandparents, but I never saw much of them. My mother's mother was the most shadowy figure of all; she died long before I was born. My mother's father, Grandfather Perry, I know only by a photograph, taken as he sits between his two youngest children. He is a small but muscular man. His gray hair is cut short and carefully parted and combed. He wears a full beard and mustache. He was a rancher and horse trader; he homesteaded one of the first ranches in the Maher country above Crawford.

Even allowing for the time (most people, including children, didn't smile in photographs then, at least not in western Colorado) my grandfather looks stern. I asked my mother about him, but I was never able to get much out of her. She was always determinedly loyal to all relatives.

"What was my grandfather like?" I asked her.

"He was a good man."

"Was he a pleasant man?"

"He was pleasant enough, I suppose."

"Did he tell jokes?"

"He wasn't much for jokes."

"Did you and he talk?"

"Not too much."

"Was he strict?"

"Yes, he was kind of strict."

I gave up then. That was the way it was with my mother. If you wanted to learn something from her, you had to ask the right questions. Like a trained witness in court, her answers were relevant, competent, and material, but not too informative. I did learn eventually that my mother's mother had died when my mother was very young, and my mother's older sister had kept house for their father, and when she married my mother kept house for him in her turn. I think he wasn't much for jokes, and I think he was strict, at least to the point of thinking that children should be seen and not heard, and that a woman's place is in the home.

And over the years, through patient prodding and from talking with my Aunt Ina, I also learned that he was brought up in the Blue

Grandfather Perry with younger children

Ridge Mountains of Virginia, and had fought in the Civil War on the Southern side, as a personal aide to General Fitzhugh Lee. Mostly I think he looked after the General's mounts; apparently he knew and loved horses. Several were shot from under him during the war, and

Aunt Ina showed me a vest once that he had worn, and a small Bible he had carried over his heart. He had kept it in a metal case, and a bullet had seared a path across the case. There were four bullet holes in the vest, but he had never been seriously injured.

After Aunt Ina married and after my mother left the ranch to work in a store in Hotchkiss, Grandfather Perry returned East, to that part of the Smokies that probably always seemed home to him. He married again, a woman I think my mother never knew nor saw, and spent his later years as a horse trader. As he lay dying, he sent word for my mother to come back to see him one last time, but she was married then, and pregnant, and did not go.

My other grandfather, Grandfather Haley, whom I actually saw in the flesh, was a much gentler man by all accounts. His daughter Addie always spoke of him in hushed tones. He was remembered with affection by everyone. He had served as mayor of Paonia, and when he died, the places of business along Grand Avenue closed as a mark of respect. Grandfather Haley had farmed in Missouri, and later in Colorado.

I only saw him once in my life. That was on a summer afternoon and he was sitting out in front of the house on Lamborn Mesa under an old cottonwood tree. He had taken me up on his lap, or I had been placed there; I was three or four years old at the time.

I looked up into that pleasantly crinkled face, hallowed in the sunlight flickering down through the green leaves. It was a very large face, as all adult faces seem to small children, and ovoid. His white hair was thin, and he wore a handlebar mustache. There were voices and laughter from somewhere near; from inside the house, perhaps, where the womenfolk were preparing a holiday meal. But I was not paying attention to anything else; I was concentrating on the face of my grandfather.

Grandfather Haley died rather tragically. He yearned after wealth, but it always eluded him. When he was in his 70's, he conceived the notion of mining for gold; a prospector had found a promising claim somewhere up in the Crested Butte country, and Grandfather became interested and involved, and the old man had gone up there, and had been treated very unfeelingly by his partner, or so my Aunt Addie and others were convinced. He had forced my grandfather to work brutally hard, had deliberately bruised his hands, and made life in general quite miserable for him. Grandfather totally exhausted himself, contracted pneumonia up there and died. Of course, in those days, before oxygen was available for treatment, contracting pneumonia in the high country was invariably fatal.

My brother cried a little at the news of my grandfather's death. He was a little older and had seen more of him than I. My father, who was barbering in Ridgway then, attended the funeral. In those days, even in these, a death in the family is of course a sad occasion, but it also provides the opportunity for relatives and friends to get away from the daily grind, and it can be germinal, enabling them to stand aside and look at their own lives. In this case the journey resulted in my father conceiving the notion of returning to the North Fork and going into fruit farming, so over the next few years I had the opportunity of becoming acquainted with my sole surviving grandparent.

Grandmother Haley was quite a different sort of person from her husband. It was one of those cases where everyone says they don't understand how people so different in outlook and temperament could ever get together. Where my grandfather had a sunny disposition, Grandmother was inclined to be moody. Aunt Addie's daughter Mary saw more of her than I did, and she said that when they were all living on the ranch together, that Grandmother Haley would get into one of her black moods occasionally, and just disappear, and then, as Mary put it, the whole family would be obliged to drop everything, turn out, and "beat the bushes for Grandma."

I must have seen her a number of times but I remember only two encounters clearly. One was in the hospital near the Methodist Church, where she was recuperating from a heart attack. She was in one of her good moods, and we had a most companionable little visit, in the course of which she let me sample a teaspoonful of the whiskey provided to her as medicine. I found it very pleasant. It was properly aged and smooth—nothing like the sort of stuff that was in general circulation in those Prohibition years, and which I did not sample for some years after.

The other time I remember seeing her was in the little cottage on North Fork Avenue, after she had moved off the ranch and down into town. She was sharing the cottage with her widowed daughter, Addie, and Aunt Addie's daughter Mary. Aunt Addie was as loving and gentle as her father had been, but an incredible housekeeper. She could never bear to part with anything. She had a particular reverence for the printed word, and magazines and newspapers stood in boy-high stacks in the living room.

The table in the kitchen, following a custom common then when there were no electric refrigerators, was a repository for all sorts of containers of comestibles, the butter dish, little sauce dishes of jams, jellies, pickles and compotes, together with various leftovers from previous meals, placed there in bowls and on platters, and with the whole chastely draped with a dishtowel or doily in the dubious hope that some of it would prove edible later.

Aunt Addie carried this thrifty habit to bewildering extremes, so that there was hardly room on the oilcloth-covered surface of her kitchen table to set plates for the ensuing meals. There was a fairly commodious pantry off the kitchen, but it was so jammed with food containers of all descriptions—full, half-full and virtually empty—that it was not possible to enter this terra incognita more than a gingerly step or two.

Occasionally, prodded by my desperate grandmother, Aunt Addie would be driven to the doleful extreme of trying to bring some order out of it all. She would then pin on an old hat, sniff sadly a couple of times in a way she had, and sit down on the floor in the middle of the living room and begin slowly sifting through the horde of old *Capper's Weekly's, Grits,* and *Pathfinders* trying to find some clearly not worth saving, but with very little success.

I had stopped in late one sunny morning at the cottage to see Grandmother. She was sitting in the living room, sharing the old wicker overstuffed with a wad of dirty laundry. The old poll parrot was holding forth on the back porch, but I knew the minute I stepped in the front door that the rest of the household was not sharing his cheerful mood. I knew it in the distracted way Aunt Addie, a dish towel over one shoulder, was moving around in the kitchen, from the covered pans on the stove to the cluttered table, to the stack of *Pathfinders* on the sewing machine under the window. Her mouth was set in a lugubrious way, and she was sniffing more rapidly and deeply than usual.

"Now you see the way I have to live, Glen," Grandma said. Her voice carried well in any case, but she was speaking this morning in good round tones that could be heard easily in the kitchen—or even in the bedroom, where, behind the closed door, Addie's daughter Mary, not yet up, was reading a movie magazine.

"Don't you envy me?" Grandma went on; "You see the kind of care I'm getting. Isn't this a fine way for me to be treated—a fine sort of care for an old lady to receive?"

But just the same, I wish I could have known all my old folks better. From a purely selfish point of view, I think it might have resulted in my having a greater sense of inner security, and perhaps a better structured personality. And at that, I suppose, I saw as much of them as many young people of today do, when old folks are apt to expeditiously disappear into rest homes.

And I have cherished their memory. My strongest memory of all, perhaps, is the voice of Grandmother Haley heard during her better days, with the dark shadings in it, and a homely graininess that somehow reflected warmth and security.

Soap, Salve, and Sin

When we were living on the Lamborn Mesa ranch I conceived the notion of going into sales. I was seven at the time, and I saw this advertisement in *The American Boy*. It was an offer from the Sun Manufacturing Company of Binghamton, New York. They would send a consignment of their soap and salve to an ambitious youngster, who could then sell these fine products to friends and neighbors, reaping a substantial profit. I remember the company was based in Binghamton because superimposed on the ad was a steaming locomotive, together with the motto,

"Binghamton pays the freight."

I sent for a consignment, with my parents' permission, of course. It arrived promptly and I was thrilled with it. The neat box was layered full of soap in wrappers of pale blue-green and salve in tins of the same color with a smiling sun emblazoned in black on the top of each, and a description of the benefits that would accrue to the fortunate purchaser.

My mother and father looked it all over very carefully. The soap was pale blue and had a pleasant scent, and the salve, a transparent green, was even more inviting in appearance. They decided it was unlikely to prove harmful to anyone, but they were a little skeptical about the claims made for the salve, which was guaranteed to help all sorts of problems, from shingles and erysipelas to warts and cold sores.

I had pretty fair luck peddling both products around the neighborhood. My mother felt duty-bound to buy the soap, having already unwrapped a bar, and she took a tin of the salve, too. So did my grandmother. There was no use stopping at the Shoemakers— everyone knew how poor they were—but Ruth Hoskins, who was going to high school in town and lived with her parents a quarter mile down the road toward the schoolhouse, took a bar of soap. Mrs. Huddleston, considered a little strange, failed to come to the door, though I was certain she was home, but Miss Lundine, our teacher, bought soap and salve. Mrs. Plake took the salve, and both Mrs. Dewoody and Mrs. Vogel claimed they were well stocked with soap and salve and weren't at present in the market.

And so, despite a fair success with "friends and neighbors," the closely packed little cardboard box was still better than half full. Another attractive feature of the Sun Company's offer was that if all the soap and salve were sold within a month and the company's share of the proceeds promptly returned, the "agent" would be in for a special surprise gift—and the days of grace were winding down.

It was plain that special measures were in order, and finally it was decided that I should have a Saturday to try my luck in town, in company with my brother, older than I and therefore deemed more responsible, to see if we couldn't clear the shelves or at least substantially reduce the inventory. I was a little reluctant, since my brother would now be installed as a full partner, and be entitled to a half interest in the surprise gift as well. Still, it was an emergency situation, and I was forced to agree.

In town we early encountered a friend about our age, a sort of shirttail relation of my mother's, Happy Harmon, who always wore a beanie and had a crooked right forefinger; he was at liberty that day and decided to make the rounds with us without making any claim for payment, but just as an act of friendship. And we did very well. The salve went first; its pleasant odor and clean clear greenness made it easier to dispose of; but finally all the soap was gone, too, and the afternoon was only half over.

Of course we were in a jubilant mood and it occurred to my brother, to me, or perhaps to all three of us, that we really deserved some little extra reward. My brother was in charge of the funds and it was decided the partnership would spring for a round of ice cream sodas for the entire crew. And then all restraints were off. Faced with the long tramp back to the ranch, it only seemed natural we should have something a little more substantial in our stomachs, so we adjourned from the drugstore to Josh's hamburger stand and found ourselves ordering, not the five-cent hamburgers, but three short-cut steaks with fried potatoes at forty cents an order, probably the first restaurant meal that any one of the three of us had ever eaten. After that, dazed at our daring and completely corrupted, we returned to the drugstore and tapered off on ice cream cones and crackerjacks.

By now the shades of evening were drawing nigh; the town clock in front of the First National chimed the hour of six; there was not only something melancholy about those chimes, but foreboding as well. My brother checked over what remained of the day's receipts—it did not take him long—and we walked with Happy to the mouth of the alley that led up past the Harmon place. Our farewell to him was subdued, and we watched him go with envy. He had nothing to worry about. No one was waiting for him with prying questions; no one would be looking down at him with accusing eyes. He could sit down at the family table and eat supper (if he had room for any) and go to bed with a clear conscience.

As we walked up the Dry Gulch road, we mumbled over together possible alibis, explanations—lies—that might work, but we could come up with nothing that sounded very convincing. The moon rose over the shoulder of Mount Gunnison and stared pitilessly down on us; the down-river wind lowered our heads and brought our shoulders in.

A lamp was burning in the kitchen as we crept in the front door, and my mother and father were both waiting for us back there. It has never been my fate to stand in a courtroom, to be faced with a serious accusation and grilled by a cold-eyed prosecutor, but the experience that night will do instead. First we had to account for arriving so late, but that was the least of our troubles. Our pockets were emptied and the discrepancy in accounts was made plain for all to see. My father took those two or three heavy, purposeful steps to where the razor strop hung behind the stove, and my brother and I performed, in turn, our little flagellation tarantella.

Then, bed without supper, which was no deprivation, since our stomachs were well-lined anyway, and our back sides were certainly much warmer than they had been when we first came in. But we bore in our consciences the burden of our guilt.

Later it was said to be common for larcenous tykes to order consignments of products, such as soap or seed packets, to sell around the neighborhood, after which (sometimes, it is sad to report, with the active connivance of their parents) they would thumb their noses at the firm which sent the products and pocket the entire proceeds. At least the American Seed Company gave this as one reason for the permanent closing of their doors. But there was never any such idea in the minds of my parents. Although money was hard to come by for my father at the time, he saw to it that the Sun Manufacturing Company, of Binghamton, New York, received their full due.

That was my first and last experience as a door-to-door salesman. And, it was about the last shared enterprise that my brother and I ever willingly undertook. In the way of many brothers, we pretty well found different paths as we grew older.

I do remember an enterprise, if you can call it that, actually more of a scientific or physiological experiment, which my brother and Happy Harmon collaborated in a year or so after the soap-and-salve caper. This time it involved pills which arrived through the mail, sent to a number of Paonia residents, and most of which ended up in the post office wastebasket. Happy and my brother each tried a few of the pills, which had a bright, candy-like appearance. I was not that adventurous. And I was glad later that I hadn't been when at their request I accompanied the pair to the alley behind Grand Avenue and observed the fascinating change the pills had wrought in one of their bodily functions, changing what was normally a pale yellow stream to one of royal purple. As far as I know, neither of them suffered any other effects, good or ill.

But, to return to the soap and salve. The company had received the returns within the month of grace, and in good time the special surprise gift arrived (freight-free, of course). It was a kite. Not too sturdy a one, but in any case, neither my brother nor I was much interested in playing with it. It reminded us too vividly of that high-flying afternoon when we proved to our lasting regret the truth of Mr. Micawber's observation in Dickens' *David Copperfield,* that when outgo equals income there is felicity, but when outgo exceeds income, misery is the inevitable result.

Up on the Mesa,
Down in the Town

During our second year on the ranch, on a bright day in early August, a little storm whipped up. It only lasted ten or fifteen minutes, but when the skies had cleared, magically, as they can after such a storm, the sun never shone as brightly again for my father. The storm had brought not rain, but hail. His crops were ruined, and his resources were at an end. He began to spend more time than usual talking to my mother in the kitchen after supper, and you could hear them sometimes, talking together in the same low, worried way, in their bedroom at night.

The result of it all was that on a number of weekends late that fall and early winter my father would drive the buggy into town early of a Saturday and work the day in a barbershop. Another indication that a change was in the wind was that individuals, sometimes a man alone and sometimes a couple, began stopping at our place of an afternoon to be taken on a tour of the outbuildings, fields, and orchards by my father, and then through the house by my mother. I recognized one of the couples. They lived on a rented farm at the lower end of the mesa and their two sons attended the Lamborn Mesa School. They were all dressed up, he in a suit and she was wearing a good coat and a flowered hat.

When my parents were called away during this visit, I felt that this couple was temporarily in my charge so I naturally laid myself out to be pleasant. And, as any reasonably bright kid knows, you can't talk to grownups about prairie dog holes or where the best mud is to be found on the ditch bank; that won't hold their attention. So, I fell back on statements and observations I had heard my father make about the place, and I could see they were interested in what I had to say.

My folks came back in a few minutes, and a little later the couple climbed back into their buggy and drove off. Afterward, I was a little nervous. It was the way my father looked at me. My mother, too. Their expressions were somewhere between exasperation and amusement. My father asked me if in the course of the conversation with the visitors I had happened to mention that the ranch had a poor water right. He said that was what the man had told him I had said. I said I didn't remember exactly. I was relieved when they smiled at each other. Not much, and a little wearily, but a little.

So, those people didn't buy the place. But Big Jim Smith did, or, rather, he traded for it. He had property in Paonia, a two-storied, false-fronted building on the south side of Grand Avenue next to the Paonia Hotel; a blacksmith shop and a livery stable up on Second Street across from the Opera House; and behind the Opera House, on Poplar Avenue, a two-storied frame house. The building on Grand Avenue contained a barbershop on the ground floor, and a storage loft abovestairs which we would have to fix up for temporary living quarters, since the Smiths could not give up their home on Poplar until we vacated the house on the ranch.

I never had the chance to make Big Jim's acquaintance, actually. I wouldn't be surprised to learn that my father was careful to see that I didn't—at least not before the trade was completed. And afterward we were all so preoccupied getting established down in the town that Big Jim's path never crossed mine. But I had seen him. He was a big man indeed, with the sort of stomach that would have looked good under a saloonkeeper's apron. And it had for many years been sheltered under just such an apron, for saloonkeeping had been his trade for many years both in Paonia and earlier in the mining town of Somerset up the valley. Now he customarily wore a white shirt with a string tie, a wrinkled gray suit, with a vest of course—all men wore vests with their suits in those days—black blucher-toed shoes with white socks, and an old gray hat with a medium brim. He had a gray walrus mustache to complete the ensemble.

Big Jim and his family didn't live on the Lamborn Mesa ranch for the rest of his life, if my memory serves. I think he found, after his two grown sons turned to other occupations, that retired life on a fruit ranch wasn't all that halcyon, and he moved back to town, or to the outskirts, and lived out his life in a brown bungalow that nuzzled the road behind the grade school playground. But at least once during the time he was living on the mesa ranch he was called upon to perform a public-spirited act which involved the use of some of the skills he had picked up at the saloonkeeping trade. I learned of it, years later.

There were in the North Fork country in those days men who had been maimed in the Great War. Some had lost limbs or their lungs had been damaged from inhaling mustard or chlorine gas, but others suffered from mental infirmities perhaps even more disabling than the physical ones.

One such man, a bright little squirrel-like individual whom I shall call Harvey, ran a ranch on the mesa, but occasionally would be afflicted by violent hallucinations. When these occurred, his wife and children would get away promptly and call in several of Harvey's old army buddies to see that he was safely dispatched to a facility in the eastern part of the state, where such cases were handled. Then, after a period of rest and recuperation he would be returned to his family. These friends took pride in not calling in the authorities to help in this task of calming Harvey and sending him away, and the sheriff understood and was willing to have this done; besides, his office was over 20 miles away in the county seat and he could not respond all that quickly.

This particular spell of Harvey's proved especially violent, and he was being extraordinarily cunning and resourceful so that after several hours he still had not been brought under control. Finally, a couple of his friends decided to call upon Big Jim for help. He agreed to lend a hand. When he arrived at the house on Harvey's place—it was a balmy night in the fall—it was easy to see that something was going on. Lights were on in every room, windows were up, doors were open front and back, and Harvey's voice, loud and denunciatory, could be heard in the living room. Jim and his two companions went around to the back and sneaked into the kitchen.

It appeared that Harvey was under the delusion that he was a corporal in charge of an army squad, and he had his troops lined up in formation and was conducting what is euphemistically known among the military as a "short-arm inspection." He was lurching and skipping and jumping about like a sparrow, waving a big butcher knife, and making lewd, uncharitable remarks about the physical endowments or peculiarities of his "squad" as well as impugning their standards of personal hygiene. Big Jim waited patiently just inside the kitchen door until Harvey came within reach, and he suddenly stepped in and put a hammerlock around the little man's neck, lifting him off his feet.

Harvey struggled and gurgled and waved his knife, but Big Jim maintained the pressure.

"Drop the knife, Harve," he advised, and Harvey finally did. But before he released him, Big Jim asked, "Are you going to be good, Harve?" and when the little man finally nodded, he let him go.

Harvey was quite calm after that, and cheerful. He came up to Jim, patted his forearm and said,

"You're a strong man, Jim," and allowed himself to be led to the waiting car.

All of this happened much later on. Meanwhile, Big Jim's sons were looking after the ranch, my father took over the management of the barbershop and my poor mother shouldered the double responsibility of keeping my brother and me clothed and fed and in school on the mesa while on the weekends she and my father were making ready the temporary quarters over the shop.

The upstairs was, as my mother described it, "A sight."

"I was just awestruck," she said. Two cluttered little rooms, partitioned off at the rear, had from time to time accommodated batching barbers, and the rest of the space was full of dust-burdened barrels, packing boxes and discarded tonsorial equipment. The stairs that led up to the rooms at the rear were rickety, and the red galvanized tin that roofed them was in tatters.

So, although my father would come up when the work in the shop permitted on Saturdays to see how things were going (with a comb tucked behind his left ear) it was my mother who superintended plumbing and heating repairs and the disposal of trash and then the scrubbing, mopping and painting. My brother and I were only available for help on weekends and then we didn't do all that much except for the running of errands.

I suppose our retreat from the ranch represented a comedown in the world, but I am sure this didn't bother my brother or me. Small children, so long as they are loved and well-looked after, as we were, are not often critical of accommodations or conscious of social position. And, after all, we were town kids before we were country kids and we looked forward to a more exciting existence than we had had on the ranch.

The front windows over the barbershop looked out on Grand Avenue, and although our living quarters did not extend clear to the front, my mother saw to it that those windows were curtained, though no one wasted much time using them. The door on the stair landing at the rear opened into a narrow hall, with a bedroom at the left and another beyond, and a curtained doorway on the right opened into the kitchen. A window in there looked out on the back yard, an expanse of territory virgin except for weeds and a clothesline, and on beyond to the alley which ran along behind Grand Avenue. This alley itself was a busy thoroughfare for drays and wagons supplying the various shops and stores; occasionally the hearse bumped along it too, bound for the mortuary in the rear of the furniture store on the far corner of the block. At night the alley was illuminated by a street light on a telephone pole.

Beyond the alley lay Main Avenue, which was even less "main" than Grand Avenue was "grand." It was bisected by the Paonia Ditch, with a row of comfortable homes on the far side of the road, but with rather shabby little houses huddled under the ditch to the northeast, where the avenue crossed Second Street and then tailed off toward the river. My father, perhaps, did feel some regret at our move into this humble neighborhood, for I heard him once, when we were all in a spring wagon returning from a drive across the river, refer to that end of Main Avenue rather glumly as "Pig Turd Alley," a remark my mother deplored, especially because it had been uttered within the children's hearing.

But although we were leaving the ranch on the mesa without any particular regret on my part, our sojourn there did make an indelible impression on me. I had begun to read, avidly, and some of the books I enjoyed most were set by my imagination on that mesa. The little patch of scrubby cedars where the creek meandered through the pasture on my grandfather's place became for all time the *Secret Garden* of Frances Hodgson Burnett. The Tabler place just below ours became for me forever the inn described in Conan Doyle's historical tale, *The White Company*. And, when a few years later I was reading *Treasure Island,* my grandfather's place became the old Benbow Inn; Captain Billy Bones and the other guests at the inn sat out on pleasant evenings under the old cottonwood where I had once been placed in my grandfather's lap; and the pirates who came to kill Billy swept on horseback around the curve of the Dry Gulch road and ransacked the dining room and the upstairs bedroom of the old house where I was born.

In fact, the last clear memory I have of life on the mesa had to do with a trip I made on foot from the ranch down to town just about dark of an early winter evening. I could have ridden down with the rest of the family, but I had hidden out to read the tales of King Arthur; and no doubt to teach me a lesson, my parents had gone on without me.

It was Friday and my head was filled with stories of deeds of the noble knights, and, besides, on the last half hour of the school day, and without fail on Friday, our teacher was in the habit of reading to us from the books about Oz, so that evening as I walked along I alternately played in two different worlds. In one, I was a knight of the Round Table, armed with a sword I had whittled out of lath, and beset with enemies (dried weeds still standing on either side of the roadway). In that role I was obliged every so often to dash off to do battle, slashing and hacking the enemy down in bloody rows. The rest of the time I was skipping down the yellow brick road with my friends from Oz. I could even see, just beyond Cedar Hill, the faint glow of the magic city.

But I could not see clearly enough down that magic road to know what really lay ahead for me. In the little school on the mesa we were all one family, and spoiled, I suppose, to a degree. But it would be different down in the town. I could not descry the coming years of hacking and slashing away at the hordes of O's and racks of slanted lines in the red-covered book of Palmer Penmanship; the multiplication swamps and the long division bogs to be waded; the perilous thickets of Latin, algebra and geometry.

And it was just as well. I think if I could have seen all those frightful hazards ahead on my quest, even my mighty warrior's heart would have quailed.

III. DOWN IN THE TOWN

Shoeshine!

With my father back in the barbering trade, our lives went smoothly enough. My parents were very busy. My mother kept the apartment over the shop tidy, saw her husband off to work downstairs and her two small sons off to school, and once a week did the family wash. Weather permitting, she did this out in back, with tubs up on apple boxes and an old electric washer wheezing away. For a time she did the family laundry and the shop laundry too, but when business improved father sent the shop laundry to the Beals Laundry in the big, rambling old building across from Union Fruit.

My father worked at the first chair during the week and on Saturdays, pulling down the green blinds on the big front windows at nine on Saturday night (though laggardly customers came around after that, shook the door handle and rapped on the glass and were usually admitted). On Sundays father gave the shop a thorough cleaning, which included hosing out the brass spittoons, a chore he detested. He had laid new linoleum throughout the shop, and installed a new lavatory and a third chair.

It was a very lively time then; with the war over, the nation was on a buying binge, the coal mines up the valley were going full tilt, and Paonia fruit, grown in orchards all over the little valley and on the surrounding mesas, was bringing premium prices. The barbering business was going full tilt, too. There was another well-established shop just up Grand Avenue run by Art Laurence, a spidery little man with a wry sense of humor who always wore a green eye shade when he worked. In both his shop and my father's, one and sometimes two other barbers worked steadily.

I was now eight, my brother was going on ten. We were required to come directly home after school to do our "chores." We brought in the coal for both the apartment and the shop, cleaned bathtubs—there were four of them in the shop, in cubicles at the rear behind a tongue-and-groove partition—took out the ashes from the stoves, went to the stores on errands, and took turns working at the shoeshine stand.

The stand was positioned against the partition wall at the rear of the shop proper. It consisted of a platform two steps above floor level with a pair of steel footrests before each of two captain's chairs. Cut into the riser of the second step were three drawers to accommodate the tools of the bootblack's trade: bottles of dye, tins of polish—black, brown, cordovan—brushes, daubs, shine cloths of green baize retrieved from the pool hall next door when pool tables had been re-covered, and an antiquated case knife and some old toothbrushes to clean and daub the mudguards.

When we first started working at the stand it was a dismal gray in color, mottled and streaked by polishes and dyes, so my father purchased some dark brown paint: "Tobacco Juice Brown," he called it. He wanted it to be dark enough to conceal the stains and streaks of polish and dye, as well as to camouflage any other soil deposited by a customer, perhaps one not too accurate in his aim at a nearby spittoon.

Both my brother and I shined shoes, but we usually took turns at the stand, since business was slow except on Saturdays, when the ranchers brought their families in to shop and the coal miners and their families came down from the upper valley.

But we also took turns at first because of Dutch. Dutch had worked for the previous owner, and my father kept him on. Dutch was a jolly sort, older than my brother and I, though we never learned his age. He was in my grade, but I think he had missed a few years somewhere. His parents had drifted away, leaving him in the charge of his grandparents, an old couple who lived in a dusky cottage down toward the river. My father said they needed the money Dutch brought in shining shoes. The grandfather could be seen almost any evening in the summer, sitting in an old rocker on the sloping little front porch, a leather visor low over his eyes, a cane made out of a length of willow lolling against his heavy leg.

Dutch taught us, singly and together, the rudiments of his art. First you tucked up the customer's trouser legs to keep them from being soiled by the polish. Then you cleaned the shoes, soaping them if necessary with an old shaving brush, and wiping them clean with a strip of old toweling. If the shoes were badly scuffed, you might try to persuade the customer to go for a dye job as well as a shine, which raised the price of the whole operation from fifteen cents to a quarter. Then you daubed the polish on the shoes. Dutch disdained the use of a daub, slapping the surface of the polish lightly with the tips of his fingers and then the shoes in a syncopated beat. And although this way of doing it guaranteed that your fingers would be stained, it was the professional way, anyone could see that, and so my brother and I usually did it that way, too.

The polish, which my father ordered through a barber supply house, came in a shallow can about the diameter of a large orange. On the cover was the name of the maker, Whittemore, along with a drawing of a shoeshine boy with a portable stand slung over his back on a strap, walking down a city street. I identified with that boy: he and I were in the same business.

With the polish on, the next two steps were crucial. The way you performed them proved whether you really knew your stuff or not. First you took the brushes, if you were good enough to use two brushes—if your hands were small and your technique shaky, you used one, as I did—and buffed the shoes all over with a rocking rhythm. Then, the climax. You laid down the brushes, picked up the green shine cloth, stepped back to whip it behind you to make it snap and then laid into the shoes, sawing across them with both hands, stopping every so often to trail the cloth nonchalantly behind you to snap it again. As a final gesture you went to the sink for a few drops of water to flick over the vamp to heighten the shine.

The main idea behind all these flourishes was to convince the customer he was getting his money's worth both in service and entertainment. Neither my brother nor I were a match for Dutch as an attraction. He kept up a patter with the customer, whistling, chuckling, joking, and on demand even stopping to perform a little shuffle or jig. Sometimes he would play the mouth organ with one hand while buffing shoes with the other. He could play the musical saw, which he brought to work on occasion, and the fiddle, though he did not bring it to the shop. And when all else failed or things were a little slow, he could exhibit his teeth—he had two complete sets of natural teeth in his upper jaw.

Dutch soon found working conditions at my father's shop a little crowded, with two shoeshine apprentices to look after, and he moved up the street to stage his act at Art Laurence's shop, where, I am sure, he attracted more trade than the Haley brothers did. Though I think he may have made the move with some reluctance, because my father and he got along well together. Laurence, though, had the carriage trade in those days—the bankers, the lawyer, the doctors with the exception of my Uncle Waldo, the mortician, and the editor of the paper. I think they felt my father's shop lacked class—and Mrs. Laurence was much more socially involved in the community than our busy mother.

But my father and his customers had more fun. He was an entertainer in his way too. He greeted everyone in a friendly way, knew his customer's eccentricities about shaving and haircutting, provided any special services required, like singeing or massaging, and kept up a running stream of friendly talk, badinage or gossip if that was what seemed to be wanted, or remained respectfully silent if the man in his chair responded better to a quiet mood.

And, now and then he called upon me for a vulgar story, my

repertoire of such having expanded somewhat since the days in the Ridgway shop, though I had no more idea of what they really meant than I had before. They were always received, of course, with knee-slapping glee but they didn't seem all that amusing to me. I found the whole idea of sexual relations between the sexes grotesque, and rather distasteful. A foolishness dreamed up for sport. It never occurred to me that it had any serious or worthwhile function. I doubt if my mother would have found it amusing to hear me tell such a story, but I was aware that it was a part of the cabal of men versus women, and I wasn't supposed to tell her about them, and I never did.

As in Ridgway too you went to the barbershop for information on road conditions, say, on the East Muddy, on localities where fishing and hunting was best, on how the peach crop was progressing in the lower valley, or on who might need help there. Then, there was the sort of information that consisted largely of speculation and rumors, bits of gossip, and claims and observations passed around among the salesmen and young-bucks-on-the-loose regarding the susceptibility for conquest of certain widows in the community or other ladies of varying degrees of attractiveness and states of availability.

And, this being during Prohibition, it was even possible for a man to learn at the barbershop where he could buy a good bottle of bootleg; but at my father's shop a man with a thirst got this information from a source other than the first chair. My father was a teetotaler, and his customers respected his attitude; never, so far as I know, did any drinking take place around the shop. And he continued to detest the tobacco habit; a prejudice reinforced for him every Sunday morning when he growled and complained as he dealt with the spittoons.

In the shop in Ridgway and to a lesser degree in Paonia, my father inveighed against the barbering trade, but on the whole, in what proved to be the last months of his life, he was reasonably content. The shop was prospering, we had finally been able to move into the house on Poplar, and on Sunday afternoons he could get out and do a little small-game hunting with my brother. He had lived in Paonia as a young bachelor and had many friends there, and he was pleased and proud when his brother established a thriving medical practice.

Now, with our new prosperity, our family was able to attend the local movie house, the Gayety, and saw such films as "A Fool There Was," which would doubtless have received an "R" rating then, if such had been given, ending as it did with the original movie vamp, Theda Bara, strewing confetti along the body of her despairing suitor just after he had committed suicide. But more to the taste of my family were the straight-arrow westerns of William S. Hart, and the early Keystone comedies for which my father, with his easy, carrying laugh, provided more than his share of the voluntary laugh track. All in all, it was a good time.

Uncle Doc

Uncle Doc, my father's brother Waldo, was a marked man. The mark was on his left temple, a circle of pure white hair no larger than a quarter. It grew over the years, spreading slowly and insidiously in the brown pasturage of the surrounding hair and finally crept throughout. But he was a marked man in another respect; a man who always knew what he wanted, and that was to be a doctor. What misdirections and disappointments he struggled through in his early years I never knew. But by the time he actually set about becoming a doctor, he was in his late twenties or early thirties, with a wife and two small sons.

Fortunately for him and the fulfillment of his dream, the wife he had chosen, Constance, was aptly named. She was the daughter of a German immigrant, Joe Roatcap, who ran a sawmill in the high hills beyond Paonia and later farmed down near the town, in Roatcap Gulch, named in his honor. As a young girl she cooked for the sawmill crew, and when she married "Doc," a nickname he received in boyhood when he looked after disabled animals, she went with him to the West Coast, he pursued medical studies, while she ran a boardinghouse for oil workers and looked after her sons.

Doc intended from the beginning to practice in his home town, but at first it wasn't possible. Paonia at the close of WWI was prosperous enough, but also freighted with doctors, five of them. Moreover, they all held medical degrees and Uncle Doc was an osteopath in days when osteopathic training was looked down upon, so there was no likelihood of joining an older man in an established practice. The best solution for the time being was to begin in the nearby village of Crawford. This he did, renting a farm on the outskirts with an impressive barn but a modest house. Both structures still stand, six decades later, somewhat the worse for wear.

To this day, recollection of that barn and farm cause hallucinatory prickles to coast around in the region just below my spine. During the time Uncle Doc and his family were on the ranch and we had just moved back to Paonia, we spent a Sunday on the ranch and my brother and I played with our cousins, James and Ralph, boys of similar ages to our own. They took us up on Young's Peak, which

Uncle Doc's barn

shelters the town, where we had the ill luck to encounter some outriders of the juvenile McKisson clan, then at the height of their power in the environs of Crawford. The McKissons closed in, emitting fearful cries, and we, outnumbered and (it might as well be revealed) completely spooked, headed for home. As we scampered madly down the hill I misstepped, lost my balance, and ended up sitting in a patch of cactus. Agony. The McKissons overtook us, but finding one of us *hors de combat,* let us off with a stern warning.

Aunt Connie, as we always knew her, also garnered a painful memory from those days. During the time she and her family lived on the farm, two milk cows were kept in the barn, and one night with Doc as usual on a call she went out to milk, and a hornet dive-bombed her, making contact right between her brows. The next morning her husband and the astonished sons looked at a wife and mother whose pretty blue eyes had completely disappeared from view.

At last Uncle Doc felt strong enough in experience and with the loyal practice he had built up in the nearby Crawford country to venture into Paonia. The other doctors there solidly banded against him, but he was younger, a clever and innovative surgeon, a skilled diagnostician, and had the further advantage of possessing a most ingratiating and reassuring presence. His practice grew steadily. As one ailing patient expressed it,

"I begin to feel better the minute I see him coming up the walk."

And, overriding all other advantages was that of the support of his wife. Because he was not a member of the local medical association, it was soon necessary for him to establish his own hospital, which he did, requiring several nurses, and Connie ran the entire establishment as well as looking after her family and bearing her husband two more sons. Both she and her husband, especially in the early days, were busy all their waking hours. Once Aunt Connie was struck low with an attack of typhoid that nearly carried her off and in the course of which she lost most of her hair. Years later Uncle Doc laughed when he told how he went in to see her when she was plainly on the road back.

"What are you going to do first when we let you get up, Con?" he asked her.

Her eyes snapped open. "I'm going to work and work and work," she said.

His practice was an exciting and far-ranging one. I rode with him on some of his many calls in later years and he would tell me of operating and delivering babies on farm kitchen tables, at first only with the help of his wife; of coming in to a lonely ranch on Fruitland Mesa to discover an old man dead of malnutrition, with a porridge of wheat flour and water still sitting on the stove.

A particular challenge was caring for the needs of minority families. He told of sharing the evening meal with a Mexican family, and watching the wife prepare the tortillas by rolling them out on the smoothest object available—her naked upper thigh. Once he went out on a mesa to inoculate an Austrian family against smallpox. He worked his way through a phalanx of children and when at last he looked up and asked, "Is that all?" The children stared at him blankly until finally an older girl spoke up.

"All but Johnny," she said.

"Where's Johnny?" he asked.

"In the chickenhouse and he won't come out."

But after messengers were sent, and after a great cackling of chickens and a tremendous dust, Johnny was routed from his hiding place, cornered, and inoculated.

Immigrant Italian families loved Uncle Doc, and plied him with "Dago Red," as their wine was locally known, and of course drank plentifully of it themselves in the process. One Italian farmer went to bed tipsy after entertaining Doc late one night, and when the farmer's wife aroused him later in the dark bedroom to alert him to the fact that there was a skunk in the chickenhouse, he slipped into his long-handled underwear to find that the sleeves seemed endless: in his befuddlement and haste he had put them on upside down and backwards.

Pay was not always prompt. Once I stood beside my uncle at a high school football game—he was an ardent sports fan—and he kept encouraging one back by yelling,

"There goes my boy! There goes my boy!" and explained to me, "He must be mine—he was never paid for."

But paid or not, he always went on any call, anywhere and at any time.

My brother and I loved to visit at his home. It was an exciting place, always busy. Every meal was an occasion, particularly the noon meal, when Doc, his wife, his sons, (then numbering four) several nurses, visitors and a convalescing patient or so, would be seated around the great oval table; in the warm summer months everyone would be drinking iced tea, and his sons would all stir their tea at once, the spoons and the ice sounding like a medley feverishly played by Swiss bell ringers.

He was unfailingly sympathetic to all, including his relatives, whom he treated for free, although sometimes he became "fed up" as he would tell me, with his older sister, Addie, a widow with a multitude of eccentricities. She came at least once a week to his office with some complaint, although she was invariably in good health, and made it a habit to appear at his table often, and indeed often appeared at our family table. At Uncle Doc's she was often accorded—or managed to appropriate—a seat beside her beloved brother. Then, sometimes she would lean in toward him with a sniff, a mannerism of hers, and lay a hand on his arm and say, confidentially,

"Doc, if you don't pass me some more potatoes I guess I'll just have to stop eating." This annoyed him, particularly when everyone knew that she would still be at table after everyone else had risen, and he would snap, only half in jest,

"Stop eating then, for all of me," but then he would pass the potatoes.

Both of his sisters annoyed him. His other sister, Hettie, an osteopath herself with a practice in Denver, came over to visit in Paonia when she could, particularly when her parents were still alive. She took after her mother, nurturing a melancholy strain the family possessed, and my own father sometimes exhibited, and which only exasperated Uncle Doc. On one occasion, a death in the family—it may have been that of my grandmother—I was riding in the front seat of a sedan following the hearse slowly up Cedar Hill to the cemetery, and Aunt Hettie sat in the rear with Uncle Doc beside her.

"Well, Doc," she said mournfully, with a perverse, almost

Uncle Doc and Aunt Connie

lubricious pleasure, "we've followed a good many of them up this old hill."

I was watching his reaction through the rear-view mirror, and I saw him pull his shoulders in, and scrunch lower in his seat, looking as if he had just bitten into a lemon.

On the other hand he seemed to get along quite well with his brother, my father, Bob. My father was very proud of him, and they enjoyed each other's success.

One pleasant midsummer evening my father accompanied his doctor brother to see a patient on Stucker Mesa, west of Paonia. I asked to go along, but my father gently refused. I didn't know until later that he had it in mind to learn to drive, Doc had agreed to give him a lesson, and I would be in the way. Besides, he wanted to surprise his family.

On the way back after the call, night had come on. My father was at the wheel. On a curve they were caught in the glare of the lights of an approaching car. My father pulled to the right and his hands froze to the wheel. Uncle Doc was a physically fit man, but my father was larger, and his brother shouted at him and pried at his hands in vain. Dazedly, my father followed the lights of the car he was driving off the grade and down into the Fire Mountain Canal. A dislodged boulder followed after, and he was immediately killed.

The respect and affection my brother and I had for our uncle, and his continuing interest in our welfare, were going to be more important than ever to our mother and us in the difficult years to come.

Lost in the Police Gazette

My mother was poorly equipped to survive and raise her two sons. She had finished the eighth grade in a Blue Ridge rural school, but that was the extent of her education. My father left her with a small life insurance policy through the Woodmen of the World Lodge, which also provided a stone above his grave on Cedar Hill where he rested with his parents and Aunt Addie's husband. Beyond the insurance, there was the house, the barbershop, an old livery stable and blacksmith shop, both jerry-built in the frontier fashion and doing poor business as the motor age was dawning. Liabilities, actually, more than assets.

Still, there was nothing for it but to go on. On the night of my father's death my mother sat in our parlor with the lights on, and women came by for hours, to weep with her.

"I'm living for my boys now," she told them.

At last we went up to bed and for the first time since babyhood I slept with her. I was unable to believe it all had really happened, and during the night I slid down under the covers until my feet encountered a small thin rectangular object. I told myself it might be some sort of a message from God, a sort of guarantee that my father was still alive. But it was only a clip on my mother's corset. He was gone, all right, no doubt of that.

On the day after his death, Mrs. Purtee came over to ask if I wouldn't like to come over to their place and play with their grandson, Raymond, a pal of my brother and me. My mother responded, wearily, at once. No, she said, I would prefer to stay there, by her side. If she hadn't spoken so promptly, I think it possible I might have given Mrs. Purtee a different answer; at the moment playing in the Purtee back yard looked very attractive.

But once the funeral was over there was school again, and there was still the work at the barbershop. No buyer was available at the moment for any of our property, so my mother put Jess Cox, a barber in my father's employ, in charge of the shop, and things went on much as before.

Not that there weren't changes. Some of them before my father was killed. At school, for instance, where on the mesa the entire student body numbered perhaps 20, a single grade school class in town was larger. I liked my fourth grade teacher, Miss Curtis, but recess proved a problem. Five boys one recess, for instance, gave me a little initiation. Some were my age, some younger, but all were larger, and I did not fare too well, showing up at the barbershop after school that day with a shiner.

This created another problem for me. My father was determined that I should learn to protect myself, particularly because I was bookish and short of stature, so he sent for a set of boxing gloves with the idea of teaching me the manly art of self defense. Suitable sparring partners were hard to come by, but he found one. It was Rex, a clumsy kid perhaps my age but a head taller, who was hanging around Grand Avenue, running errands, many of them the same sort of errands my brother and I had run in the Ridgway shop. The game where some sport with a keen sense of humor bribes a kid with a dime to go down to the restaurant to borrow a pie-stretcher, or to the hardware store for a left-handed monkey wrench, or to the bookstore for a bottle of striped ink. My brother and I had grown wise but Rex was always willing. He was so willing, in fact, that the sponsors of the game concluded he was only in it for the dimes, which of course spoiled the fun, and they gave over playing.

But one day my father persuaded Rex to put on the gloves to go a round or so with me. I wasn't all that enthusiastic, but before a number of shop idlers I felt I couldn't back down, so Rex and I donned the gloves and squared off. With my father's encouragement, I sailed in, arms flying; Rex put up a token defense and contributed some half-hearted haymakers, but it was over soon enough. He backed off, stumbled and went down. I have always had the opinion that the fight was fixed from the start. As I remember, my father paid him a quarter after it was over, and, anyway, how would it look for a boy his size to flail the barber's small son?

How would it all have turned out for my father and me if he had lived? I have no doubt that he would have continued his campaign to make a man of me. Perhaps I would have done better in the battle of life. There were occasions afterward in my life where I accepted abuse that was corrosive to the personality of any boy growing up in a male-dominated world; if I had had more confidence in my ability to take care of myself, who knows? Would I have felt better about myself, been more secure, or would I have had my brains knocked loose?

But my father died, and certainly my mother had no desire to foster aggressive tendencies in me. She was too busy holding together the little estate my father had left to her to know or to worry over how my brother and I were getting along in school or out. She assumed we would be doing our best, and it is to my lasting regret that I was not. In the barbershop, of course, things were easier. We were supposed to do whatever Jess, or the other barber, Ben Campbell, asked of us, and for the most part we did, but neither of them was apt to be as critical of our performance of sweeping and cleaning tasks as my father would have been.

We still took turns working there during the week, and both of us came in on Saturdays. It was much less of a bore for me than for my brother, who needed space and air. I enjoyed listening to the talk, much of it about professional sports—baseball, boxing, wrestling— and I was free to read the *Police Gazette,* a lurid, pale pink sporting weekly to which my father had subscribed. Perhaps partly because of my triumph over Rex, I became fascinated with ring lore and the back pages of the *Gazette* were full of it. My father let me read it grudgingly, but it was different after he was gone. I was reading everything by this time anyway, except of course my school assignments, though even there I made it a habit to bring in my readers and other school textbooks, and I became the shop sage and wunderkind, an eminence that would have astonished my grade school teachers if they had heard of it, because in my classes they were getting less and less from me.

I was deferred to particularly by Ben, who made a sort of game out of attempting to stump me with questions on assorted subjects, including history and geography. Some of the answers I actually knew, but it was no problem when I didn't. I always came up calmly and promptly with an answer, and since he had no way of proving me wrong, he would shake his head, impressed, give the chair a quarter turn, and go back to snipping hair.

The *Gazette* was the boxing and wrestling bible then. On its cover almost invariably appeared a photographic reproduction of a gorgeously bedizened Ziegfeld Follies beauty, but I didn't waste my time on that. I flipped to the tales of the pugilists of old, going back to the reigns of the first Georges in England, when men fought bare-fisted, often illegally, hustled here and there to avoid the law, even up into modern times, like the great John L., America's own bare-fisted hero, who fought against the likes of Jake Kilrain and Jack Sharkey— the original Jack Sharkey, a true son of the ould sod, not the peevish Lithuanian who fought the second Jack Dempsey—and turned to complain to the referee at exactly the wrong time.

And from the pages of the *Gazette* I learned about the black race. The only blacks I had ever seen were in the newsreels, and once very early those in the minstrel show in Ridgway, and they were wearing grease paint. A black man was an exotic sight in western Colorado then. Once the Fiske Jubilee Singers appeared in a church in Paonia. In the post office the next morning I saw an older black man standing at a desk addressing a card. When I approached he apologized and moved away, as if he thought this small white boy intended to usurp the desk. I don't think he believed it really, but he was taking no chances. And I never forgot the resentment in his eyes, and the sad half-smile that told of a lifetime of indignity and rejection.

But in the *Gazette* I read about other black men, beginning with Peter Jackson, the Australian, whom John L. refused to meet and conveniently scorned to fight. There was the Boston Tar Baby, Sam Langford, who, when middle-aged and nearly blind, could beat almost any man of any weight foolish enough to get into the ring with him. There was Battling Siki, the Senegalese who had learned to box in the French army, who lived and dressed as extravagantly as a modern rock star or a Manhattan pimp; who liked fast cars and fast women, and strolled down Paris streets with a lion on leash.

But the stories I liked best in the *Police Gazette* were about the little men, perhaps because it was becoming increasingly apparent that if I lived long enough I was destined to be a little man myself. I read about flyweights, bantamweights, lightweights; black, brown, white, and all shades in between. Joe Gans, Whirlwind Harry Greb, and Young Griffo, so fast with his hands that he could catch a fly on the wing between his thumb and forefinger. But my favorite was the lightweight champion during the twenties, Benny Leonard, who was called "Mama's Boy," because of his affection for his mother. Once he met another lightweight, Leach Cross I think it was, who was known to have a terrific punch. Benny took one full in the mouth in the first round. It broke some of his teeth and filled his mouth with blood. He swallowed the blood and concealed the broken teeth in his glove, clinched with his opponent and scoffed in his ear,

"Is that all the harder you can hit?" and went on to win.

A good story and one that travels well. I learned later that it was first told about a Greek pugilist, Eurydamas, fighting before the time of Christ. Another good story I read in the *Gazette* was the one about the younger Dempsey. He had a vicious right hand but was said to be otherwise a bum until Doc Kearns, his legendary manager, tied his fighter's right hand behind him and put him in the ring with two middleweights told to go after him with everything they had. Dempsey learned to bob, weave, and use his left. Dempsey said it wasn't true, but that didn't make much difference. It was the stuff of legends and was told much earlier about a bare-knuckled fighter in Ireland.

Dempsey, Colorado's own champion, was the most talked-about fighter in my father's barbershop in the twenties. And it was true that he had bummed around the West, including western Colorado, to this town and that mining camp, issuing challenges before pool halls and saloons in his high-pitched voice, fighting for nickels and dimes. He was said to have come up to Paonia during peach harvest and fought in the street and passed the hat afterwards. One Saturday night when I was out of the shop Fireman Jim Flynn, the Pueblo heavyweight, passed through, and to my brother fell the honor of shining the great man's shoes. Flynn had the distinction of having won a fight from Dempsey, a fight in which it was generally claimed that Dempsey, like my fistic opponent, Rex, had taken a dive.

Flynn had been touring the valley with some admirers from Somerset, the up-valley coal mining town. Back then a boxer, wrestler, or baseball player with a little talent could always find generous friends in the mining camps, especially the big camps in remote mountain locations, like Silverton, Ouray or Telluride. They were full of lonely, foot-loose men, some single, others like an uncle of mine, my mother's brother, down on their luck and working to support families living in the valleys below, most of them hungry for entertainment of any kind, at any price.

Big summer holiday celebrations were held in the hard-rock mining camps of the San Juans on the Fourth of July and Labor Day. Sprints, tugs-of-war, contests between fire-engine companies, jack-hammer contests, these were all the order of the day. In the evening, especially on the Fourth, there would be fireworks and afterward, before the big dance, the Smoker.

The Smoker consisted of a succession of bouts or matches, boxing or wrestling or both, leading up to a semifinal, which was followed by the Main Event. Often the first match of the night would be a Battle Royal, a real crowd-pleaser, where rugged local boys, a half dozen or more, some in sock feet and overalls, would crawl through the ropes and trade haymakers until only one was left standing.

These entertainments were popular everywhere in the West, and in Paonia as well. Always, in these local smokers, there had to be a ten-round main event, but there wasn't enough money to bring in a well-known fighter. At the time the only local fighter capable of going that distance, and with the necessary claim to pugilistic skill, was Charlie Elston, a young butcher. And, the only fit opponent for Charlie was a beet farmer from near the county seat, probably in his early forties, who had fought professionally in the ring as a young man. His name was McCarthy. Charlie fought as a welterweight and McCarthy may have outweighed him a half dozen pounds and possessed slightly more reach. McCarthy would show up the night of the bout looking as if he had just finished the farm chores, which he probably had; he would shuck his outer clothing in his corner and he and Charlie would have at it.

Charlie was always the aggressor, at least in the early rounds, moving in cautiously and paying a good price for every punch he landed. There were no knockouts that I remember, and I don't remember that Charlie won many of those bouts.

Once another opponent was found for Charlie—Johnny Kid West—perhaps the best fighter living on the Slope then, and one of the best who ever did. He had fought title contenders in his class—he was a lightweight—but as he began to age a little and tire of training, he settled down in Ouray with his wife, Sadie, did a little mining, a little gambling, peddled a little moonshine, fought an occasional fight, and played in the infield of the baseball team. Baseball was close to Johnny's heart, and because of it he restricted his moonshining to the latter part of the year. That way, if he was caught and had to spend several months in the cooler, he would still be out in time for spring practice.

I had a cousin named Mark who stayed with Johnny one fall and worked at the mine. One day when Johnny was out a customer called, and Mark, ever the gentleman, went down in the cellar to tip the barrel for Sadie. The customer turned out to be a revenuer and Mark received several months free board and room.

The smoker in which Charlie was to face Johnny Kid West—all these smokers took place in the old Opera House—generated a lot of interest, with ringside seats going at the unheard-of price of a dollar each. I had made it to most of the other smokers, sometimes even paying my way out of hoarded shoeshine receipts, but I had almost despaired of seeing this premier event when I ran into Tood Conine, an old rounder down from the hills. Feeling flush and having had a few snorts, he bought me a ringside seat.

Charlie was in his usual good condition, and Johnny was plainly drunk. But the trouble where Charlie was concerned, was that he didn't know how drunk Johnny really was, and he knew enough about boxing to realize that he was in the ring with a man, drunk or sober, who knew the game far better than he and possessed great natural gifts. It was a discouraging night for him and a dull one for the spectators. At one time he looked over to his corner where his father was acting as his second and moaned,

"Papa, I can't fight."

This earned him hoots of derision from the crowd.

But Charlie persevered at his avocation, working out on the heavy bag, skipping rope, using the storage area above the barbershop after Mama had sold to Jess Cox. He was clean-living and dedicated, and was never properly appreciated in Paonia. Once I went up to watch him work, and the extent of his neglect was plain in the way he seemed to appreciate having anyone, even a small boy, before whom to demonstrate his skill and conditioning. And it is good to report that later he boxed professionally out on the Coast, won consistently and was well regarded.

The match that was most painful for me to watch was between a local coal miner named Owens and an out-of-town fighter. Owens had never fought professionally, but he was in top shape and confident. So confident that he persuaded his wife, a retiring, studious girl still in high school, to attend. This was most unusual; women never attended and here were two of them—Mrs. Owens had persuaded a friend to come with her—seated prominently down front. Owens was wearing black trunks, and waved and winked reassuringly at his feminine gallery, but as the fight progressed the black trunks proved a sinister touch. Owens was hopelessly outclassed and unfortunately in such good shape and his pride was such that he would not be persuaded to throw in the towel. The match went on, round after bloody, weary, punishing round. And, overcome with pity, many of us watched Mrs. Owens more than the action in the ring as she seemed to quiver and pull inwardly, her handkerchief to her mouth, at every blow her husband received.

After the barbershop was sold, my brother and I found other employment, mowing lawns, delivering milk, and later working in the orchards roundabout and at the packinghouses in the fall when the fruit crops were being harvested. Then we both became more involved in play with friends and with school activities. Besides, our mother found work for idle hands; she had to give up on the livery stable and the blacksmith shop; they were torn down and replaced with two neat cottages built by old Steve Morgan, a retired carpenter who sympathized with her plight. And two outbuildings on the back lot where our house stood were converted to rentals and we were often involved in cleaning and painting tasks. She had known all along that working at the barbershop was not conducive to teaching good work habits or to much of anything else that would help provide for a secure future for her sons, but there hadn't been much help for it.

I worked after my brother had given it up at the shop, into my early teens, but only on Saturday. *The Police Gazette* began to change character as the twenties waned, and Jess stopped subscribing to it. But I was patronizing the WCTU library by then, the library at school, and borrowing books from friends. I hardly missed it.

Christmas at the Ranch

It was always good to be going over to the ranch, but the best time of all was at Christmas. That was my Uncle Henry Elmendorf's ranch up Clear Fork outside Crawford. To get there you had to cross the Dobies, drive up through Crawford, down over Smith Fork, up Yarnell Hill and out to Goodwin's Corner, then turn east up the long grade past the Vandenberg's, on past the schoolhouse, and then wend your way through the ranches of the Carters, who had a regular colony in those days on Clear Fork, until, on a lane that looked like it led straight to the foot of Cathedral Rock, the old white frame house with the red trim slowly rose into view on the left.

One time my mother's brother, Arthur, who for a time ranched on Fruitland Mesa, came over and picked us up—my mother, my brother and me—to deliver us to the Elmendorf's. The buggy had a top and was enclosed with isinglass curtains on the sides, but it was a pretty cool trip, especially across the Dobies. My Uncle Arthur chewed tobacco and just when you thought you had squeezed out the shivers for the time being, he would pull back the side curtain to spit, and that cold wind off Saddle Mountain would snake around your back again.

The best Christmas of all was the one when Uncle Henry's oldest son, Fred, came over and picked us up in his Graham Paige. That was really going in style. Even when the big old car stalled and boiled over on Yarnell Hill, it was just part of the fun. Fred tugged his overshoes on over his button oxfords (he was still ranching at the time, but later he was a candy salesman and he was always a snappy dresser) and went up to Yarnell's and came back with a pail of water, while we just lolled there in Graham Paige luxury.

It didn't seem any time at all after that until we were turning in at the open-frame gate. Attached at the middle of the top two-by-six was a piece of board with my uncle's name seared on it, and under that his brand, the Open-A Lazy L. (One time Uncle Henry wintered a brindle heifer for my mother because the heifer was dry and not due to calve until spring. He warned the boys not to get Mama's heifer mixed up with the other stock, so they didn't put the ranch brand on her. Instead, they printed MRS. FANNIE HALEY on her, a brand that ran clear across the side of the poor cow.)

Anyway, we drove up to the old gate that Christmas, and Fred got out and tugged it aside while two young dogs and old Shorty, who was about twelve and getting pretty hoarse, gave us the big greeting. Fred parked next to his brother Kenneth's Star pickup and we got out on stiff legs and prickly feet and walked up the path along the creek to the back door of the house.

I was relieved to see that there weren't any tracks in the snow alongside the house; that meant that Uncle Henry's pet billy goat was tied in the barn and couldn't bully small boys as he liked to do. Aunt Ina opened the door, rubbing her floury hands on her apron, and she and mother embraced, with Aunt Ina welcoming everyone in that over-strong, carrying voice of hers.

Aunt Ina and my mother were separated in age by thirteen years, and my mother never told me until she was very old why that was. Her parents had raised a whole family between Aunt Ina and my mother—four children—and they all perished in a diphtheria epidemic.

There were hugs all around for my mother, my brother, and me, and from Kenneth's wife Jenny, Fred's wife May, and Aunt Ina's two daughters, Marva and Cena. Then, led by Kenneth and Jenny's two small girls, we children all scampered through the dining room to the front room to look at the tree. Both of Aunt Ina's and Uncle Henry's daughters were still at home then; Cena was going to high school in Crawford and Marva to normal school up at Gunnison, and they really had outdone themselves this year. They were taking art and domestic science courses, and I think they wanted to prove to the old folks and the rest of the family how much they had learned.

That tree was a fantasy forest of little red Santa figures in papier-mache, brown reindeer baked from dough, and everywhere were strands of tinsel, glittering balls of red, gold, silver and blue, strings of popcorn and dozens of colored candles. And, of course, the most important decorations of all, the presents banked in their bright wrappers all around the base of the tree.

It was still a while before dinner, and the men lounged in the washroom just off the kitchen, staying out of the way of the women as they basted, stirred, whipped and sliced, and the air throughout the house, even in the front room, was warm and full of the odor of spices and roasting turkey. But we four children wandered through the rest of the house, bemused by the tree, and gobbling candy and cookies, which had been set around on stands and tables in decorated paper plates; plates of homemade rich brown fudge, dazzling white divinity, transparent red and green gumdrops dusted with powdered sugar, and cookies in fancy frostings. We children helped ourselves generously to everything in spite of the warnings called out of the kitchen:

"Here, now, Rhoda, that's enough," or "Mildred, you'll spoil your dinner!" or "Glen-n-n-n, I don't care what Harold's had, you've had enough; now I don't want to speak to you again . . ."

All the men were dressed in their best. Kenneth's suit was a blue pin stripe and Fred's a brown plaid. Their white shirt collars were starched, and the ties were luminescent. The pants of the young men's suits were peg-topped and the shoulders of the coats padded. Both suits were mail order, from Crews Beggs in Pueblo. Uncle Henry's suit of heavy dark wool, though, wasn't as heavily padded in the shoulders and the trousers, uncuffed, flared out a little at the bottoms. The boys liked to tease their father about his "Granddaddy suit," but he had the last laugh; he wore that suit (the three or four times a year when he felt the need of it) clear through the twenties and into the early thirties, and when the bell-bottoms came in, he was right back in style.

Fred had not seen much of his sister Marva for the last several years, and he couldn't get over how she had filled out and turned into an attractive young woman. He persisted in staying near her, and they kept an arm around each other, and he squeezed her once in a while, so that the other women, Kenneth's wife Jennie, and Aunt Ina in particular, professed to "feel sorry" for May, Fred's wife, for the way Fred was "honeyin' around" his sister, and May went along with it, saying that she was worried too, and getting pretty jealous.

By this time the meal was ready, and we all came to the long table in the dining room where the west window looked out on the snow-covered yard and to the barn and corrals beyond. Most of the year only the end of the table nearest the kitchen was in use; only at holidays and harvest time was it fully used. On this day it was.

Uncle Henry sat at the head, with Aunt Ina on his left, where it was easy to get up and check anything on the stove; my mother sat next to her, and Kenneth's wife and her two children. Then there were May, Cena and Marva. Uncle Henry's sons sat at their traditional places at his right, and on their right were my brother and I, filling out the men's side—and as far away as we could get from our mother.

There were all the usual staples of the Christmas feast, as well as apple salad, hot rolls, pickled beets, pickled peaches, bread and butter pickles, sweet pickles, jam and jelly. Then there was the pumpkin pie topped with sweet, thick, golden whipped cream—Uncle Henry never missed the opportunity to point out the color of the cream and to brag about the richness of the milk his Jersey cow Maud provided. He said she had established herself as a phenomenon around the country, and her milk tested higher than that of any other cow.

"Wy, when they first seen the results of that test in the creamery, they wouldn't believe it. Martin called in everybody from the front to show it to 'em."

"I've heard those folks at the creamery don't know straight up about measurin' butterfat," Fred said.

"That's a lie and you know it," his father said.

"Dad," Fred protested, "I'm just tellin' you what I heard."

"You never heard nothing of the kind," Uncle Henry said. He got up and went into the kitchen and returned with the bowl in which the cream had been mixed.

"You ever see color like that on cream?"

"Mama," Fred said, "I seen you over at the bowl with the yellow cake colorin'. Didn't you put in a little too much?"

Uncle Henry glared at him and returned the bowl to the kitchen.

"Shut up, Fred," his wife May said. "Now just shut up."

Then there was talk about the weather . . . "awful lot of snow for this early . . ." and about the price of sugar . . . "terrible high" . . . and the new women's styles. "If they keep on," Aunt Ina said, "those young girls' dresses will be clear up to their hips."

"I can hardly wait," Kenneth said.

After all had eaten as much as they could hold, and my mother had refused to permit the delivery of a third piece of pie to either my brother or myself, Uncle Henry leaned back and rubbed his stomach. "Mother," he said, "I just wish I had a rubber stomach so I could eat some more of this good food."

"Well, Dad," Fred said. "If you did have, I'd sure hate to jack you up and repair a puncture."

This caused a general laugh and cries of disapproval from Fred's wife and his mother.

"Why is it," Uncle Henry said, "that you just blabber on with your mind outa gear? Why is it that you have to come up with something disgustin' all the time? Can't you ever act like a grownup man?"

Both Fred and Kenneth could hardly contain themselves. They snickered together like the two mischievous boys they once had been.

"I'm sorry, Dad," Fred said.

"You ain't sorry," Uncle Henry said. "As long as you get a laugh, that's all you're after. You ain't a bit sorry."

Afterwards the women cleared the table and washed the dishes. Then they went outside briefly and when they returned the men went. The men sat around the table again, the women sat around the work table in the kitchen, and we four children went into the front room.

This was one of those rare days when we were freely allowed to go in there. The curtains on the window—the front window facing the road, and the side window looking east toward the Wynants' and Cathedral Rock—were drawn as a rule to protect the oatmeal

110

wallpaper, but on this day they were open. We could sit on the "good" chairs and the love seat, all framed in dark wood and padded, seat and back, in red and black tapestry. We could look through the books in the bookcase, or turn the leaves of the family Bible on the stand by the side window. And we could even sit at the organ in the far corner and pump away and pull out the stops, each with a strange name in old English script printed on its ivory face.

Aunt Ina, her two girls and the other women went into the downstairs bedrooms for a nap. The men went out to do the chores, and we four small children were left to entertain ourselves. Patterning my behavior after my cousin Fred's I began hugging and kissing Kenneth's youngest daughter. She had blonde hair and blue eyes and full red lips and I got a sort of a tingle out of it, but she wriggled and laughed so much that I gave it up. When we all began playing tag around the tree, my mother and Jenny came out; the girls were taken into the bedroom with their mother, and our mother took us upstairs to lie down in the "boys'" old bedroom.

Just inside the door of the room was a closet, and on its wall hung a great gaudy mane of dress ties, relics of many a birthday and Christmas in the past. The room's main wall sloped down to a west window, and we could see the sun sinking in streamers of deep red. We crawled under the patchwork quilt to the rustle of the cornshuck mattress.

We had dozed off when a car was heard in the yard. It was Boyd, the youngest of Uncle Henry's boys. He had taken his folks' car and had gone to dinner at the home of his best girl, Helen, whose folks lived up the road. Helen called out "Is anybody home?" as they came in, and we all came to the dining room again.

Food was laid out on the table in the kitchen, where plates were filled and carried into the dining room. All the grownups said they couldn't eat another bite, and everyone did in spite of that. Aunt Ina's girls replenished the candy and cooky dishes.

Then it was time for the presents. Embroidered washcloths and handkerchiefs for the women, scarves and neckties for the men, dolls for Kenneth's girls, games for my brother and me. Each rustling package was opened to "oo-oo-ooh's" and "a-a-a-ah's" from the women.

My brother and I got a checker game and another board game called "Touring." A number of us tried "Touring," laying the board out on the dining table under the white buzzing glare of the gasoline lamp. It was played with little cars. There was a dial you spun to see how many spaces you could move to advance your car along the road to "home":

"I did not spin 'four'—I spun 'five'" ... "Woops! 'Jail'" ... "You mean I have to go clear back to 'Start'?" ... "Mama, he was s'posed to be in the mudhole; make him play fair" ...

Now Kenneth and his family had to go home to their own chores. The other two couples bundled up to go out to a "kitchen sweat"—an impromptu dance held in private homes out on the mesas.

"At the Clarence Carter's?" Aunt Ina asked unbelievingly. "You right sure they invited you?"

Fred grinned wickedly. "Right sure they didn't. That's what'll make it fun."

When they all were gone, Aunt Ina brought in a coal-oil lamp from the kitchen, and the gasoline lamp was moved from the foot to the head of the table, where Uncle Henry looked through *Capper's Weekly*. Mama and Aunt Ina visited. Aunt Ina's girls were going through the Montgomery Ward sale catalog.

My brother and I played checkers; I lost all three times and didn't take it all that well. The girls retired to their bedroom and although both my brother and I declared we weren't in the least sleepy, we, too, were taken upstairs to bed.

The dogs were barking and Uncle Henry went out and settled them down. We heard him stamping the snow off his boots at the back stoop. We were sated with food and the good times, and settled down into the rustling bed and looked up at the sloping white ceiling as my mother took up the lamp and the shadows bobbed along in her wake, until the door closed behind her and we heard the slow creaking of her footsteps on the stairs.

The Chocolate Cave

Luke Skywalker and Indiana Jones were still to be heard from when I was young on the North Fork, but we had Captain Nemo and his marvelous submarine from Jules Verne's *Twenty Thousand Leagues Under The Sea,* and a considerable roster of other heroic figures from fantastic fiction. Prince Valiant was not yet on the scene, either, but there was Tarzan of the Apes, and John Carter, Warlord of Mars. John won the beauteous Dejah Thoris, princess of Barsoom, and—there's no more delicate way of putting it—*fertilized* the egg which would hatch as his son, Carthoris, decades before Superman was a gleam in Marlon Brando's eye.

And, although we youthful antagonists did not face each other off with ray guns in our war games, we did have the Colt 45, the old frontier peacemaker serviceably rendered in wood, and the sterling examples of William S. Hart and Tom Mix to emulate, and we could base our bloody battles on the West as revealed by Zane Grey and Max Brand, which we did in such locales as the old fruit-drying plant on the corner of North Fork and Second, and in the virtually deserted livery stable my mother owned further down Second Street.

The plant was a lost dream of my uncle, Albert Rose, Aunt Addie's husband, who had died before he could bring his plan of drying North Fork fruit commercially into being. The huge old three-story structure sank into ruin for over a decade, with mummified peach and apricot halves still spread on drying screens on the top floor. On days in summer when our mother could not contrive to keep my brother and me meaningfully employed, we joined with other youthful adventurers in the old plant and waged our feuds through the basement clutter of rusting machinery and the dust-ridden sorting tables on the main floor, and, invariably, in moments of extreme peril, one side or the other would be driven to flee to the freight elevator. It was still in working order, and the beleaguered and bloodied company would be slowly hoisted up to the floor above as our shouting pursuers closed in. Once I remember being late in arriving at the elevator, and it had rumbled and creaked upward several feet above floor level before helping hands could drag me aboard.

My mother never learned about such adventures, of course. We never told her anything more than we could help of our pastimes. I never told her, for example, of being isolated at the cupola on the roof of the drying plant, clutching at the eave of it with my fingers and inching around it while below me at ground level two boys—one my brother—chuckled uncontrollably while they flailed away at me with pebbles and clods. And I never told her either about the time when I walked—and even trotted, finally—along the top of the old iron bridge fifty feet above the waters of the North Fork, on a beam no more than eighteen inches in width.

We always assured our mother that we would not go far when we went out to play, but we interpreted that promise very liberally as covering almost any location within town or immediately out of it. And, even though my mother was not a robust woman, nor the possessor of a strong voice, she could be heard at surprising distances in the quiet air of evening in a town still fairly free of noise-making gadgetry.

When she did call I usually didn't answer right away. It gave me a mean, obscure sort of pleasure to go on with whatever I happened to be doing, on beyond the third or fourth summons, and always denying when I at last arrived at the house, that I had heard her calling more than twice. That was a common ploy then and probably still is among children being summoned. A small female cousin of mine, in the course of being spanked by her father for such a transgression, wailed,

"I never even heard you when you called from the back door; I only heard you when you called from the front."

When my father was alive I must admit his calls conveyed more urgency. I was reading one evening on the fire escape at the side of the old Opera House which is next door to the house in which we then lived, and I stopped to depict a scene from the book to my cousin Mary and a chum of hers who happened by as my mother called me to supper.

"You better answer your mother," one of the girls said.

"I'll let her call five more times and then I'll answer," I said airily, and went on with my story. But then came another voice, heavy, and flat:

"Glen!"

I broke off in midsentence, the girls recall (I myself have only the dimmest recollection of the incident). "I gotta go," I said, and scrambled down and away.

With my father dead my mother did the best she could in demanding obedience from us. No longer could she threaten, "Just wait till your father comes home," so she did the best she could, and with continued practice eventually wielded the razor strop very effectively.

In the twenties the gangster movies came into vogue, and once a

114

memorable gang war centered around the old livery stable. Our gang consisted of the Tiptons, the Halls, and the Haleys. The father of the Hall brothers was a teamster, poor but honest; the Tiptons and the Haleys were widows' sons; I suppose you could say it was sort of an uprising of the lower classes. The opposing gang recruited its members from the middle class residential streets east of Grand Avenue.

The opening battle of the war was set for midmorning of a summer Saturday. At the appointed time the enemy swooped down the alley from the north in full cry, scions of the Crawfords, the Smiths, and the McKees, past the town maintenance building on the alley behind our home, past Steve Morgan's home facing on Second Street, on they came, while we crouched up in the hayloft behind the big double doors that opened on the corrals to the rear. Clods and rocks rained on the weathered walls of our fort; through the substantial cracks in the clapboard walls, we could see the enemy loosely deployed below us. It was the time we had been waiting for. We had our missiles and weapons in order, sticks and wooden guns for close combat, clods

The brothers in Paonia

115

and rocks for artillery, but in addition we had close at hand an apple box half full of a secret weapon provided by the Tipton brothers from the family ranch—rotten eggs.

With answering shouts we swung open the doors to the loft and began to let fly. The annals of warfare prove that comparatively few projectiles in a barrage inflict casualties, and, for a time, our new weaponry did not. But standing over at the side of the enemy's ranks was a sort of an auxiliary, or supernumerary, one Harvey Kosmont. He was obviously dressed for some family occasion, probably an impending outing, in freshly laundered and ironed bib overalls and spotless white shirt, and had probably been instructed by his parents, noted for their strictness, to stay out of trouble. But he had been swept up in the excitement of the attack, and was doing what he could to provide moral support, shouting and waving his arms, and he presented a fine target.

Struck by a very ripe egg, he stared down at the mess of yellow and brown goo positioned on his left chest like a medal and giving off, doubtless, a most foul and repellent odor—not unlike that encountered in other types of chemical warfare—and he broke out in a bellow of agony and dismay.

All action ceased. We were all frozen by the sound. The world of mock war had suddenly sleeved into the real world, of adults and laundry and commitments. Harvey turned and ran back across the street to the alley, wailing and threatening as he went, and although he had not suffered physical injury at our hands, we all knew he shortly would at the hands of others.

Hostilities were not resumed. The spirit had gone out of the action for both sides. The attackers shouted accusations and re-criminations and vowed vengeance, even as they beat a retreat. The battle was over, and, for that matter, the war, but the odor of the victory stank in our nostrils.

We played more organized games, like pump-pump-pullaway and hide-and-go-seek, and kick-the-can. One summer night in the alley behind Grand Avenue, well after the eight-o'clock curfew, we were still playing kick-the-can and I was hiding out and getting set to make a dash for the circle to kick the can when I saw an ominous shadow against another building up the alley, in the light cast from a street lamp. It appeared to be the silhouette of an ancient face under a hat brim, grim and still; at first I thought it only a product of my imagination, but then I saw Bobby Crawford, a participant in our game, creeping slowly along the shed wall on which the shadow was cast, and the shadow suddenly flickered and lengthened, as Hanks, the old town marshal, the nemesis of all curfew violators, reached out and clutched Bobby by the collar. All games have dangers, imagined or real, and most particularly childhood games.

Caves hold a special fascination for young adventurers. Our fifth grade teacher gave full play to her Missouri accent by reading to us from *Tom Sawyer*, which contained a marvelous cave adventure, and many of us were reading pirate stories like *Treasure Island*. All this brought on a spate of cave building for a time in the community. In the vacant lot across the alley from K. Kohr's tiny tailor shop a number of us dug a cave by hollowing out a pit and covering it over with old tree branches, sheets of cardboard ripped from packing boxes abandoned behind Grand Avenue business houses and then covering it all with layers of earth.

This cave became a pirate cave. Meetings were held. Candidates for membership in the pirate crew were given the choice by candlelight of signing up in blood or skulking away to await delivery of the dreaded Black Spot. Vows taken were vague, though the language they were couched in was grim, and the signing did carry with it an element of real danger that we did not recognize at the time: the blood for the signature was obtained by pricking the candidate's thumb with a safety pin, exposing him to the possibility of contracting blood poisoning.

The acknowledged paragon of caves at the time was one that two families of boys on Bone Mesa had dug in an alkali-infested pasture. The cave was a complex of tunnels meandering all over the field, tunnels consisting of a trench covered with brush and made light-tight by an overlayer of earth, and I once spent a major part of an afternoon crawling the length of the maze, arriving finally at the secret core and then finding my way out again, impressed and fulfilled by that monument to boyhood industry.

Still, the cave that remains most fondly in my memory was the one dug halfway up the northeast face of Cedar Hill by Albert Macklin and me. It was not much as caves go, being little more than a dugout scooped from the hill-face a few yards below the ditch. It was concealed from view by a cedar tree and a thicket of sagebrush, goldenrod and wild roses, and over the entrance we had improvised a door of old boards camouflaged by willow branches brought down from the ditch bank.

The furnishings were plain: two apple boxes filched from the loading yard of the Union Fruit Company, and a crate set into the earthen rear wall with a lid wired across its front, which functioned as a sideboard or hutch to contain necessary supplies. These supplies were always the same—a carton of Camel cigarettes and another of Eline's chocolate bars. The supplies came from the back room of the grocery store which Albert's father ran in a long, low wooden structure on Grand Avenue. We could see it from our cave when we moved out and took the sun in the late afternoon, a cigarette between the fingers of one hand, and an Eline's chocolate bar in the other. Albert explained that these particular items were the only ones he felt safe in lifting, due to a fortuitous arrangement in the supply room, and I never questioned his judgment nor had the bad taste to complain about the monotony of fare.

I don't recall that much philosophizing or even conversation went on at the cave; it was enough to be there, alone in our retreat, sampling forbidden fruits. We told no one about our refuge, and we were extremely careful to conceal all signs of our arrivals and departures, brushing out all footprints in good woodsman fashion, and avoiding the establishment of a recognizable path.

I don't remember how long this halcyon life went on. Whenever we ran low on cigarettes or chocolate bars—the chocolate bar supply in particular always seemed low—Albert would come up the next rendezvous afternoon, the shirt under the bib of his overalls and over his thin chest bulging as if he were an asthma victim, and there would be another carton of Camels and another box of chocolate bars.

Pleasures are fleeting, and an end to our days at the chocolate cave came soon enough. As the weeks went by I began to notice that the demeanor of my friend Albert, always so carefree and sunny, had altered. We would meet at the cave and make ourselves comfortable but then, more and more often, I would see Albert in a brown study, looking off at the ground to one side, and at last he confided in me that the reason for his sadness was that his father and older brother who helped tend the store, were preparing to take inventory. Up to that point I had never known nor cared what an inventory was, in or out of a grocery store, but when Albert explained, I saw the problem soon enough. From then on, in the dwindling number of days left to us, our meetings were even more subdued.

And I trusted Albert; I hoped that even in a worst case, I would not be involved (I think now that it is very likely that I might have been, and of course I would have deserved to have been).

Anyway, there was nothing to be done, and even with the threat of discovery hanging over us, I found that my pleasure in eating chocolate bars did not noticeably subside. It was all in the laps of the gods.

And the gods came through. One night I awoke in bed beside my brother at home as the town whistle warned of fire. We ran out to see a great illuminated orb of smoke and flame rising from down near Grand Avenue. It was the Macklin store, and it burned to the ground.

I didn't see much of Albert after that. It was hardly a time to express feelings of relief or congratulation. We never again met at the cave. The Macklins moved away not long after. All that remained of a material nature to remind me of the days in the chocolate cave was a compact little dictionary issued by the Eline's people as a promotion. I gave it to my mother, fashioning an appropriate falsehood, and she kept it all the rest of her days among her few effects, not because of any sentimental value it had for her, but because she never threw anything away that could be potentially useful, and because of her worshipful respect for the written word. The cloth cover of the little book was done in a sort of Persian intaglio, the same design imprinted on the chocolate bar wrappers, a design the memory of which still gives me a nostalgic if guilty pleasure.

Years later when I was visiting at my aunt's home in Denver, I was sitting on the top step of the front porch watching the traffic. The cars streamed by, on this or that commercial or social errand, no more identifiable than so many ants trundling to and from a nest, when I suddenly made out in the ruck the unmistakable little green-sided flatbed truck the Macklins had owned and driven when they had lived and worked in Paonia. Mr. Macklin was at the wheel but there was no one with him, and the truck bed was empty. I did not try to gain his attention; after all, there was nothing I had to say to Mr. Macklin who probably would not even have remembered me. On the truck went, a fleeting vision from the invincible, the irretrievable, past.

Apteekki, Apoteka, Farmacia

It is true that children are not all that concerned with whether their parents are poor or not when they are quite young, but I was concerned after the death of my father. As small as the town was, and as ethnically uncomplicated—there were no Orientals, no blacks, and only one or two Mexican families—there was still a range, both social and economic, from the leisured few at the top of the scale to the families of day laborers and widows at the bottom, struggling always to make ends meet.

One day my mother pointed out to my brother and me that "Vacations are not just for play; they are times set aside to earn extra money and get the clothes and books to go to school again."

Of course in our case she was right, but this view of the vacation struck me as arid and disillusioning. It certainly didn't conform with the way other children and their parents viewed vacation. It wasn't the way the family of Mrs. A.V.S. Smith who lived in the mansion next door to us on Poplar viewed it; it wasn't the way it was viewed by the sons of R.F. Rockwell, the leading citizen of the town and a state senator; or even the way it was looked upon by our two cousins, the sons of Uncle Doc. They looked upon the vacation as a time for going fishing or swimming or playing tennis and finding other pleasant ways to keep from getting bored.

The best summer source of employment for my brother and me was in the fruit orchards on the mesas around the town. Sometimes we got work through the good offices of Aunt Polly, everyone's favorite telephone operator. From the time I was able to pick up a ladder and even before, I was picking cherries, apricots, peaches and pears. On Saturdays there was shoeshining in the barbershop. Late in the fall when I was large enough to wield a pushbroom, I got a job sweeping out the grade school.

For several years too I worked for old Mr. Redwine, delivering milk around town. After supper in the long evenings of summer or in the early dark of winter, I would walk out to the dairy at the edge of town. The dairy consisted of a corral and an old barn in the dale along the river, and although the drainage should have been good, the corral was knee-deep in all seasons and weather for Mr. Redwine and much deeper than that for me, so I seldom ventured down there. The milk was laboriously carried up to the house by my employer, an old man who was never unkind but never kind either, and who lived a work-filled life looking after his cows and seeing to the needs of a paralyzed wife in those days before Welfare, pensions, and Social Security. Mrs. Redwine was mute and completely helpless, and I always found her sitting in her chair on the front porch of the gray little house, staring grimly out to the road, her frozen hands in her lap. But the flowered cotton dresses of somber hue that she wore always looked clean, and her gray hair, bobbed short, was always neatly combed.

The milk and cream were poured into pint and quart bottles on the Redwine back porch, and arranged in a pair of five-gallon lard buckets which I picked up by the bails and carried into town and delivered around the streets. One winter night I remember seeing a group of children from my fifth-grade class across a snowy inter-section under a street light, laughing together, dressed for an outing in the snow, and I was ashamed to be seen by them and felt that the distance across that intersection was very wide indeed.

But there were diversions. A cat would occasionally decide to come along on my milk delivery route, sniffing at the milk and scampering around my feet and in and out of yards for a few blocks. One night a drunken cowboy lurched to a stop at an intersection as my cat companion for the evening loped by.

"Look here, kid" he said, "you get that black cat back across my path or I don't budge." And he stood wavering there until I coaxed the cat back and cancelled out the threat of misfortune.

Then there was the summer night several years later when my friend, Tippie, who had contributed the rotten eggs for the famous "Battle of the Livery Stable," made my rounds with me. As we passed the Friends Church, Cecil spied Billy Bangs, son of the manager of the furniture store, peeking into the church through a raised window, watching choir practice.

"Here," Tippie said, going over and lifting Billy, a boy of ten or so, down from his perch, "what are you doing there, kid? Don't you know you ain't supposed to peek into churches?" and he gave him a light whack on the seat of his overalls, and as Billy ran off, insulted and crying, he called after him,

"And I don't want to hear of you of doing anything like that again."

That seemed to be all there was to the incident and we went on down the sidewalk under the dense shade of the box elder trees, but then I looked back to see a large, unmistakable form approaching us, swinging along, huge in the dark under the trees but huge in any aspect, for it was Henry Bangs, Billy's father, a man over six feet tall and of great girth, weighing well over three hundred pounds. It was said that for a late afternoon snack at Josh's hamburger stand he would eat eight full-sized onions.

"Did you strike my boy?" he roared at Tippie.

"I just gave him a little lovepat on the seat," Tippie said, and I said "He didn't do him any harm," but Henry was in no mood to listen to reason. He moved in on Tippie, a slender boy of perhaps five-foot six; since it was impossible for Henry to bring his great arms to play across his enormous belly, they churned back and forth at his sides like the breaker arms of a locomotive. Tippie, who never backed away from any challenge, moved to meet the attack. He looped a great haymaker at Henry's chin, but the force of his charge, coupled with the resilience of Henry's paunch, caused him to lose his balance, and he fell at Henry's feet while Henry's arms, bigger than Tippie's legs, continued churning fruitlessly. Once Tippie had regained his feet the battle easily could have gone on, but Henry seized the opportunity—since technically he could claim that he had achieved a knockdown—and he turned and lumbered away, only looking back to promise darkly,

"And if you ever lay a hand on a son of mine again, I'll knock you cold to the earth."

My brother and I saw quite a lot of Tippie in those days. His house was not far from ours, his mother was a widow of slender means like ours and we made fudge and popped corn at each other's homes on winter evenings. Sons and daughters of the poor—and not-so-poor— enjoyed such simple entertainments then. And we had other resources. My brother and I had a good sled which our father had bought for us, a Flexible Flyer, the Cadillac of sleds in its day, which we grudgingly shared with each other. Then we had ice skates, and when Harold was in the first years of high school he made himself a pair of skis in Manual Training and he acquired traps and trapped for muskrat along the ditches and streams feeding into the North Fork.

In the summer many boys and even young men spent long, luxurious hours in the swimming hole above the town bridge—and just above the town sewer outlet—but I was never attracted to that particular diversion. It was not for the squeamish. The big round rocks imbedded in the sandy approaches and the broken branches of cottonwood and willow were easy to bruise your naked feet against, and everywhere there was the odor and the evidence of dog and human feces.

The school, the twin bastions of learning, I looked upon with some ambivalence. The bell in the grade school steeple rang the hours, the half hour and the quarter hour before school and again at noon, and then a five-minute warning bell for the grade school children to heed and to form up into a military procession and march up the front steps and into their various rooms from the dark lower hall, while the

122

teachers on playground duty stood, arms folded, and watched us go by. The sound of the bells was not a pleasing sound to me and yet not altogether unpleasing. It meant penmanship and arithmetic, but it meant reading, too.

For years I swept out the grade school, usually in the company of another boy or so, and once, for a while, another boy and I, hired as sweepers, formed a compact to break into the grade school on weekends. We would leave a window unlatched in a rear room on the lower floor and that looked out over the coal yard, and crawl in through it over the coal on a Sunday afternoon. We would then walk through the cool dark halls and up the main staircase and around the banister to the enclosed library on the second-floor front. There we could loll in the overstuffed chairs and leaf through the illustrated and beautifully bound set of books dealing with the agricultural and botanical triumphs of Luther Burbank, or work the crank that controlled the elaborate scale mechanism of the model solar system, or trace explorations on the large, rotatable globe of the earth.

We were never caught because we didn't continue doing it for very long, and also because it never occurred to us, as it does to present-day miscreants, to "trash" the place. We didn't have that

Grade school

desire to wreak vengeance upon the school or society; on the contrary, we referred to the school between ourselves, as our "Castle," and it was a treasured privilege to enter there. There was little pillaging of public property then, except on Halloween and that was a different sort of a thing, permitted or at least tolerated. The only destruction of school property that I remember, other than the obligatory literary and artistic efforts on the walls of the boys' restrooms, occurred on senior sneak day when a misguided youth of our class threw two large dictionaries out of the windows of the high school. The class was castigated for that by an indignant superintendent, and we all felt, I think, guilty over it.

Winter held a long sway over the North Fork in those days, when the roads were channels of mud and frozen ruts, and toward spring, going out of the warm classroom at recess to wander the playground in sleet and slush was more ordeal than pleasure. The ground around the swings, teeter-totters, and the Giant Stride was heavily cindered and those pastimes were well patronized, but for the rest of it, there was only one area of the yard that presented any possibilities, and that was the zone of dry ground running across the playground between the two school buildings over the buried pipes that carried heat from the boiler in the grade school basement to the high school. In February the zone would be only a foot or so in width, so that there would be room only for the more aggressive children to play hopscotch or marbles there, but as the days grew warmer it would widen and soon all comers could be accommodated.

During the February thaw and from then on, there was that other restricted space downtown which became the special province of older boys, and that was the vacant lot at the northeast corner of Grand Avenue and Second Street, convenient to the drinking fountain and next door to the drugstore. On a sunny day in February, boys from thirteen or fourteen and on up would assemble and play step-and-a half, a form of leapfrog entailing running at a mark and taking off and vaulting over the back of the boy who was "it" until someone missed and had to take his place. It was exhilarating to run out into the middle of the street and look forward to where, across the gutter and sidewalk the mark was drawn, and beyond that the denim-clothed rump awaited the vault. Above it all on the side of the drugstore was painted a mysterious legend—like that written by the disembodied finger on the wall of Nebuchadnezzar's banquet hall:

APTEEKKI
APOTEKA
FARMACIA

Magic words. I murmured them over to myself as I looked to the long jump ahead as the distance between the mark and the waiting back

Beside the drugstore

lengthened after every turn.

Of course, I found out eventually that the "magic words" were only names for a drugstore in three different languages. But then, magic words are only magic if you believe in them, anyway. And growing up on the North Fork was a time of magic even though I sometimes felt abused at being "poor" and having to work when there was work of any sort available.

There were differences, social and economic, among the town's citizens, but I felt welcome almost anywhere. The community was a true community, and we were all, widows' and paupers' sons and all, little brothers and sons to most of the inhabitants. It was home from one end of town to the other and up on the mesas and into the hills where everywhere friendly and hospitable people lived.

Those times seem far away indeed, and things since have not turned out exactly as I had hoped, but perhaps it all might have gone better if I had not forgotten, some time back, to murmur over to myself those magic words when a decision had to be made or a trial to be run. Maybe it would have helped. Maybe it still can.

Clothes Make the Boy

Clothing was not a problem for my brother and me when my father was alive, but even then our mother did a lot of sewing for us. She even made us shirts, and once she made me an overcoat, which I lost coming up the lane from the Lamborn Mesa school one evening. She went back with me to look for it, but it was never found and I paid the painful penalty for my carelessness.

Another time, after we moved to town, she made me another coat which I contrived to lose in a unique fashion. I was with a gang of boys one Halloween before citizens were given the option of providing treats, and trickery was rampant. A real triumph involved the upending of an outdoor toilet, and our outriders had located one on the end of the lot of a residence just east of the Christian Church. We had all got into position and put our shoulders to the task when the owner suddenly appeared from inside the structure. Mouthing threats and imprecations, he pursued us up the alley, and it was every boy for himself. I was moving as briskly as my little legs would carry me, but I heard his heavy tread behind me and felt the tug as his fingers closed on the tail of my coat. I flung back my arms, shucking the coat, and with the added inducement increased my speed. At that he gave up and retired from the chase, but I was faced with another crisis; how would I explain to my mother? In my extremity, I made my way disconsolately back down the alley, and found that our pursuer, who may have been up to similar tricks in his own youth, had left the coat where I had shed it.

Once my father began to do well in the barbershop money was a little easier. My brother and I each acquired a suit then. There is a photograph taken of us in the Walker Studio; we are scrubbed, suited and necktied and bending over a checkerboard, engaged in a game— or, rather, my brother is engaged in a game and I am looking on at the slaughter. But I never felt those suits really counted. They were worn under protest. They consisted of a jacket and knickers, and underneath you wore a demeaning supporter arrangement to hold up the black-ribbed full-length stockings. Such an outfit marked you as a boy and not a man, and a rather sissified boy at that, or so we always felt. Still, even big boys like Paul Hofer wore such suits, often even to school, and I remember seeing Earl Thaxton, suitably knickered, thundering through his version of the Turkey Trot with some girl at a junior high school party.

After my father's death it was a struggle for my mother to provide clothing as well as food and shelter for us, particularly presentable wear for social occasions. Neither my brother nor I was much concerned about the problem, though, until junior high school, when it became acceptable to show an interest in girls. And it was just about that time that the great emancipation was taking place—even younger boys were acquiring long trousers. Apple-cheeked lads in long pants lounged through the pages of the Montgomery Ward and Sears, Roebuck catalogs, and sons of prominent citizens, boys of my age, began showing up at church socials in the new garb.

I had saved some money shining shoes in the shop and around my freshman year I was able to send off for a long-pants suit. It was gray, a color which my mother approved—she always insisted on colors that would go with everything, and observed this criterion when buying or making clothes for herself. My suit arrived at last, and fitted me well, and I couldn't wait to wear it downtown. On a sunny Sunday morning in spring I strolled down Second Street in my new suit and sporting a gray cap. I casually approached a little knot of young men standing by the water fountain talking about Paonia High School's basketball prospects and I joined in, though all were several years older than I, and Ham Bryan, a recent graduate now working as a barber in the Laurence shop glanced slyly at me and said,

"Well, now, look what we got here—a fella lookin' pretty spiffy in a new suit with long pants."

A proud moment, that.

I don't know what that suit was made of, but it lasted a very short while, and as a high school sophomore I was in the market for another. My mother was determined that this second suit would "have a little more wear in it." I wasn't entirely willing to submit to her judgment, and I certainly wouldn't let her make measurements that required that she violate my maleness, like the inseam measurement, so a third party was brought in. This was my Uncle Henry Elmendorf, who had ordered suits for his sons when they were growing up, and was therefore a qualified consultant.

Uncle Henry took over the tape and did a thorough job, while my mother wrote the numbers on the order; he added a half inch for growth here, an inch there, three inches there, and the order was placed in the mail. The suit arrived at last. It was a three-piece job; coat, vest, trousers. It was tan in color—my decision—with a vertical chain design in a darker brown. I remember everything about that suit more vividly than any I have ever owned.

Uncle Henry's generosity in the measurements was at once evident. The coat sagged down over my shoulders, the shoulder seam halfway to my elbow. It was good and full along the bottom of the coat, in the zoot style that was to become popular on the West Coast some twenty years later, but didn't help me at the time. The trousers were not so bad for length—by raising them to a point at the inseam just short of inflicting pain, and so that the belt loops rested along my second ribs, I could keep the cuffs off the floor. It was the waist, where Uncle Henry had thrown in an extra inch or so, that gave me real trouble.

Depending upon the occasion when the suit was to be worn—whether I was going to have to be moving around or could just sit quietly nursing a cup of cocoa—I had to make a decision as to what to do about the extra material at the waist. If I was to be active, I usually preferred to hide the spare goods in a fold under my belt at the rear. If I could remain seated somewhere I would divide it into a pair of pleats running casually down the front, on either side of the fly; that rear fold could be murder over an extended stretch of sitting on a bare bench or in a smooth-bottomed chair.

Actually the only way I could manage to feel halfway presentable in that suit was to maintain a slight crouch forward with my shoulders in, while I clamped my arms to my sides to keep the sleeves pulled back and the coat from bellying out in front. That way, an observer had the option of thinking I was either ill or the victim of an anatomical defect.

A photograph was taken of me during the days when I still wore that suit. I was sitting, naturally (or, rather, unnaturally, naturally) slumped like Quasimodo, with a feeble and apologetic grin on my face.

My mother tried making a number of tailoring adjustments, but nothing worked. I wore it for a while to Sunday School and to family dinners, but that was about it. And it was good material; it lasted well. Exiled to the rear of the closet, the brown-chain pattern glimmered accusingly out at me for years.

There was no question of either my brother or me having another suit to wear while we attended school. He was growing too fast and I had already had my chance. So my mother allowed us to buy "dress" sweaters at Norval Bruce's Toggery. Mine was a black job with a sybaritic stripe of gold around the waist and at the collar, and this, together with a good pair of wool trousers, was my costume for the high school dances and other dress occasions over the next two years.

School clothing wasn't as much of a problem. Bib overalls were practically the uniform for boys of all ages. Boys with the desire and the means for keeping up with trends bought striped overalls, and later on came jeans with red gores sewn at the ends of the legs to make them flare—bell-bottoms. I didn't have the means or the desire to keep up with fashion trends, but I did inherit a couple of pairs of dress trousers from my cousins, the doctor's sons, which my mother altered to fit—unfortunately I was smaller than any of my male relatives and was thus at the bottom of the pants chain.

Then there was the costume with which Mrs. Thomas, the banker's wife, provided me. One of her sons had attended a military school a couple of years, and had brought home a powder-blue uniform of the World War I type with rolled leggings and with a black stripe running down the sleeves of the blouse and along the sides of the trousers. It was a good fit and looked pretty dashing and romantic so I accepted the gift and wore it to school one day. It turned out to be a minor sensation. Up and down the main stairway of the old high school between classes, I was the cynosure of all eyes. As the day wore on, however, word got around that I really was not newly enlisted in some form of junior ROTC and I grew more and more reluctant to answer questions about where the uniform had come from and why I was wearing it. The next day I was back in mufti.

At graduation I did acquire another suit, a blue-striped one that fitted well and cost somewhere around twenty dollars in Grand Junction, but by the time I entered college at Western State two years later it was threadbare and shiny. Still, the dress code at Western as at Paonia High School was extremely relaxed and I got along well enough through the first two years. As a junior, though, I had been dragooned into a fraternity which was going national and each of the brothers had to have a dark suit for the group photograph. Fortunately one of the fraternity sponsors was working at a men's furnishings store, and in this crisis I was extended credit. The suit I chose was in a rich shade of oxford gray with a three-button coat. It was not long before I was made aware that the suit, of good quality and fit, was a bit old-fashioned. Fred Kuypers, a dressy emigre from California, gave it to me straight:

"They must have seen you coming when they sold you that suit, Haley."

And it was true. The top button on the coat was about four inches below my Adam's Apple, and the suit would have looked great with a wing collar and a Prince Edward cravat. But this was 1934, not 1904, and other lads were wearing coats with lapels that homed on the navel, and the coats could be left casually and elegantly open to reveal perhaps a double-breasted vest.

I tried pressing the lapels on the suit to broaden and extend them down to the second button, but that didn't work. And there was nothing else for it; I couldn't afford another suit. I couldn't even afford the one I had. For the next two years I didn't get much mail, but every several weeks two letters could be depended upon: one from my mother, and one from Miller's Men's Furnishings.

I was able to dress better later. As an enlisted man in the Army, though, there were problems—shoes as long as training skis (when I grumbled to the supply sergeant about all the spare space beyond my toes in those shoes he only said, "They fit you where it counts."). And then there was a pair of dress pants issued me made of army blanketing, that stood away from my legs like armor—and wore like armor, too.

I don't worry all that much about suits now. And I have a lot of company. It's nothing nowadays to see celebrants of the most sacred rites—attendees of both sexes at christenings, weddings and funerals —dressed in sports clothing.

My mother gave me lots of advice when I was growing up, and much of it I ignored or scoffed at, but in my mind's eye I can still see her as she bent over the old White sewing machine, making shirts for my brother and me, and one morning when I was in one of those receptive moods that can occur once in a blue moon when a parent talks to a child, she told me,

"Always take good care of your clothes."

And that, Mama, I have tried to do.

The World of Uncle Henry

My Uncle Henry Elmendorf was a man of parts. Loyal to friends, considerate of all relatives. A gentleman—if a little rough-hewn—and a loving son, brother, husband, father.

As a son, he spoke of his mother in epic terms. All of Uncle Henry's tales were epic, or at least those that were recounted in my presence, and the earliest ones began with his recollections of growing up on his mother's homestead, later included in the Elmendorf home ranch. His mother was widowed early, but with her half dozen stalwart sons ruled on at the ranch, dispensing wisdom and justice to her little kingdom. As well as I was able to understand she was eminently fair in her dealings with her sons and with everyone else, but stern.

Aunt Ina, too, had apparently enormous respect for her mother-in-law, and accepted the older woman during her lifetime as the head of the family. It was only natural, I suppose, that afterward she took on something of the aura and became the decision-maker often in her own family, and was the one to whom all turned in a crisis.

Uncle Henry reverenced his mother's memory and patterned his behavior on the principles that she had laid down, as the other sons must also have done. Once when I was at the ranch one of Uncle Henry's older brothers came for a visit, and their conversations were conducted on an elevated plain, it seemed to me; there was none of the familiar give and take between them that I have observed between other brothers. There was dignity, respect, and affection, but neither took liberties with the other.

Uncle Henry was a big, broad-shouldered man with a head of luxuriant dark hair peppered with gray, and a black mustache underlining his heavy German nose. In middle age he was afflicted with stomach cancer and went to an osteopathic doctor in Salida, where the D&RG railway had a renowned hospital and treatment center, and was there operated upon. I remember lying in bed one night in the boys' room upstairs at the old ranch, and Uncle Henry, just returned from the operational wars, laid aside the upper half of his long johns and revealed the long red scar that traversed his mid-section for his sons' edification. I just happened to be there at the time, but I was awed, not only by the scar, but by my uncle's broad muscular chest and shoulders. He was physically a match at least in appearance still, for any of his grown sons. He went on, of course, to describe in stately terms the operation, and what he had said to the doctor and the nurses, before and after, and what they had said to him.

Outside when working around the ranch, Uncle Henry wore a stockman's hat, bib overalls and a denim shirt and workshoes. But on any appropriate occasion he would don his one suit, a dark one, with a white shirt, and a tie.

He was polite with strangers, courtly with women, but among men with whom he felt comfortable enough—and those aspiring to be men like his sons or small male relatives—he was apt, at times, to be forthright.

I first became aware of this trait of his when he and Aunt Ina came down to the Hotchkiss station, the nearest railway depot to the ranch, to pick up my mother and me when we appeared there on a visit from our home in Ridgway—my brother Harold was already visiting the ranch at the time, and our father was unable to get away from his barbershop. This was a dress occasion for Uncle Henry in that several female relatives and friends accompanied my uncle's party on the trip to the station and back to Clear Fork, and he looked most impressive to me, a six-year-old, in his dark suit and stockman's hat, with the pipe he always smoked firmly between his teeth.

On our way back to the ranch, when we arrived before the Clear Fork school, Uncle Henry abruptly pulled the car to the side of the road. Then the ladies in their long dark coats and flowered hats retired into the cedars up beyond the schoolhouse, while Uncle and I walked down into the brush below the road.

The stop had been made without any words being exchanged that I was aware of, and I was bewildered. "Why are we stopping, Uncle Henry?" I inquired.

"Because, Nephew, Uncle's got to pee," he said, suiting the action to the word.

That was another quirk of my uncle: he liked to use the family designation, not only for himself, but when addressing all relatives; he commonly addressed my mother as "Sister," and his daughters and daughters-in-law, individually, as "Daughter."

Although he could be frank with men and boys, he was almost never profane around women; there was only one occasion, when driven by exasperation, that I ever heard him speak in a vulgar way to any member of the opposite sex. This occurred one evening when his daughter Cena, immersed in her eighth-grade homework, shared the light from the gasoline lamp at the end of the long table in the dining room with him. At one point, she turned to him for help in interpreting a passage in her agriculture textbook.

"Papa," she asked brightly, "it keeps talking about manure." The word was obviously unfamiliar to her and she pronounced it as "man-yoor," with the accent on the first syllable. "What is man-yoor?"

Uncle Henry looked up from *Capper's Weekly* and over his half spectacles, his wide mouth stretched in a way that showed his embarrassment and discomfort. "Daughter," he said, "it's a substance that's used on ranches."

"Do you ever use it?"

"Oh, yes, sure, I use it," Uncle Henry said, abruptly turning a page.

"Well, what is it, exactly?"

"It's a kind of a fertilizer."

"A fertilizer," Cena repeated dreamily. "What kind of a fertilizer, Papa?"

"Oh, it's just a—just a fertilizer." Uncle Henry's voice rose somewhat, impatiently. He grew testy. "And I won't say any more than that."

Cena was rather enjoying herself. All the children liked to annoy their father—he was a good subject for teasing. "Papa," she said, "I got to know more about it for my lesson. What is it, Papa, what is man-yoor?" Uncle Henry responded evasively a couple of times, and then remained silent. Cena continued her inquiries, and at last said, "Papa, I'm beginning to think you don't even know what 'man-yoor' is."

By now, her father's short fuse had run out. Besides, this was a taunt he could not ignore. He was a well-informed man despite a very modest education, and he took pride in the fact. He crunched the newspaper down and glared at his youngest.

"Goddam it, Daughter," he said, "it's cowshit."

Cena stared at him, astonished and affronted, then she leaped up and ran into the kitchen where her mother was setting up a batch of bread:

"Mama," she cried, "Papa's cursing at me!"

Another time when Cena managed to drive her father across the line occurred at an evening meal when I was staying at the ranch. Cena had passed her sauce dish for a second helping of canned peaches, and her father inquired, serving spoon poised, "How many peaches do you want, Daughter?"

"A few," she said.

"How many," he asked, "is a few?"

"Oh—you know. A few is a few."

"I *don't* know." Uncle Henry lowered the spoon and the sauce dish. "How many peaches do you want, Daughter?"

This was more than Cena had bargained for. So far, the evening had been rather dull. She smiled roguishly, and looked casually out the west window, evidently caught up in admiration of the sunset. "Just give me—a few."

Uncle Henry stared at his daughter for some time. Then he picked up the spoon and began ladling plump halves of bright yellow peaches into his daughter's sauce dish. Two, three, four—Cena became alarmed. "That's enough, Papa, that's enough!"

Uncle Henry stopped at five.

"I can't eat all that many, Papa!" she wailed.

"You can, and you will, or I'll strap you," Uncle Henry promised. Aunt Ina was called in, while Cena wailed, "I only asked for a few peaches, Mama, and he just loaded them on. Everybody knows that a few peaches is two—everybody knows that."

"Everybody doesn't know that," Uncle Henry growled, "I asked her several times to tell me how many peaches she wanted, and she just smirked at me. Now she's going to eat what I dished up for her."

Aunt Ina could usually be depended upon to intercede in a matter of this kind, but this time she did not. She retired to the kitchen, muttering something about "childish behavior," and Cena bent to her task, between bouts of tears and cries of "One, two—a few . . . one, two—a few . . . "

But Uncle Henry got along with everyone, even his children, for the most part. Of course there were the usual problems. One involved the automobile. In the twenties right after World War I, when wheat, hay and cattle were bringing good prices and Uncle Henry had the help of his husky youngest son on the place, he and Aunt Ina felt they could splurge on a really fine machine. Big new touring cars were just coming on the market. Uncle Henry bought one, maroon, with wheels with wooden yellow spokes, and a thermometer for a radiator cap. The running boards were wide enough to accommodate a man lying down—a stunt that was part of the standard sales pitch which every car salesman relied on in those days.

"Looka here," he would say, removing his straw skimmer and laying it and his suit coat on the radiator, "Look at the running boards on this car—wide enough to lay down on." And he would lie down on it to prove it.

The sedan my uncle bought was an Elcar, made by the best buggy makers in Indiana claimed Uncle Henry, with running boards second in width and length to none.

Uncle Henry at the helm of his Elcar was an imposing sight. A broad-shouldered man, he sat well back with a big muscular hand clamped to either side of the wheel, his chin tucked in and his face grim under his stockman's hat, and he drove at a respectable speed of from seventeen to twenty miles an hour.

Boyd was the problem where the car was concerned. One morning over breakfast when he was complaining as usual about not being allowed to drive the car by himself, his father said,

"If you want to know why I won't let you take the car by yourself, Boyd, I can tell you easy enough."

"Well I just wish you'd do that, Dad," Boyd whined, "I just wish you would."

"You remember that time last week when I let you drive into town after groceries?"

"What about it?"

"You came up over Yarnell Hill and Al Goodwin was out irrigatin' and he seen you go by and he said you was doin' at least 45 miles an hour."

"That's just a damned lie," Boyd wailed, "I wasn't goin' no 45 miles an hour, nowhere near it."

"You was," his father shouted, "Al Goodwin don't lie. You was doin' that if you was doin' five, and I'd bet on it. I know how you drive."

But on the whole he and Boyd got along quite well. He was young and his judgment was not always to the liking of his parents, but he was steady and strong, a good worker, and it was their hope he would remain on the ranch after they were gone. There were four other sons and all had drifted away—owning, perhaps, all of them, something of that restlessness in their natures that had spurred their father's brother, Sid, to seek his fortune in the Klondike.

Uncle Henry read extensively in newspapers, and was well up on the Bible. He had an inquiring acquisitive mind. When as a small boy I followed him around the place, he often stopped to explain things to me and elaborate on the qualities of various materials—at the woodpile he told me about ironwood, which the Indians had used, he said, to make their war bows from, and about greasewood which burned nearly as readily as paper. His shop was part museum; on the walls, high above the log-supported counters and the forge, hung a wide array of harness, tools, and odd pieces of equipment. Across one wall were hung Boyd's traps—each of Uncle Henry's boys had taken his turn with the traps—when a boy was of an age to want things that cost money, he was led to the traps and told to line his own pockets.

On a rainy day, when work in the fields was not possible, work could go on in the workshop, and often neighbors perhaps lacking a forge or some specialized tool, would stop by for Uncle Henry's help and advice, or, one was apt to suspect, partly for the entertainment of hearing Uncle Henry hold forth on early days around the country when it was not settled up, or of the times he had freighted goods and equipment over Black Mesa from Gunnison, and stories of what he had seen in that then wide-open mining camp; about the legendary

"Doc" Shores, frontier peace officer; the big poker games in the saloons, or of waking in a rooming house and looking out into the alley and seeing a Mexican strung up on a telegraph pole after a drunken argument.

Uncle Henry was also an authority on the ills of livestock, and what native plants had to be watched out for and avoided. He had a store of medicines for all sorts of illnesses, in both animals and humans, and was generous in dispensing both medicines and advice to anyone who solicited either.

He had strong views, too, on religion, and followed with approval the sayings of Judge Rutherford, a prominent evangelist of the day. An area of inquiry which interested the judge, and in turn fascinated my uncle, was that of the question of whether there was life on the other planets. Both he and the judge were of the opinion that there was life, and at the time there was much popular and scientific interest in Mars, the red planet, with its prominent canals that were generally believed to prove that thinking beings had laid them out. Uncle Henry looked forward to a time when there would somehow be communication with those beings, and he seemed certain that they would be well-intentioned, incredibly intelligent beings, and once in contact, life on earth would be marvelously advanced and improved.

On Sunday evenings after dinner, when even Aunt Ina would have an hour or so of precious leisure, Uncle Bill and Aunt Ina and whatever children or guests were present, would all go out to the screened-in front porch, and sit down and stare out into the friendly dark, with the stars brightly shining in the clear mountain sky, and Uncle Henry would lead a discussion of what might possibly be going on in the universe. He told of how there was no atmosphere beyond that surrounding the earth—where space took over, but the argument then, and he went along with it, was that something had to be out there, in the great spaces between the planets, and that something, although no one knew what it was, had been dubbed "ether;" Uncle Henry tried to explain to me that it was a tasteless, odorless substance, but always in my mind, the vast reaches of space were for me informed with a slight odor; that of the ether I had inhaled when my other uncle, Uncle Doc, had removed my tonsils. Uncle Henry assured me that there was no connection between the ether in space, and the ether I had breathed in for the operation, but I could not entirely erase the relationship from my thinking.

I never felt closer to my Uncle Henry than I did when one time he took me along after a load of coal from the Farmer's Mine above Paonia. We drove over in a freight wagon, and on the way back, night came on. We were provided with a lunch, which we ate, and out in the wastes of the Dobies below Crawford, a storm overtook us. Uncle

Henry had a slicker and had brought along another for me; we drove on through the quiet countryside, and through the sleeping town and on up the road towards home. The rain soon subsided, and the night sky was brilliant again with the stars above the silhouette of the West Elks, and Cathedral Rock looming up in the distance like the seat of some medieval or fairy-tale prince. And again we talked about the stars, and hearkened to the old song, later said to be Franklin Roosevelt's favorite, "Home on the Range," with the lines,

> How often at night, When the heavens are bright,
> With the light from the glittering stars,
> Have I stood there amazed, and asked as I gazed,
> If their glory exceeds that of ours.

The two daughters of the family, despite Uncle Henry's occasional problems with Cena, in the end fulfilled all his hopes for them, marrying dependable men and settling on ranches in the Hotchkiss country to raise their families, but the sons had difficulties in settling down, and all, eventually, with the exception of Boyd, were involved in separations and divorce actions. Uncle Henry once observed, sadly, that his sons had "done mighty poor jobs giving me daughters-in-law."

And all of the boys, again with the exception of Boyd, had antic dispositions, and enjoyed playing jokes and teasing their sisters and their father (their mother was a different proposition; she 'could see them coming,' as it were, and was seldom taken in by their shenanigans).

The acknowledged leader in such trickery was the oldest son, Fred, who was a brewer of mischief all his life. Fred had difficulty in making a place for himself out in the world. After a try at cattle ranching which ended in his first divorce, he drifted into hotel management and then into selling. At one time when he was at loose ends, he stayed with his sister, Cena, then living in Paonia, where her husband was working on the county road crew. Fred's brother, Kenneth, bossed the crew, but there was no place there for Fred, so he looked after the barn for Kenneth, fed and groomed the teams of horses and a stallion which Kenneth kept there at stud. Fred liked to tell anyone who inquired about his work, that he was "pimping for a stud horse."

And, for entertainment, he teased his father. This was after Aunt Ina and Uncle Henry had retired from the ranch, and bought a little home on the outskirts of Paonia. Not long after, Aunt Ina was carried away by pneumonia, leaving Uncle Henry at loose ends and disconsolate. After a while, he became interested in a widow, the Widow Manfield, who ran a small, neat restaurant on Grand Avenue.

As is often the case in families, the grown Elmendorf children had ambivalent feelings about seeing their father interested in another woman. Only Fred claimed to be absolutely impartial, and even voiced encouragement; but his father was, properly, suspicious of his oldest son's assurances of support.

This was at a time when I was away at college, and I saw or heard little of what was going on except when I came back to Paonia at intervals between quarters. It was then I learned of some of the efforts that my cousin Fred had put forth in furthering his father's romantic interest in the Widow Manfield.

For example, one morning when Uncle Henry was grumping around in the house, Fred helpfully bustled up to the widow's restaurant, where a number of customers were seated at breakfast, and inquired

"Excuse me, Mrs. Manfield, but Papa's in kind of a state this morning. He can't seem to locate his upper plate anywhere—he didn't by any chance leave it up here, did he?"

Mrs. Manfield was of course annoyed, and Uncle Henry was enraged, and paid no attention to his son's apologies. "Dad," Fred assured him, "I was only tryin' to be a help."

"I can do without any of your damned help!" his father shouted.

By now, Uncle Henry was the possessor of another sedan, an Essex, and occasionally inveigled Mrs. Manfield into accepting a ride of a Sunday afternoon. He piloted it in his usual dignified fashion, head back, hands firmly on the wheel, and drifted as serenely as if in a yacht, around the streets of the town. Except of course for the afternoon when Fred slipped a cushion of the type commonly called a "whoopee cushion" into the front passenger seat.

Still, the affair went on—until the time came for the district ball to be given by the Odd Fellows in Cedaredge. Fred wondered aloud at the house if his father would ask the widow to go, but Uncle Henry maintained a dignified silence about any such intention. Fred had acquired the habit of stopping in at the widow's restaurant for a cup of coffee in midafternoon when he was certain his father was at home having a nap, so on one such occasion, he remarked to the widow that he approved of his father's interest in her. She was embarrassed and annoyed, and Fred apologized.

"It's none of my business, that's for sure," Fred told her. "But I couldn't help noticin' that it isn't all on one side, and I wanted you to know that that is fine with me."

"What do you mean by that?" she snapped.

"Well, it's gettin' to be pretty plain that not only does Dad favor you, but that you kinda favor him."

The widow had grown children of her own—one, a daughter, often helped out in the restaurant, and Fred had chosen a time when the daughter would be present, assuming probably correctly that the children of the Widow Manfield also looked a bit askance at this winter

138

romance. So the widow, partly perhaps to reassure her daughter, said,

"Mr. Elmendorf's all right, I suppose, I have nothing in particular against him."

"Oh, now, Mrs. Manfield," Fred snickered, "that's certainly putting it mild. The truth is that you're pretty stuck on my dad."

"Would you care for some more coffee?" the widow inquired, glaring at him with the pot raised in her right fist. The color had risen in her cheeks. Her daughter was listening from the kitchen.

"You don't have to hide it from me—matter of fact, you can't— why, it's written all over your face when my dad's around that you—"

She took the pot back to the hot plate and then returned to face Fred, smiling as easily as she could manage. "I don't behave any differently towards Mr. Elmendorf than I do toward any other customer, and I don't feel any differently toward him than I do toward any other customer," she said.

"Oh come on, now. I expect you've heard that the Odd Fellows are having their big annual blowout over in Cedaredge in a couple of weeks," Fred said.

"I may have."

"Dad's already asked you to go, hasn't he?"

"The subject," Mrs. Manfield replied curtly, "has not come up."

"I'll bet you must be on pins and needles, then ain't you?" Fred asked sympathetically.

"I'm not on pins and needles about anything."

"Well if he does ask you, you're going to go, ain't you?"

"I might, and I might not."

"That's a good one. When Dad gets around to askin' you—*if* he does—you'll jump at the chance."

"As a matter of fact," the Widow Manfield said evenly and coldly, "I've got other plans for that weekend and I wouldn't be able to go even if I was asked."

Uncle Henry did get around to asking, and the Widow Manfield turned him down. Worse, she would give him no reason for her refusal. Fred expressed the opinion that she was seeing somebody else, and his father thanked him to keep his opinions to himself.

How the affair would have ended no one would ever know, because the cancer that had attacked Uncle Henry's stomach a decade earlier returned to plague him again, and this time in earnest. He began to fail, but although the doctor and his daughter urged him to take to his bed, and even when he was so weak that he could not sit up he refused to undress. He would remove only his shoes and lie down on the bed with the coverlet not pulled back, in his stockinged feet, and with his hat in easy reach, as he shaded his eyes from the morning light pouring in the windows with a hand that had turned yellow and scrawny.

Fred wandered on, into other employments and another marriage. When this wife ran away with another man, who had in his turn deserted a family in Denver, Fred, true to his trickster nature, went to see the abandoned wife, and found a pleasant, pretty little woman with whom he at once fell in love, with a family ready made; so the tricks that he enjoyed and that usually ended in annoyance for others, brought at last to Fred the most fortunate gift life could hold for him. He settled down in earnest, by this time well into middle age, and they lived happily together for the rest of their years.

Certainly Aunt Ina, and even Uncle Henry would have been pleased.

The Enjoyment of Ill Health

In her eighties my wife's grandmother had a slight indisposition and was taken to the doctor. He was reassuring.

"You seem in good health, Mrs. Hall; when did you visit a doctor last?"

"Oh, it must have been six or seven months ago."

"What was the problem then?"

"A pregnancy."

He looked startled.

"Not me," she said, "It was my granddaughter's. I just went along."

In all her life except when she approached death in her middle nineties the old lady never was examined except that one time, but she had "visited" a doctor on a number of occasions. In remote farming communities such as she had lived in, going to the doctor was an event, and one not to be missed by an ailing woman's female relatives and close friends; one of those rare dress-up occasions when one could conscientiously get away from the monotony and drudgery of the farm.

That was the social sphere in which my own mother grew up, and I'm sure she would have seen nothing strange in the practice and probably followed the custom herself when she lived on her father's homestead in the Maher country as a young woman.

We saw the doctor rarely when my brother and I were young but more often than we might have otherwise, because Uncle Doc didn't charge for the visits. Still, we tried not to make a practice of it. Once I had what seemed to me a suspicious lump on my wrist. I went to him about that. He talked to me as he commonly did, giving generously of his time to a boy no doubt hungry for a little fatherly attention, and then he received my hand into his, examined the swelling, reached for a small book on a nearby table and hit the swelling with it. The swelling promptly went away.

But for the most part we did our own family doctoring like any family of slender means. My mother had a book with a red cover that she kept in the front room secretary. It was full of vague and evasive statements on a variety of common diseases, a dull book almost never referred to; and there was that larger and more authoritative book with copious and fascinating colored illustrations on female diseases hidden away in one of her bureau drawers. For day-to-day family emergencies, there were clean cloths in the drawer of the washstand to take care of small cuts, and behind the bathroom mirror several shelves displaying a motley of jars, bottles, cans and packages for the treatment of colds and digestive complaints.

My brother was in rugged good health and had fewer complaints than I. I was prone to sieges of tonsillitis until my uncle removed my tonsils, along with my adenoids, when I was seven or eight. I remember listening to him explain the surgical procedure to my father a few days before the operation took place. It was the fashionable minor operation of the day, and not in as good repute now, I think.

My mother was one of those girls in delicate health when quite young. She was never "strong," and told me that she overheard her folks talking about her case more than once, and giving the opinion that "that girl will never live to be grown."

I think she never really looked forward seriously to marriage and childbearing, thinking in her state of health such a life and such responsibilities were beyond her. She certainly would have thought so if she had known what she was in for, raising two active boys without the help of a husband. And when these burdens came to her, and with the sort of upbringing she had had, it was all doubly hard. On cold winter mornings she would stir up the banked fire in the front-room heater—my brother and I slept upstairs and she in the rear downstairs bedroom—and when we came downstairs she would be dressing behind the heater.

If, as was often the case, she was suffering from a headache, a continual low, grunting groan would arise from her throat which never failed to annoy me. I always resolved that whatever ailments I would be cursed with, I would not take up my mother's habit of groaning. I understand her state of mind better now. She was alone and depressed, overwhelmed with her responsibilities; she had always favored herself because it was assumed she was sickly, and now, with all the duties and worries forced upon her, illness was a sort of refuge. There was no adult nearby to confide in, only two careless, growing boys. A daughter might have helped.

We did not have the money to waste on nostrums and remedies of which there were then a great many. My mother favored only a few and these were not exotic concoctions or painkillers. Cough drops she resorted to, but they were hard to keep on hand because her sons used them for candy. That left Vapo-Rub, Mentholatum, iodine, and a militant representation of laxatives and purgatives, ranging up the chain of command from Ex-Lax through Cascara and Sal Hepatica to

Epsom salts.

To my mother, I always felt, the human mechanism was a simple one. It consisted of two systems: lungs and bowels. Nearly any ailment other than infectious diseases, rheumatism or cancer, was apt in her view to be the result of clogged passages—a pumping problem, essentially. If one kept the pipes clean, washed them out regularly, everything would come right. And she was perpetually at this task, not only with her own "system" but with my brother's and mine. He was active and hard to pin down, but I was often around the house reading, so it was easier to worry about my health.

Besides, I slyly traded on this attitude of hers. I hated school, particularly when in the third grade I failed to master the multiplication tables and later on gave up division as an occult art. And I had had tonsillitis, which gave me an edge. On a morning when I could not stomach the thought of going to school I would make it plain that I was not feeling very well. Nothing in particular, maybe a little discomfort in the stomach. I would eat little breakfast, a necessary sacrifice, feel pale and wan and actually begin to look that way. My mother would question me, the symptoms would add up to a diagnosis, and she would usually decide, as the school bell dimly pealed the quarter-hour before nine, that maybe it would be better if I stayed home. I would remain listless, concealing my exultation, while my mother pondered treatment. The least I could hope for would be Sal Hepatica, the torture of choice for a run-of-the-mill disorder; Epsom salts was called for if she determined that my condition required blasting rather than just pick-and-shovel work.

Afterward, properly purged, with my insides in a state of shock, my mind torpid and miasmic, I could turn to the real business of the day—reading whatever Tarzan book or issue of the *American Boy* or *Amazing Stories* or *The Golden Book* that I had on hand. I had, however, to be circumspect until after the noon hour—a too startling improvement could send me to school for the afternoon session. Around 1:30 I could begin to show improvement, sometimes miraculous improvement, which my mother of course credited to whatever preparation she had dosed me with, and in an emergency I might even be able to undertake a shopping errand. One time I was on such an errand when I saw approaching me on the street my sixth grade teacher, apparently on some errand of her own during a free period— and I swiftly hid behind a billboard as she passed by. I thought she hadn't seen me, but I was to learn later, under excruciatingly embarrassing circumstances, that she had.

It was during the next week when she was reading to the class from some favored book that she stopped abruptly and asked,

"Glen, what were you doing behind the billboard across from

Wade's Grocery last Thursday during school hours?"

I really don't remember what reply I fumbled out for her. I'm sure it wasn't at all adequate. But the impression that remained with me from the incident was that Miss Hazlett was exceedingly devious, and with a little streak of malevolence in her makeup. Besides, she was the daughter of a doctor who was a business rival of my uncle, and I always believed that that had something to do with her attempt to shatter my defenses and expose my malingering in so public a way.

And although often my illnesses were fakery, there were those times when I really was "out of sorts" as my mother would say, and for such emergencies she reserved the ultimate treatment: an enema, or an "injection" as she called it. Actually, given the choice of attending school or submitting to a colonic irrigation, just stated in those bald terms, my resolve might have wavered; but if given time to reflect a little on the alternative—the torture of penmanship, the battering of the psyche inflicted in arithmetic—I would still have chosen the enema.

I think it only made a philosophic sort of sense to my mother that one must suffer indignity and pain in order to achieve a state of good health. It was the catharsis, the purgation—comparable on the spiritual level to the Confession. And even Gandhi, that modern saint, would not have quarrelled with that. It was not with her an emergency measure but a periodic antisepsis basic to good health.

But if she hoped to inculcate this conviction in me, she failed. I never forgot, for instance, one evening when I was "out of sorts," and she demanded that either I go to bed or submit to an "injection." I naturally chose bed, but she warned that if I lingered a single minute after the hour of ten o'clock I would pay the penalty. Naturally this challenge could not be ignored and I purposely trimmed the time as closely as I dared, only closing my book a half minute before the critical hour. But as I rose from the chair at precisely 9:59:30, she and her niece who was staying with us that winter to attend high school, descended on me, laughing and giggling, set up the rubber bottle filled with warm salt water and set me on that disgusting phallus, an act of treachery I never forgave.

My experiences with ill health were not always so unpleasant. I enjoyed the attention I received while I was recuperating from the tonsillectomy. This was in the old hospital in the brick house beside the Methodist Church. There was the discomfort in my throat right enough, but matched against it were the meals cooked by country women and the lazy afternoons lolling in bed reading. Years later my uncle removed my appendix in his own hospital and this was even less of an ordeal than the tonsillectomy; during the operation I was under a local anaesthetic, and I could hear my uncle whistling to himself as he worked. But there have been other experiences since, not so brightly colored by memory. I no longer entertain any affection for hospitals.

I suffered quarantine at least twice, once for smallpox and once for whooping cough. Both times the disease lingered longer with me than with the other members of the family, and I can conscientiously say that in neither case was this through any fault of mine. And, both times the quarantine was lifted from the house, freeing my mother and my brother, but leaving me exiled to a one-room cottage at the rear which my mother rented over years to bachelors or couples but which often stood vacant.

The whooping cough quarantine when I was in junior high was all right for the first month but it went on for so long that I became bored with it and actually yearned to return to school. Dr. Hazlett, my uncle's sworn professional enemy, was on the quarantine board and I seemed to have become a pawn in their ongoing feud. When I had been out of school for six weeks, my mother appealed to my uncle to request that I be allowed to return to school and he provided me with a note to submit to the school authorities. Armed with the precious note, I appeared at the office of Superintendent Wubben, who was also the son-in-law of Doctor Hazlett, for the all-important interview.

I was nervous, and the office was small and seemed uncomfortably warm. Mr. Wubben took his time reading the note. I became more and more uncomfortable. An itching crept into my throat. I stifled it. It grew worse. At last I coughed a small cough. Mr. Wubben looked up, startled and wary. As he stared at me I coughed again. And again. And again. Soon, out of control, I was whooping away. Back to square one I went for another week.

On the whole I quite enjoyed the smallpox quarantine which came along a couple of years later. At least I did once the initial discomfort subsided—there is nothing quite like the feeling of having smallpox pustules cloaking you, front to back and toe to scalp, as if you had been thoroughly rolled by torturers over a bed of nails. But during the weeks of recuperation I was my own boss. I had my own bed—in the main house my brother was larger than I and shouldered the covers away on cold nights, and since this was in January I was particularly relieved to be away from him. Then, I had a stove, a table, and my food, three squares a day handed into me through the front window, and I was free to do exactly as I chose.

My school books were made available but I wasted little time on them. I did read *Literature and Life,* Book II, but this only proved an annoyance to Miss Santarelli when at length I did return to class, since there was nothing left to hold my interest for the rest of the semester. I read popular biography, Elbert Hubbard's "Little Journeys to the Lives of the Great;" the Mars books of Edgar Rice Burroughs;

various magazines, and if I wanted to read well into the night there was no one to object.

I had done this occasionally in the main house on those rare occasions when the front bedroom was not rented out and I had a bed to myself, but it was always a dangerous practice. My mother continually warned me about it so I conceived the shrewd plan of reading under the covers by flashlight, but she prowled up the steps one night and dug me out like a cornered prairie dog and strapped me.

In my quarantine retreat there was no such problem. And although I had to accept a laundry tub and fill it with hot water brought in pails from the kitchen stove reservoir for the Saturday night bath, I didn't have to have my wrists, knees, and elbows examined or anyone looking behind my ears—I decided how much soaping I had to suffer, and where it would be applied.

Whenever reading palled, which was fairly infrequently, I played solitaire; I was never really bored, even when I had recovered to the point that I felt the need for some exercise. I walked around my cell, comparing my lot favorably to that of the Prisoner of Chillon, and eventually, after establishing the regimen of taking long naps in the afternoon, I would wait until my family and indeed the entire town had gone to bed, and I would dress and walk swiftly along the streets, enjoying my splendid solitude and the daring of the lawless act. I liked best of all walking up the broad pavement leading to the quiet doors of the high school and looking in, the glass giving back the reflection of my sardonic visage with the help of the street lights. These tours made me feel that I had a town of my own, completely depopulated, all the residents taken off by a medieval plague.

But the most vivid of my recollections of the smallpox quarantine was not of these nightly expeditions which were real enough, but of a dream. Again I was in a virtually depopulated town—only three survivors, the superintendent of schools, Verne Trobaugh, and myself. It would be hard to find a pair of men as different from each other as Superintendent Wubben and Verne Trobaugh. Mr. Wubben, one of the best superintendents Paonia has had, was a man almost prim in appearance and attitude, and Verne Trobaugh was an itinerant cowboy, careless of dress, with a game leg as a result of a roping accident, bowlegged into the bargain, possessor of a speech impediment, butt of pool hall jokes, often unemployed at his chosen trade.

It is said that whenever three individuals are isolated together, two will team up against the third. And in this dream it was Mr. Wubben and I against Verne, and for a desperate and horrible reason. Verne had gone mad and had killed everybody in town but us, and was searching for the two of us high and low along the dream-dim streets, nosing us out of one hiding place after another, waving his bloody

146

hatchet (it was approaching Washington's Birthday in real waking life and I assume that that accounted for the hatchet). Mr. Wubben and I, all animosities on my part or reservations on his destroyed by our common terror, scrambled and huddled away until at last we arrived at the high school, knowing obscurely that it was the last possible refuge.

Once inside we were confronted with an interior in which there were no longer rooms, but only long strips of flimsy, whispering material, brown or white or gray wrapping paper depending from the high ceiling to the floor. We made our way through passage after passage of this paper, with Verne insanely crying out behind us, dragging his game leg, up one set of stairs, up another into the attic, coming at last to the outer wall, with Verne dragging his leg along the passages, the hatchet thumping as he inched it forward. It was then I awoke safe in my bed, bathed in sweat, with a blind rustling and bumping restlessly across the sill of the open window above my head.

My health throughout my life has been reasonably good, though I have known the heartbreak of psoriasis and my teeth are shot, but my mother did manage to instil in me the conviction that I was doomed to bouts of intestinal irregularity. In the Army at a North Carolina basic training center one Sunday I was feeling "out of sorts" and spied an army doctor lounging out under a tree with a soldier companion. I went up to him and told him I suffered from constipation and wondered if he could recommend a corrective.

He did not take kindly to my request.

"Don't tell *me* you're constipated," he said. "You're not a doctor. And I am, and I'm telling you that you are not. You're leading an active life in the open air, with plenty of wholesome food including plenty of roughage. You're not constipated, so just forget about it."

My feelings were hurt, but sure enough, my constipation was cured. I took no more Sal Hepatica, no more Ex-Lax, no more Cascara, and never again did I have to mount that hideous throne and undergo an "injection." My mother did not argue with me when I told her of my miraculous cure. I think she thought of it as just another example of that falling away into error children are prone to when they leave the parental nest.

I was with my mother or near her often during the rest of her life, and that delicate girl whose parents had despaired that she would ever live to be grown, lived on into her nineties. She had her share of health problems, suffering from glaucoma and cataracts and plagued with an arthritic back. This last-named affliction was not truly crippling until her last years, but even then, stooped by osteoporosis, and hobbling on bunioned feet which she had abused in her youth through thriftily wearing "perfectly good" shoes that didn't fit her feet, she still managed to go out to dinner with her family.

When the pain in her back became acute, she visited doctors, but with little success. One doctor recommended a corrective corset, but she fought the use of this device with might and main, partly, I think, because it made her feel like an invalid. Once, after a session with the doctor and a couple of nurses, she submitted to the corset but she only allowed them to put it on her backwards, with the laces along her spine, which meant that the device was merely supporting her abdomen and was not helping her back at all. Everyone was upset and exhausted by this ordeal, and it ended with her crying out to me,

"They just don't understand the case!"

My mother is gone now, and I miss the calls from her apartment, usually on weekends, those mysterious calls which would begin so innocuously,

"What's the matter, Mama?"

"Nothing's the matter—just calling..." until I could finally worm from her the "little problem," the emergency that had come up, consisting of anything from a leaky water closet, the need for new carpet slippers, or a sudden shortage of milk or bananas.

To enter her apartment was to enter another world. A darker world, and redolent with the odor of eucalyptus oil, a sovereign remedy for colds and neuritis that she had taken to her bosom upon moving from Colorado to Southern California. And the heat in her apartment was a palpable presence, even in midsummer, making up for all those frosty Colorado mornings when she dressed trembling behind the heater.

I'm having more trouble with the cold nowadays myself. The house often seems chilly and I put on an extra sweater and jacket in the evening and my wife and I sometimes meet at the thermostat in the hall; I to turn it up, and she to turn it down.

"How can you stand it in here?" she will ask. "You're getting more like your mother every day."

There is something in what she says. I'm having a bit of a back problem myself now. And when it troubles me I can occasionally feel, rising in my throat, that self-pitying grunt-groan of my mother's which always annoyed me so much.

Bunkhouse Blues

The old bunkhouse on my Uncle Henry's ranch sat beyond the creek. You went by the narrow wooden footbridge and followed the path straight ahead, not branching off left to the junk heap and woodpile, nor right to the cellar, to arrive at the bunkhouse door.

It was not much of a bunkhouse, but that was because my Uncle's ranch was not a large operation as ranches went. He had anywhere from two to three or four grown sons helping him on the place during his last years there, so there wasn't that much demand for extra hands except during haying.

The bunkhouse accommodated two large bunks, one on either side of a narrow aisle. Between the bunks at the back wall sat an apple box, turned on end and camouflaged with a gingham curtain cut from one of Aunt Ina's castoff aprons, to serve as a cabinet. On top of it was a kerosene lamp. There were no windows in the bunkhouse, but no ventilation was really needed; if you tried, you could look out through cracks in the clapboard walls. In the evenings and nights the air inside was apt to be bracing; on a warm afternoon it was redolent of Prince Albert smoking tobacco, with a faint tinge of the odor of mice and eau de soiled socks.

But the place was kept reasonably clean; when it was in use, Aunt Ina or one of her two daughters went out at midmorning to tidy up. This presented a minor problem because there was usually some literature lying around or filed in the lower shelf of the apple box which were not fit for ladies to see. These consisted in the main of back copies of *Captain Billy's Whiz-bang,* a compilation of coarse jokes and crude cartoons, and a well-thumbed sheaf of vulgar poems laboriously copied by hand and contributed to the bunkhouse library by workers of other years or errant Elmendorf sons. After breakfast before going to the fields, bunkhouse residents tucked these publications away along the walls behind the bunks.

In the years after my father died, I spent as much time as I could on the ranch, and in those years the bunkhouse was in fairly steady use. This was chiefly because of George Parsons. George was a man in early middle age, a bachelor, and his parents had a little place down near Crawford, but George did not like staying there. He didn't get along with his parents for reasons that I never understood. But he adored Aunt Ina and swore that the ranch was his true home. During hay harvest or when there were cattle on the range up in the hills to look after, George was paid; but even after the work was done he stayed on, doing whatever there was to do—repairing equipment, shoeing horses, helping with the milking—just for his board and room.

George was a tall man, broad-shouldered and narrow-hipped, but he was not very well. He had tuberculosis, or consumption as it was called then, and was quite thin. His complexion looked healthy enough—slightly flushed, perhaps as a consequence of his disease— but his face was gaunt and his dark hair was thin though he kept it carefully combed. He had a wide thin-lipped mouth and when he smiled, a slow, infectious smile, he revealed too much of his big, healthy teeth.

He had a brother Alvin whom he loved, a man in his early twenties, not "all there," as Aunt Ina said privately, who came up occasionally to visit his brother. For someone without all his marbles, Alvin seemed remarkably assured. Perhaps part of the reason for this was George's attitude. George found his brother a remarkable person, and was always quoting him, or describing something that Alvin had done. Alvin's most notable accomplishment and indeed the only one that was ever confirmed for me, was his skill with a beaney or slingshot. He could knock a bird off a telephone wire, or destroy a glass insulator on a power line by simply pulling up his weapon and, without aiming apparently, hit the target. He was a skinny man with the same sort of frame that his brother had, but he was smaller. He wore a disreputable black hat but otherwise he was always in clean if threadbare bib overalls, blue cotton shirt and tennis shoes. I felt certain that he was well looked after and cherished by his parents, and Aunt Ina confirmed that this was so. As young as he was, Alvin had false teeth, and when he smiled, as he did infrequently, he smiled like George, and revealed his uppers clear to the top of the pinkish blue gums.

George was my particular friend, and we spent many happy hours together. He never teased me as Uncle Henry's sons and even his daughter Cena occasionally did, and he was full of stories of his travels. He had been in the Merchant Marine, he said, and had once gone to China. He knew the Chinese system of numbering, he said, and helped me to memorize the primary numbers:

"Lee Bee, Beanet, Tripasol, Solaset..."

I have come to suspect that George was yarning a bit, and didn't really know the Chinese system of numbering and may have never visited China, but I had no such troubling doubts at the time. Perhaps because of his state of health, George had temporarily retired from life in the Merchant Marine, and become a foot-loose cowboy. There were other such saddle nomads, drifting around the country, working in haying and roundups, and settling down for the winter months on some ranch where extra help was needed—with an older couple like my aunt and uncle, or looking after chores for a rancher laid up with illness or an injury. And failing that, a man might just visit around in the off season, stopping at remote ranches overnight, to pull up a chair and plant his boots under a friendly supper table.

Such men were always sure of a warm welcome from Aunt Ina and Uncle Henry. One of these loners was a big, raw-boned boy named Rhiny Mays. He had been orphaned early, and was more or less adopted by the ranchers in the Crawford country. He stopped at the ranch one evening in late fall and I sat at the dining-room table after supper was cleared away and looked on while he and Uncle Henry went over some points in the Old Testament together. Rhiny made light of the whole exercise and said that he didn't know anything about scripture, but when he had retired to the bunkhouse with George, Uncle Henry told me that Rhiny in fact knew the Holy Book very well indeed. The next morning, after breakfast, Rhiny was gone again.

George did quite a bit of reading too, and not just in the pages of *Captain Billy's Whiz-bang*. He had a small library of acceptable books reposing on the upper shelf of the apple box in the bunkhouse. He, too, was well informed on the Bible and even had some familiarity with the classics, such as Shakespeare; he was a great reader of poetry, but his taste didn't run to sonnets. At the top of his list of favorite poets were Robert W. Service and Rudyard Kipling. George and I read and enjoyed such poems together as Service's "The Cremation of Sam McGee," with its humorous bent and strong rhythms, but the ending of the "Killing of Dan McGrew," perhaps the best-known of Service's poems, which describes the lonely death of McGrew's killer, always brought a crooked grin to George's face:

> The woman that kissed him
> —And pinched his poke—
> Was the lady that's known as Lou.

Cowboys were not handsomely paid then (or now) and were often improvident and loners besides, which made them unattractive as candidates for marriage. But they often were also sensitive and proud and wore their hearts on their sleeves, so most of them had had at least one unhappy love affair and were cynical about women, young single women at least, which accounts for the bitterness and self-pity implicit in many a cowboy ballad.

George I think was no exception in this regard. He didn't confide any of the details of his failed romance or romances to me, but he tended to linger over cynical passages in the ballads of his favorite poet, Kipling, who appeared to have assigned to himself the post of advocate for the wronged male. Among his works were whole poems about the changeableness of women, their unreliability or their downright treachery, and George delighted in these. Nothing that could be said about the fair sex was devastating enough to suit George, always with the shining exception of Aunt Ina.

He gloried in such refrains as

"I learned about women from 'er,"

and "For the female of the species is more deadly than the male."

Then there was the bitter poem, "The Vampire," beginning with

"A fool there was, and he made his prayer...

To a rag, a bone, and a hank of hair..."

But even more to George's taste was the poem in which the writer leans back in his lonely den and fingers through his extensive collection of fine cigars, ruminating over the prospect of choosing, as his unfeeling fiancée had ruled that he must, between her and the weed, and concluding in favor of cigars with the line that George always liked to repeat triumphantly with his wide-open smile,

"For a woman is only a woman, But a good cigar is a smoke."

Although George tried to be fair. Kipling's American-born wife had penned a clever and wicked answer to this poem, and George quoted it appreciatively, too.

The year that Mr. Lhassie stayed in the bunkhouse was an exceptional one. Second cutting came on early and rain threatened, so that the usual crew had to be augmented. This caused Uncle Henry to 'phone around for extra help. He brought in his older son Fred who was running his own place below Crawford and also hired Mr. Lhassie, a relative of a nearby ranch family who happened to be on hand at the time. Mr. Lhassie was a comfortable sort of man, middle-aged, blond-headed, with a slow smile and an easy way about him, polite to ladies and a good yarn-spinner who naturally received a cordial welcome in the bunkhouse from George and me.

And, Uncle Henry also hired Jeffrey Macklin. Jeffrey was my cousin Cena's boyfriend, or "best beau" as the relationship was described at the time. Cena was petite, with intense, large dark brown eyes. She liked to tease me, and sometimes when Aunt Ina would send me upstairs to help Cena make beds (in order to get my nose out of a book) she would bug those large eyes out at me, pretending she was a witch. I was very frightened of witches at the time. And once when the three of us, Cena, my brother Harold and I, were all aboard old Nellie out by the haystacks, Cena pretended she was going to put me off and leave me there for the coyotes to get me. I later decided one of the reasons she teased me the way she did was because her brothers so delighted in teasing her.

It was indicative of how strongly smitten Cena was with Jeffrey that she went to the trouble—and it was considerable—to get her father to hire him for the haying that year.

"Daughter," Uncle Henry protested, "Jeffrey is a town boy, with no experience in haying, and I need a good trained hand."

"Oh, Daddy," Cena cried, "you don't know Jeffrey. He can do anything he sets his mind to, and he's a good worker, ask Mr. Clark in the packinghouse if he's not. Jeffrey works there every fall, and—"

"Well, it's more than that," her father said, "Fred's going to come up to help out, and you know Fred. He'll make the boy's life miserable, and yours too. You know how he can go on."

"Fred can just mind his own business," Cena snapped. "I've told Jeffrey about him, and all my brothers, what clowns they are. Besides, he's going to have to meet them sooner or later."

"I don't know, daughter, I don't know," Uncle Henry said, but relented in the end.

"He's awfully good with his hands," Cena once said at supper when Fred happened to be there. Jeffrey was a frequent subject in her conversation about this time.

Fred lowered his fork and sat back and regarded his sister solemnly, until Boyd, the youngest of the Elmendorf brothers, snickered. Even Aunt Ina couldn't forbear a smile.

"Oh for heaven's sake, Fred," Cena said disgustedly. "You know very well what I mean."

"I certainly hope I do," Fred said, "for your sake and the sake of the whole family I certainly hope—"

"All right, Fred," Uncle Henry said, "that's enough of that." But he looked pointedly at Cena. "I told you, Daughter, how it would be."

Jeffrey came the next week, driven over by his father in the family Model T. The Macklins were a quiet couple living in a small house in the eastern end of the town of Paonia, and surviving by Mr. Macklin performing clerical jobs down in the town, augmented by Mrs. Macklin working in the fruit in the fall, and doing sewing and baby-sitting as the occasion presented itself. Jeffrey was out of high school a year, but hadn't decided on any line of work as yet. This was during those years when Cena stayed at our house in Paonia during the winter and went to high school. She and Jeffrey had met at Epworth League. There were snapshots of them, out with friends on winter Sundays, standing beside the Macklin's Model T, Cena bundled to the ears in her coat, and Jeffrey in the sort of suit fashionable at the time, coat pulled in at the waist, peg-top trousers, pointed-toe oxfords, and with a large wool cap setting on his ears and shading his prominent nose.

Jeffrey did not make the mistake of arriving in the suit, though he did wear the cap, but rather in denim work shirt, jumper and bib overalls and serviceable working boots, and with a bundle of extra clothing in a leather grip. His father greeted Cena and her parents pleasantly, was invited to stay to supper but declined, saying he was expected back by Mrs. Macklin. But he did promise to bring Mrs. Macklin over for a visit when he returned in a couple of weeks to retrieve his son.

Jeffrey was a little more than average height, with sandy hair and light eyes rather close together in a narrow face. He was quiet, and courteous, and took his time in answering questions. Cena's parents were favorably impressed with him. He offered to sleep in the bunkhouse, but Cena had insisted that he be put up in one of the boys' vacant rooms abovestairs, thus raising him to the position of a guest. Her father had objected, but Cena had insisted, her mother had taken her part, and so it was decided.

At supper, though, Fred saw to it that Jeffrey was seated next to him on the righthand side of the table with the men—George, Mr. Lhassie, Boyd and himself. He also saw to it that the guest was well supplied with food—"better have some more beets, *Jeffrey,* more potatoes? Here, let me help you to some meat—" all under Cena's suspicious glare, and guided the conversation, giving a certain emphasis to the guest's name:

"Well, *Jeffrey,* Sis—that is, Cena—tells us that you're pretty handy with your hands—"

Quiet descended on the table. Jeffrey sat back and laid down his fork. A slight flush of color suffused his cheeks. Cena had opened her mouth to speak but before she could say anything, Jeffrey spoke up.

"I do some woodworking," he said, and calmly bent to his food again. Cena looked triumphantly to her father, and she and Jeffrey exchanged looks. Obviously Jeffrey had been primed for just such an emergency, and had passed the test with flying colors. Fred seemed impressed, and asked further questions, eliciting the information that Jeffrey had made a chest for his mother in manual training at the high school, and a bookcase ("just a beautiful bookcase," Cena could not help adding) and that he was now at work in his spare time at home on a desk.

On the following morning Jeffrey further established his right to be accepted on his own terms when Uncle Henry made working assignments for the day. It turned out that Jeffrey had gone to the trouble of brushing up on handling horses and volunteered to help with the raking. And he curtly refused Fred's offer of help in harnessing up, which earned him renewed respect from Boyd, who knew that Fred had planned to plant a burr under the collar of Doc, the right-hand bay of Jeffrey's team.

In the following days the work went smoothly, except for the time when Fred sneaked out just before the noon break for lunch, and forked the ditches full of hay in a field that Jeffrey had just finished raking, and took his father over to show him the careless work the new hand was doing. Uncle Henry was initially concerned enough to mention it to Jeffrey, who took it in good part, and promised to do better, although Cena, well aware of the true situation, indignantly accused her older brother that evening when the other men were still in the barn milking. Fred denied it all with a hurt look on his face.

"I can't believe you'd think I'd do a nasty trick like that, Sis," Fred said mournfully. "That fella is just breaking up our family, and if this goes on I don't see how in the world—"

"Just shut up," Cena snapped, "Just shut up and stop your stupid tricks. Everybody knows you and you're not upsetting anybody, so just quit it."

And from then on, as the haying wound down, Jeffrey had his accepted place on the crew. He and Cena walked out occasionally in the evening when he had finished with the milking and she was done helping her mother in the kitchen, but they were suitably discreet, never staying out long and comporting themselves decorously, not even holding hands, or at least not where they could be seen. Jeffrey finished the raking and shocked hay and even took his turn on the stack with George and Mr. Lhassie, and it was not until the day before the last of the cutting was in the stack that any incident involving Jeffrey occurred that was at all unfortunate.

It was that quiet time of the evening. It had begun to grow dark, and the setting sun had picked out the rimrock on the hill beyond the ranch to the north, and the turkeys were settling down on the threshing machine in the shed beyond the blacksmith shop, conversing more or less amicably together, when Jeffrey, Boyd and I walked up the path leading to the kitchen. The women were still busy in the kitchen, and Uncle Henry had just lit the gasoline lamp and set it on the dining-room table so he could look through the new copy of *Capper's Weekly.* Mr. Lhassie had lighted his pipe, and was lolling on the front stoop of the bunkhouse with George Parsons beside him, swapping stories about their travels.

Everyone was in a relaxed mood. Boyd was shying pebbles from the gravel in the path at the willows along the creek, and Jeffrey picked up a few and did the same. He had a strong arm, and just as a further diversion he and Boyd began throwing stones up into the sky, to see which could outdo the other. Jeffrey easily bested his rival and picked up larger stones to see how much further he could throw, and finally scooped up a rounded pebble nearly as large as a baseball and let fly. Up the rock sailed, and fell out of sight beyond the willows of the creek.

An instant later there arose a bellow of mortal pain from the direction of the bunkhouse. Stunned, the three of us hurried on up the path. I ran over to the bunkhouse and George met me at the door.

"Mr. Lhassie's been injured," he told me. I heard Fred inside, talking to the groaning man, and I followed Fred as he bustled by me across the footbridge to the kitchen, where Aunt Ina and Cena stood aghast inside the screen door, making inquiries about the stricken Mr. Lhassie.

"A rock came out of somewhere and hit him," Fred said. "Get me some warm water in a pan and a towel."

"How on earth could such a thing happen?" Aunt Ina asked.

"I don't know," Fred said darkly, "but maybe Cena's beau has some inkling."

"Jeffrey wouldn't do a thing like that," Cena said, "at least not on purpose."

"On purpose or not it hurts just as bad I expect. Have you got some kind of painkiller, Mama?"

"Well I suppose I have, if I just knew what was actually needed. Where did the stone hit Mr. Lhassie?"

"On the front step of the bunkhouse," Fred said, taking the pan of warm water and the cloth from his mother's hands and hurrying out.

By now Uncle Henry had gone out as well and the two women and I waited for more word from the bunkside. Fred came rushing back across the bridge.

"Where did the stone hit him, I mean on what part of his body?" Aunt Ina asked.

"Give me a pan of cold water this time, and another towel," Fred said.

"Where is he hurt? Will you just tell me where he is hurt?"

"Maybe a little tonic of some sort would help," Fred said, "something with a little zip in it. And have you got some mentholatum, maybe?"

"*Where is he hurt?*" Aunt Ina demanded. Fred hesitated. Even he was lost for an appropriate answer. And then it came to him.

"In the crotch, Mama," he said. "In the crotch."

No one, not even Fred, thought that Jeffrey had injured Mr. Lhassie on purpose. Jeffrey went to the bunkhouse and apologized profusely, and was reassured by Mr. Lhassie, who by now was resting fairly comfortably. But even Uncle Henry agreed with Fred that it was "a damn-fool trick," and spoke to both Boyd and Jeffrey about it. The absurd nature of the accident operated against Jeffrey despite Cena's warm defense of him. And, somehow, still another rather ridiculous incident which occurred after Jeffrey's parents arrived that Sunday for a visit almost made it appear that the fates were against the young lovers.

The elder Macklins had driven over in the family car, and had brought along my mother, who intended a few days' visit. But with the exception of my mother and myself, the group which gathered around the big dining table that evening consisted only of the immediate members of the two families. This was not purely accident; Cena with her mother's help had arranged it. She was evidently determined that the Macklins and her parents should become acquainted under the best of circumstances. Fred had returned to his place below town, taking with him George Parsons who had been persuaded by Aunt Ina that he should no longer postpone a visit to his own parents; a subdued Mr. Lhassie had returned to his relatives; and even Boyd was away, courting a neighbor girl.

The Macklins proved to be a quiet couple of approximately the age of Cena's parents, polite and pleasant people. Mrs. Macklin in particular had a comfortable look about her. There was a mole on her right cheek that somehow added to this impression, and her voice contained deep harmonic patterns that indicated an inner security. Her graying brown hair was arranged in a bouffant style, and she was wearing a becoming voile dress with a lace collar. Jeffrey expanded in her presence, seeming much less stiff and more genial. Cena's dark eyes shone; the evening was going well.

After supper we men adjourned to the front porch where my uncle lit up his pipe, and various subjects were addressed, from the Teapot Dome scandal which was surfacing in the public prints about that time, to discussing the possibility of life on Mars, a favorite topic of my uncle's. From the kitchen could be heard the chatter of the women and the clatter of plates and tinkle of silverware. At last the guests concluded they must go, and we all walked out with them down the path leading out of the yard to where the Macklin car was parked near the main gate. It was a clear and starry night, with a crispness in the air promising fall.

The women were in the lead, walking leisurely, still talking animatedly, and we men brought up the rear, quiet for the time. As we approached the yard entrance I looked down to discover, trailing after Mrs. Macklin, something ghostly white in the gloom, and at first I thought she had dropped her shawl, but I looked up to see that it was still around her shoulders. She stumbled slightly, and now it was plain what the object was; Mrs. Macklin was in the process of losing a petticoat.

She was speaking at the moment, and she went on with whatever it was she was saying, meanwhile regally reaching back a hand and swooping up the petticoat, draping it sedately over her arm, and the procession continued with hardly a pause.

The Macklins departed, Cena, claiming a headache, retired shortly afterward, and the rest of us remarked, with admiration, about the presence of mind that Mrs. Macklin had shown. But of course Boyd and Fred, naturally, learned of the incident, and when Fred spoke sympathetically of it to Cena a few days later, she answered him with a vicious request that he mind his own business.

These two events should not, and perhaps did not, have anything to do with the flagging of the relationship between Cena and Jeffrey. But each went on to other attachments, and Cena finally brought home a slender, quiet little cowman, hard-working and even-tempered, who accepted Fred's pranks good-naturedly, and he and Cena were married.

With the arrival at the ranch of my mother, my nights in the bunkhouse with George Parsons came to an end. It worried her that he had a lung disease, and I was told to inform George that my tonsils acted up when the weather turned cold, and henceforth I must sleep in the house. George was not fooled, and said so.

Soon my mother and I returned to our home, and I prepared to return to school. I never saw George after that. Uncle Henry and Aunt

Haying on the ranch

Ina were slowing down, and that was the last winter they spent on the ranch, giving it into the care of Boyd, who had married, and were moving over to Paonia where they bought a small house. So George lost his "home" and took up his wanderings again, and my good times in the bunkhouse with him were forever over.

Spring Madness

In the merry month of May
When the jacks begin to bray
And the jennies come and
Gather round the barn—

Anon.

Winter can drag along like a wounded snake on the west side of the Rockies. Snow, hail, mud, rain, frost; they come, and come again, but when spring truly arrives you know it. Once in the early twenties it seemed to my eyes that spring came in the middle of one particular morning. Bedazzled, I walked up the Lamborn Mesa road. The air was suddenly warm and the icy ruts were streams of gurgling brown water. Snow banks seemed to shrink before my eyes. I turned off into a muddy path on Cedar Hill, where little blue and yellow flowers were opening. The air was filled with clean, clear scents; the soft wind brought the sound of lowing cattle and the rumble of farm machinery from the valley below.

And as the bawdy old song tells it, jacks, jennies and all living creatures are affected by urgent longings at such a time. This ardor was beyond my comprehension then, but that didn't prevent my peers and me from having a lively curiosity about it. On a warm Sunday afternoon in spring several of us were playing up by the depot when a couple tramped by, headed up the tracks, a young girl and an older, determined-looking man. She wore a simple gingham dress and a cloth coat, and her brown hair was pulled up in a bun from her slender neck. He wore an old suit coat over a denim shirt, Levi's, and heavy shoes. He was bare-headed, his shaggy hair disheveled.

I didn't make much of what the girl was thinking or feeling, but it was easy to tell that the man had something on his mind. His face was set, his jaw jutted, and the cords on his neck stood out. There was about him a wild urgency that fascinated me and my playmates as he tramped doggedly along the ties, pulling the girl by the hand, and when he saw the troop of small boys following, he snarled threats and waved a fist. This caused us to drop back a respectable distance, but, to say the least, piqued our interest. Nothing could have prevented us from following.

When he realized that he was still leading a procession, he not only shouted threats, but released the girl's hand and picked up rocks and cinder clumps to throw at us. Finally he made snorting, growling charges in our direction. We scattered, but regrouped each time and when we arrived at a section of track which passed between high banks, we dispersed Indianlike and pursued our quarry from the heights.

At this point the man's tactic changed. The couple sat down, he removed his coat and looked up at either side for his tormentors; his mouth assumed a trembling, altogether unconvincing smile. He fished inside his coat and came up with a bill in his fist. His voice turned pleasant.

"If you boys go on away and leave us alone," he wheedled, "I'll give you this dollar."

We didn't take the offer very seriously. For one thing, no one of us wanted to get within arm's reach of him. For another, we were all so fascinated that we felt the entertainment was worth more than the bribe.

It didn't end well. After more snarling, rock-throwing and chargings, he gave up and dispiritedly led the girl back to town. I've always felt a little guilty about that escapade; later I knew more about where the man was coming from, so to speak, and his dream of lying alone with his love, on a sun-warmed slope among the spring primroses, seemed so appealing that it was as if I too had suffered the loss of a dream.

Then there was a night in spring, a Saturday night, when several of us were loafing about the door of the old Opera House. A dance was taking place inside. A couple came slowly up the street, hardly distinguishable as two people so closely did they walk together, and paused at the base of the steps. For a moment they stood motionless in the circle of yellow light thrown by the green-shaded lamp above the entrance. Then they languorously mounted the steps to the foyer and whether they had originally intended to go inside and dance or not, they wavered over beyond the black iron grating that enclosed the entry stair and melted into a dark corner of the foyer where they remained, embracing and nuzzling. There were a number of lookers-on, but this in no way inconvenienced the lovers. They seemed to take pleasure in having witnesses, so overcome with their passion that they wanted to share it with everyone.

The next day was a sleepy Sunday, with the streets free of traffic, and this couple made the town their rendezvous again, dazedly wandering along the streets, lolling unashamed on the Opera House steps, and eventually reaching the old Nelson Packing House. There, they seated themselves at the edge of the loading platform, their legs swinging idly. He folded his coat and she lay back upon it, and he kissed and fondled her throughout the afternoon.

Romance in the spring. Entrancing. Illogical. Bewildering and amusing to those not involved.

But sometimes others were involved. A man living in town then had returned maimed from the war. He had been inoculated in a training camp and the serum was contaminated. This man, Morgan Donaldson his name might have been, was still able to walk, but he carried himself with his trunk forward, his elbows out, his withered legs making each stride a stumbling one.

Before the war he was a rancher, and he still wore Levi's, boots, neat gabardine shirts with two mother-of-pearl buttons at the cuffs, and a medium-brim light-brown Stetson. He was a pleasant, friendly man. And, he had friends. For that time and place and for the circle he moved among—day-workers, seasonal workers—his army pension made him well-to-do. You could see him almost any summer afternoon sitting forward—apparently the only comfortable position for him— in the neat little black Star touring car. It would be parked either on Grand Avenue or under friendly shade in a nearby street where Morgan and his little court could pleasantly pass the time away.

One companion was a cousin, well enough physically but "work-brittle," some said, and another a drifter called Tex, like Morgan a neat dresser in the cowboy style, a cheerful, laughing man with cheeks as plump as a thrifty squirrel's. Tex liked to spin stories and one of them was a fantasy that it pleased Morgan to hear. Before Morgan left the service he was told by a doctor that there was a possibility that some day his disability might suddenly lift, and Tex liked to dwell on that.

"Some day it'll happen, just as sure as the world," I heard Tex say once. "And what a day that'll be." He gave a low whistle and laughed and the others laughed quietly with him. It was warm, and Tex removed his gray Stetson and ran an index finger along the front of the sweatband before settling the hat back on his head as if facing into a pleasant wind. "It's going to happen. It's bound to, and when it does, I aim to be around to see it."

Morgan roomed at the old Commercial, and his cousin and Tex stayed there, too, probably at his expense. They ate some of their meals at Josh's hamburger stand, and when they weren't sitting in the car or driving around somewhere, they were in the pool hall, watching the games. Sometimes on Saturday nights Tex drove the Star out to kitchen-sweats on one of the mesas, or to one of the dances up in Somerset, or down to the pavilion near the hamlet of Read. Morgan couldn't dance, but he enjoyed being with others who did, and he naturally provided the bottles of bootleg to keep things amusing. A fellow named Fred, younger than the others and temporarily out of work too, began tagging along, enjoyed the good times and the booze, of course, a sort of fourth musketeer, and as summer sleeved into fall, room was made in the Star touring car for another passenger, Amy Ausman.

Amy's life was hard. Her parents had died, and she looked after three younger brothers in a little tumbledown house near the river. The oldest of the brothers worked at anything he could find to do, and so did Amy, doing housecleaning and washings and whatever came to hand. There was something a little hard and resentful in her thin face, but she was not the complaining type and everyone admired her for the way she looked after the family. Morgan and Amy enjoyed each other's company, she was kind to him, and then loving. In the fall they were married, to the delight of all their friends.

Morgan moved into the little house; a room was added on. Now Amy had a fourth to look after, but there was no doubt that her life had improved. She had new, bright dresses instead of the old, slatternly gray ones. She tried one of the new permanents; it added a little warmth to her face. And, instead of the couple settling down into dull married life, Morgan's friends still gathered around, and there were parties at the little house and the Star would be packed with laughing guests to go along the winter roads to country dances which Morgan encouraged his wife to take part in, though he could not. Fred, youngest of the gang of four, always seemed to dance the waltzes with Amy.

Spring came and a saddening spectacle unfolded. Amy abruptly neglected her household, and walked everywhere along the streets of the lower town with Fred, arm in arm the two of them, as careless of the attention they received as other spring-smitten couples could be, moving only within the gauzy walls of their mutual desire. Morgan's friends and acquaintances looked on indignantly, but he could only turn wearily away, as if from a vision too hot and bright for his eyes.

Amy and Fred left town together, to drift apart soon enough; and Amy's brother, the oldest of the three, became the head of the family. Morgan was no longer well enough or of a mind to enjoy sitting around town in the back seat of the Star. He moved out on the ranch to stay with his aged parents. His cousin took a job and married. Tex drifted on.

The passion that a love can arouse does not always seep away as marriage begins. Often it lingers on, imparting a glow of affection to the partnership. But sometimes it turns into something dark and strange, gripping the vitals of one or both of the lovers. There was this man with a good business down in the town, an ambitious man, hard-working, who bought a home on the heights and planted new young orchards around it, working his long hours down in the town, and in the evenings, sometimes even after dark, he could be seen

163

weeding, irrigating, pruning in his young orchard. His energy and drive were the wonder of those who knew him.

His wife was a pleasant woman, looking after the house and their two young sons, inclined to overdress but not unduly extravagant. But she was placid, and did not own the sort of fierce energy that was her husband's. With her boys down in the school and her husband away, winter and spring days must have stretched out endlessly for her. It was not surprising that one spring she began looking forward to having a neighbor, a man, stop by her kitchen for a cup of coffee in midmorning, on his irrigating rounds.

Was there more to it than that? Very likely not. But whatever the husband knew or thought he knew—perhaps it was only that someone, a rustic Iago, told him of a shovel leaning beside his kitchen door—it was more than the husband could bear. There must have been thundering scenes between him and his wife, and what the community knew was that one warm spring afternoon in the center of the town, in front of the drugstore, two men were fighting, the husband and the neighbor. The general reaction was astonishment and disbelief. A crowd gathered, and the struggle went on, the husband attacking, and his neighbor fiercely defending, until the town clerk crossed the street and came between them, speaking to them like two errant children, breaking the spell.

The husband remained in town that afternoon, became roaring drunk, and drove wildly up to his home. He did not get out of the pickup to open the gate this night, the gate he had proudly put together with his own hands, but crashed straight through and drove out into the orchard until the car's wheels mired and the engine died. He must have wandered up and down the rows of young trees, full of white bloom, and shouted his despair and rage at the dark house and the moon, and then he took a last drink, this time from a bottle of corrosive poison, and died a desperate death.

Romance never quickened my pulse in spring more than at any other time, but I do remember one glowing spring when I was attending Western State. In Gunnison, the coming of true spring is even more of a delight than it is on the North Fork. The broad valley permits the northern wind free play, and in the desolate early months of the year it moans around the house corners, arousing memories of old wrongs and sorrows, and when spring at last arrives it is like a rebirth of the earth and of all living things. Once on such a spring day four of us, fraternity brothers, contrived to borrow a car and drive up to Ouray on some sort of fraternity errand, through the pleasant weather.

Ouray, beautifully cradled in the San Juans, was just emerging from winter. Snow lay on the heights all about, and every cry of child, bird, or bark of dog, seemed to mount quickly up into the air, as if swallowed up in memory. In the rear of an old bar, two men danced to jukebox music—not as if they were gay, but in the old, shambling, friendly way of the mining camp, where women were once in such short supply.

Our business done, we acquired a bottle of moonshine, easier to find in Ouray then than a cup of tea, and drifted back down the road toward Montrose.

The bootleg was smooth, and before we left the lower end of town the car was moving along a foot or so off the surface of the road, elevated into a dream of spring. The Ouray cemetery, behind its white palings, lay in a pale green smoke of young emerging leaves. When we had navigated Cerro Summit beyond Montrose, and Blue Mesa, and wavered by Sapinero and on into Gunnison I was so full of moonshine and the worship of spring that I had to call a little red-headed girl I was seeing, not so much out of love for her, but because of the absolute need to tell someone what I was feeling.

She wasn't all that pleased to receive my call. She had spent the day having her hair done, and made it plain she wasn't up to seeing anyone, and particularly not anyone drunk, as I plainly was, but that was all right. I only needed to talk.

I asked her the next day what I had said, but she told me she couldn't make any sense out of it at all.

The Summer With the Cows

The summer between my freshman and sophomore years in high school I spent at the dairy belonging to Pierce Elmendorf. It was on a farm at the end of Ballard's Lane, about a mile out of town. It was a miserable farm; it lay not too far from the river and was half seep. About all it was good for was pasturage and not much for that. It had a big old barn that had never known paint but was reasonably solid, and a neat, two-story house. The house was all there was to the place that was really worth anything.

Pierce was the son of my mother's older sister; he was a man then in his early forties. He had married a woman fifteen years younger than he, a nervous, energetic woman of Irish parentage. Her name was Shana. She was shapely and had a very pale skin, lightly freckled, with fine red-gold hairs on her arms and legs that gleamed in the sun and in the lamplight—she only wore stockings when she went to town. They had a three-year-old daughter, Dora.

Pierce had taken me on for the summer for board and room and a very modest wage to help him to deliver milk from his dairy at night and herd the cows in the daytime. He had the idea that I could drive them out every morning to feed on the alfalfa, sweet clover and other grasses that grew along the fences in the nearby country lanes. He had a herd of beautiful cows, most of them Guernseys, reddish fawn in color, with some white markings, and always the inverted white triangle on the forehead, the distinctive marking of that aristocratic breed.

He had acquired the whole spread, the house, barn, cows, a purebred bull and some milking equipment in exchange for a pool hall he had owned in Crawford, some fourteen miles away from the dairy across a stretch of hilly wasteland known locally as the Dobies. He had grown up on his father's cattle ranch above Crawford, on Clear Fork, under Cathedral Rock.

Several of Pierce's brothers were big—or they seemed big to me then—though Pierce was not big himself, and his ankles were weak, but he was strong otherwise. He had done a little of everything—hard-rock mining, work on the country road, he had drunk more than his share of bootleg, and had more than his share of fights. He had big, heavy fists, and was handy with them.

Shana had not been happy in Crawford with Pierce running the pool hall. She was a local girl, and Catholic. Pierce made the exchange for the dairy, he said, to save his marriage.

I was no great help with the milking chores. Pierce was a good, strong milker and tried to teach me to do it, but I never really got the hang of it, and have never regretted it. But I did feed the three calves and helped carry the milk to the house where Shana poured it out in crocks to cool on the screened back porch under clean cotton towelling. Then, after breakfast, she would hand me my lunch and I would take the cows out to graze.

At night, after evening milking and supper, Pierce loaded up the milk that Shana had poured into bottles from crocks and we, he and I, were off to town to make deliveries. I had delivered milk around Paonia for Old Man Redwine and considered myself something of an expert in that department. Pierce and I really worked it down to a science. I sat beside him in the front seat of his Star touring car. The back seat was removed and the bottles positioned back there in two rows of wire baskets. At the few houses where we had to leave off more than two quarts they were carried in the baskets, but for most deliveries of say a quart, a quart and a pint, or two quarts, I would reach back with both hands and get a firm grip on the cool necks of the bottles and with the right-hand door always swinging unlatched, I would shove out and leap off the running board before the car had come to a stop.

Sometimes there would be a set of front steps leading up to the porch, sometimes two sets of maybe four to a half-dozen steps on each landing, first to the lawn level and then to the porch. I could negotiate four steps in one leap without too much trouble and, on a good night, at the I.M. Huddles place, with four steps from the sidewalk and eight on beyond, I could make it in three leaps. Pierce seemed impressed with my agility and cheered me on. He liked to keep up my enthusiasm for the work.

And it was pleasant driving around the quiet streets, with the lamps on the tall poles at the street corners besieged by moths and shivering slightly in the down-river breeze, and the light filtering down greenly through the great cottonwoods. Almost no one would be on the streets, but sometimes we would encounter Mildred Barber out in front of her parents' place, watering the lawn. Pierce always liked to stop, tip his hat, and exchange a few polite words with her. She was a quiet girl, a little younger than I, well-spoken, who had no attraction for me. Pierce called her "a fine young lady," and constantly encouraged me to show a little interest, but I wanted more glamor in those days.

We would be done about nine or so, but we never went home then. Instead, we drifted down to Grand Avenue and bellied up to the counter in Josh MacIntyre's hamburger stand. I don't remember that Pierce ever bought us hamburgers, though once he did buy pie. Mostly it was coffee, one cup, and Pierce would talk. He liked to talk to men. He liked to astonish them, or make them laugh. Among men he talked in a good, carrying voice, using round language. Declaiming is what it was. He told jokes, or bragged about fights he had had or witnessed. This would go on until he ran out of material or hearers or both, around ten-thirty, if he was in good form. Then he would make some excuse or other, get up, tug at his hat brim—he wore a well-blocked old tan fedora—run his thumbs down along his overall bib, and we would strut out into the quiet street with toothpicks in our mouths.

Usually we would go home then but some nights he would take a notion to drive back up into town and turn at Second and Poplar, kill the motor and ease up to the curb across from the Gratton house. The Grattons had a daughter called Hubba because she was always in a hurry, a big, giggly, lively girl with heavy breasts and a wide bottom. She had an upstairs room and she never pulled down her shades. Pierce and I would wait across the street there in the dark, sometimes seeing Hubba remove a sweater or a dress and walk across in front of the light in her slip, and then when the room went dark we would drift back down to the dairy.

I had a room in the back upstairs all to myself and I really liked that. At home I didn't have the luxury of sleeping alone and of lying awake and reading in bed. I did this every night at Pierce's no matter what time we got in. Pierce would go straight to bed but often afterward I could hear Shana's low, keening reproaches, and Pierce's quiet, self-justificatory responses. He always spoke to her in a considerate way, even when, sometimes, she would be really angry, or half hysterical. I understood that she was leading a lonely life and that she wished he would come home sooner at night; I even suggested that he do so, but although he would agree that he should, he only did so once that I remember of.

Pierce had trouble getting me up of a morning. He would call up to me from the back yard, standing there with a milk bucket in each hand, on the way to the barn in the feeble light of the coming day, and I would respond, but sometimes I would not be up by the time he had returned from milking and he would have to come to the bottom of the stairs and call again.

Once up and washed I had breakfast, Shana handed me my lunch, I tucked a book under one arm and Pierce and I went to the barn to let out the cows for the day's grazing. As Pierce undid the leather fastening at the corral gate, I could look over to the left and see, from where he was penned behind the barn, his neck stretched out so his great head rested on the topmost rail of the corral fence, the titular head of the herd, that rebellious and thwarted monarch, the pedigreed Guernsey bull.

It is only fair to speak of him first, though I saw less of him, by design, than of any other creature on the ranch. He was a large and handsome animal with swelling muscles on his shoulders and along his mighty back. In his great head, marked with the princely inverted triangle, were large defiant eyes that never reflected friendship for any living creature. He was a fine figure of a bull and sired many calves, but he was short on stamina because of his cramped life in the corral, as I learned later on.

His life, generally speaking, was a depressing one. He was continually irked and occasionally driven to berserk rage by his confinement in the corral away from the cows, and constantly irritated by the presence of the human beings who trespassed into his domain. It was a never-ending contest between the bull (he was never called by any other name although he had one, pompous and long, on his registration papers) and the man who owned the herd. Pierce never walked through the corral when the bull was out without carrying a pitchfork. On most days this protection was enough, but on other days when the bull felt the injustice of his imprisonment keenly enough, he would dare the sharp tines on the off-chance of doing the man harm. He was never able to injure Pierce, but the combination of momentarily destroying the man's dignity, and perhaps even the sharp pain of the tines in his shoulder or flank seemed to provide him with a catharsis that would give him comparative peace for a few days.

Of course, there was a truce between man and bull when cows of the herd or from some other farm were brought in on errands of *amour*. There was a tractability, a certain willingness to be as cooperative as possible in the bull's demeanor from the very moment a shy but willing paramour came into view. The human panders were ignored or even grudgingly accepted as *maitres de chambre*. But otherwise in the dull dream-plain of his existence he appeared as baffled, defeated, and sulky as, judging by photographs in the press, members of royalty or celebrities often seem.

Royal the bull was, but he was completely removed from the social and workaday hierarchy of the herd, which was inevitably matriarchal. Indeed, even if he had been in a position of real leadership, he did not impress me as an animal of judgment or of the temperament to command wisely, and the herd was definitely better off under the leadership of Lady, the Queen Regent, the mother of the bull.

Lady's breeding was evident in the clean, delicate lines of head and jaw. And beyond her appearance, she was aristocratic in the imperious way in which she assumed command. When the corral gate was opened in the morning and the cows rushed guiltily out to freedom, she was nearly always first through the gate. The yard opened out on the river lane, and Pierce would stand in the middle of the way to prevent the cows from heading left toward the river, though with Lady there was little likelihood of that. Head up, the bell she wore ringing rhythmically, she moved swiftly and purposively along, up to the entrance of the river lane into Ballard Lane, and turned right at the corner of the fence, to wait for her charges to assemble in the little swale before the house.

Even with her good offices, though, the first crisis of the day was apt to occur here, occasioned by Brat, Lady's daughter. Brat was a handsome cow, with the imperious energy of her mother. She was the only member of the herd who had escaped dehorning; but one horn was broken, giving her an erratic, malicious appearance that was not at all misleading. She would graze swiftly along the lane from the river, her eye on me, and if she saw what seemed an opportunity she would rush forward and attempt to lead the herd up Ballard's Lane in the direction of town, and I would have to lay down my lunch and my book and run ahead of her and head her off. She would scamper back then and create a tumult in the herd, sometimes facing off Lady and hooking at her with her good horn. Lady would not be dismayed and after Brat had shown a little fight for appearance's sake, she would hastily scramble out of her mother's way.

There in the swale before the house the herd would then assemble and move out in an unvarying order. First Lady, then Brat, and behind them the herd's bourgeoisie. Buzz, of rhinoceros strength, came first, followed by lumpish May. Had Buzz desired to strongly enough she could have bested Brat—when sufficiently aroused she could overcome Brat in spite of the devilish horn—but like many another seeker of middle paths, Buzz lacked the sustained desire to better herself. I never learned what significance, if any, attached to her name.

As for May, she was the most contented member of the herd. Much of her energy went to milk—she gave the most of all the cows save Lady. She was an unintelligent, thoroughly undistinguished creature with her large, ungraceful frame covered with dowager-like flesh. She was pure Guernsey in breeding, but all the fine markings in her were blurred.

The remainder of the herd, the proletariat, were, several of them, not Guernseys. Brownie, a brindle, probably part Durham, was a responsible, well-behaved cow who contented herself with following after May. She wore the other herd bell. Behind her came Holstein, a heavy cow with the black and white markings of her breed, a good milker and reliable in every way. The rest of the herd trailed along in nondescript fashion. Cherry, so named for her distinct coloring, was graceful, handsome, and empty-headed, a scatterbrain of too unsettled a temperament to have any established place in herd society. She was continually moving along the flanks of the herd, occasionally colliding with May or dodging Brat's wicked horn or even foolishly duelling with Buzz. She had always to be watched.

The two remaining herd members bore the unmistakable signs of fine Guernsey breeding but had no standing in the cow community. Two years before May had given birth to twin heifers, one of whom was born crippled, with a rear foot twisted so that she limped heavily. She was unkindly known as Cripple. Her sister was sold, but Cripple remained. In the beginning of the herding season when grazing was good in nearby lanes she was allowed along, but she always dawdled and made as much of a nuisance of herself as she could manage, wincing pitifully if approached in a threatening way, eyes rolling hysterically, but still causing trouble whenever possible, turning off into byways or entangling herself in fences or in gates.

Dummy was the other dawdler. She was a handsome, incredibly stupid cow. All the other cows butted her whenever the opportunity presented itself. In contacts with other herd members her chief aim was to stumble, wide-eyed, out of the way as soon as possible. No amount of encouragement could cause her to accelerate her pace above a swinging walk. Even towards evening with the herd turned homeward, when other herd members had to be discouraged from walking too rapidly, there was no such problem with Dummy.

I learned how difficult she could be quite early. In late June it seemed a good idea to save the easy grazing along the main road until later and turn off into potentially promising byways. One day I took the herd up a back road leading past the cemetery. This involved negotiating a dry hill grade and crossing over a creek by means of a plank bridge, but once beyond the bridge the grass appeared good.

The cows were reluctant to cross the bridge, testing it with their hooves and sniffing it warily, but Lady, tempted by the smell of the damp grass along the ditch bank on the other side, went boldly forward, and the others clattered after. All except Dummy. I missed her and went looking for her and her head jerked up from a patch of willows below the bridge. I drove her up to the bridge. She smelled it, her eyes wide, and lunged away. I lost my temper and belabored her back side with a willow club. Harder, and still harder. Her only reaction was to snuff at the bridge and then to look back at me with a reproachful, stubborn expression. I rounded up the other cows and drove them back so she could see them, but this didn't help. Finally nothing remained but to drive the cows back across and stampede Dummy into returning with them. After this I was careful to see that she was well up with the rest of the cows by the time we arrived at the bridge.

The sweet clover grew rank along the lane outside the cemetery, and I was able to relax and read. I had that summer acquired a gift of a number of books from my uncle, my father's brother, a doctor with a practice in Puerto Rico, who had come to Paonia to visit relatives and friends. Some of these books turned out to be rather strange and helped me to understand when, years later, my uncle became involved in voodoo.

The first work I tried was a well-worn two-volume set of Morgan Robertson short stories, called *The Grain Ship*. In every story, the two leading characters are identical twins, and due to some strange circumstance shortly after birth they are separated and grow up not knowing of each other's existence. At last they meet, and it always turns out tragically, as on the grain ship itself, beleaguered in a storm, with the two brothers slowly climbing up into the shrouds side by side, one soul in two bodies, fatally inimical to each other, inevitably driven to mutual destruction.

I was pulled out of that black maelstrom of rain and terror one sunny morning in cemetery lane by the realization that everything had become extremely still. The sound of cowbells had grown faint. I was overtaken by a terrifying surmise and rushed up the lane. Sure enough, someone had neglected to close the gate and my charges were grazing busily among the graves. At my shouts they raised their heads and stared at me with the usual expressions of scorn and amazement they reserved for the antics of human beings, and then raced about, bumping into gravestones and galloping across graves. I had a breathless and frantic time getting them back into the lane. I closed the gate behind them and returned to brush dirt carefully into hoofmarks on the mounds, and to straighten the spilled offerings of flowers. Even in the bright sunlight I half expected a thunderbolt from on high.

From that day I kept the cows out of the cemetery lane and we moved along the road leading over Lamborn Mesa. When I tired of reading I could look out across the mesa to the West Elk mountains and further to the right over the Dobie wilderness to the tall hill that sheltered Crawford. In the blue haze of distance stood Cathedral Rock above the ranch where Pierce and his brothers had grown up.

A closer object of interest in the landscape was a large white farmhouse across the hollow below the road. It had a red roof and a veranda extending around three sides. To the left, a short distance away, was the big red barn. I stared at the place often, but never saw anyone around. It seemed curious to me that so fine a house should be without tenants, and I remarked on it at supper one night. I learned from Shana that the owners had died, and although the house was unoccupied the Catholic Church had the use of it, and some orphans in the care of an order of nuns were coming to stay there for the summer. I stared at it often, wondering about the orphans. On the night my father was killed my aunt bent over me, cried over me, and called me an orphan. I felt a strong kinship with these children who were coming to stay in the big white house.

One day I was thrilled to see the figure of a slender girl standing before the house. She seemed to be looking in my direction. I concluded she was probably a fellow-being starved for romantic companionship as I conceived myself to be—a young person of unplumbed capacities, unappreciated by the world. I stood up and waved to her. She waved back. Then, for several days we each, I am sure, looked forward to this communication. I never saw her closely enough to form any conception of her at all. And, one day she did not appear at the usual time and I never saw her again. It never occurred to me to try to learn more about her, but the little I knew of her has caused her to remain in my memory: it is one of the most satisfactory, or at any rate least disappointing, relationships I have ever had with a member of the opposite sex.

Grazing along the cemetery road grew sparse and we moved on along the mesa road. One afternoon a shower came up, swift and cold. The cows, subdued, stood head to tail in little clumps, and I took shelter under a scruffy cedar just inside a fenced field. We were across the road from a farmhouse and I heard the voice of an old woman call out,

"Don't you want to come and stand on the porch, young man?"

"No, thanks," I called back, but a few minutes later the old woman appeared at the back door of the house, a shawl pulled over her head and shoulders, and ran out through the gate and in my direction. I felt certain she was coming to renew her invitation, and I had a vision of sitting in a dark front room in a rocker with an antimacassar on its shiny back, and drinking hot cocoa and eating cookies, but that vision was soon dispelled. She did not speak as I met her at the fence, but in one bony hand extended two little religious tracts, pulled the shawl over her head again, and ran back to the house.

So much for summer encounters with humankind. For the rest of it there was just Pierce and his family, except one Sunday afternoon when my mother came to visit. Sunday was always a quiet time at the dairy. The cows were given hay and grain, Shana fixed a good Sunday dinner, and we just lay about and read or napped. In the afternoon I usually looked through a magazine to which the preceding owner of the dairy had subscribed and which kept on coming, *Hoard's Dairyman*. It was full of stories about other dairies and photographs of broad cool barns and fine farm homes, of beautiful cows and rolling green pastures. Here dedicated men put together thrifty little kingdoms in which they built up their herds over years, improving the breeding stock, making careful records of their cows' performances and eliminating those animals that did not measure up. The cows gave milk, their manure fertilized the fields, from the fields came their sustenance; nothing went to waste. A calm, uncluttered way of life.

In the late afternoons I would lie in my room and journey to the homes of the great with my mentor, Elbert Hubbard; this was from a set of books my Puerto Rico uncle had also given me, but which was beautifully bound in leather and not suitable for reading while out with the cows. And, from the window in my room, I could watch as occasionally some vehicle would move by on the river road. Perhaps it would be Erma Baumgartner, returning home from Bible study in her parents' old Ford pickup. She was a skinny young girl with sunburned cheeks, who wore dark dresses handed down by her mother. She was "built like a beanie," as Pierce said, but seemed sufficiently attractive to cause me to indulge in erotic fantasies about her, laid in the loft of Pierce's barn.

By July, grazing on the Lamborn Mesa road was playing out, but grass still grew luxuriantly along the main road south of Ballard's Lane. Lady, the belled queen of the herd, led her charges triumphantly from the corral in the morning, and as triumphantly back in the evening. I sat under a succession of old cottonwood trees and read dark stories of star-crossed twins. Pierce was in good spirits, and felt confident enough of the success of the dairy to invest in milking machines which aroused the curiosity of Shana and their small daughter, who came down to watch them in action, and farmers came from miles away to watch and admire. One night at Josh's hamburger stand Pierce bought us pie, and at the unheard-of time of ten o'clock he stood and stretched.

"Guess we better be gettin' on down the road," he said.

"What's your hurry?" a young fellow, Frank Carver, asked.

Pierce had been waiting for this. "My wife's plannin' on makin' a baby tonight," he said, "and I'd kinda like to be in on it."

By mid-month we had made our way along the road, the cows and I, to Coburn Switch, just below the Chinn Ranch grade. Along our route on each side the succulent alfalfa had been nibbled short, and timothy and sweet clover grew scarce as well. Even the swamp grasses were turning brown. But each day on the road as we crossed the railroad tracks below the Patterson ranch, we could look down the right-of-way to where the old packing shed sat at the switch and

174

between there and where we stood, on both sides of the tracks, were literally acres of tall grasses alive with the hum of bees; purple-blossoming alfalfa, white-blossoming sweet clover, flickering seductively in the down-river breeze, just begging to be ripped away and gulped down. Unfortunately, rows of serried iron teeth had been laid down between the rails by the D&RG, buttressed on either side by stout wooden barriers. And a sign warning against trespassing was stoutly planted just beyond.

Even after we crossed the tracks to go down toward the switch by the road, the cows yearned disconsolately along the barbed-wire fence enclosing the right-of-way, shoving their heads between the punishing strands, eyes protruding with the strain, to wrap their drooling tongues around the grass within reach, tormenting themselves the more. Every morning as we passed the barriers at the track one or another of the cows would test the iron teeth between the rails and pull up trembling hooves and lurch away.

The right-of-way Eden seemed hopelessly out of reach, but I noticed that between the rows of teeth and the rail on either side there was a space perhaps six inches wide in which a cow's foot could fit, assuming she could walk Indian-style, with one foot placed directly before the other, a way of walking foreign to any cow. And Brownie, the other belled cow, who had calved not too long before and was especially ravenous, gave the problem (with, I confess, my encouragement) her soulful attention. One day she managed several short steps with her front hooves, but the back feet gave her trouble and she was turned away. But then came the day when she placed her front feet with the usual care, her muzzle low, her nostrils distended, her breath whipping away the cinder dust between the ties, and after painfully, clumsily, and tremblingly raising one hind foot and then the other, she placed them between the teeth and the rail, her front hooves came free beyond the barrier, and with a final lunge she was through.

The other cows now accepted the feat as possible. Brat and Lady negotiated the obstruction, then Buzz, and that concluded the matter. The other cows now followed, even Dummy, at first accepting the pain, and then learning how to avoid it. Pierce's only comment was that it would be well to be out of the way and better still out of sight whenever a train came through, so daily I drove the cows further on down the right-of-way and sequestered them behind the packing shed at Coburn Switch for the afternoon siesta. I worried when an occasional freight would pull by as we trailed back up the right-of-way in the late afternoon, but no complaints were received, and since the one daily passenger and mail train made its scheduled run after we had already departed for the dairy, all went well.

So as August came we were literally in clover, feeding in the hip-high grasses, and early every afternoon repaired to the rear of the packing shed where the cows would lie down heavily and chew their cuds and I could go up on the shadowed, echoing platform of the shed to eat my lunch. The shed was no longer used for packing fruit, and was falling into ruin. A conveyor belt ran the length of the shed with some machinery at one end, half covered by decaying canvas. Here I made my nest.

I had finished *The Grain Ship* and had started another book provided by my uncle. My mother would have been scandalized if she had known how far some of the stories I was reading diverged from the high moral tone of Elbert Hubbard's little journeys. This book was called *Limehouse Nights* and all the stories in it concerned the Chinese living in the Limehouse district of London, down by the docks; tales of murderous tong wars, of opium dens, of struggles over prostitutes. Above me where I lay in the shed the wind whispered through the loose tin roofing, sometimes a bumblebee planed crankily through the half-gloom, or there would come a light rustling caused by a mouse tunnelling in the piles of discarded boxes and tangles of picking harness. The odor of rancid machine oil and decayed apples hung in the quiet air. But none of these sensations disturbed my reading. I was far away, walking the dangerous, narrow, twisted streets of old Limehouse.

But prosperity is treacherous. Just when all seems well the seeds of destruction are sprouting. One day I had lingered long over lunch, reading of how an ancient Chinese had cunningly snatched a beauteous little blossom from the hands of a warrior tong and, that night, by the light of a candle in his little room was laying aside her garments, one by one, and kissing lingeringly each exposed limb, breast, and the pale yellow orb of her stomach, when a sound, at first faint, but growing ever louder, impinged on my consciousness. At first I mistook it for the groan of a foghorn off the West India docks or in the Limehouse Cut, but it dawned upon me finally that it was not a foghorn—it was the whistle of a train, in the real world, approaching Coburn Switch.

I flung down the book and struggled up, looking off to the right into the bright sunlight where the cows had bedded in the dust of the parking lot. They were gone, but I heard the bells. When I rounded the corner of the packing shed it was to see the cows busily feeding along the right-of-way. Except for Buzz and Cherry. They were butting heads in the middle of the railroad track.

The freight train loomed up, just beyond the crossing below the switch, and I could see the engineer in the cab of the locomotive, looking out and tugging away at the whistle. I raced to separate the combatants, and Buzz stumbled away; but Cherry in a spirit of deviltry, galloped directly up the track in front of the chugging engine, her tail up, rump high, for the better part of a quarter mile, and I knew from that moment that our halcyon days on the right-of-way were numbered. Pierce heard from the depot agent in town that same evening.

Now the herd, banished from the right-of-way, fell upon hard times. We tramped weary miles in the mid-August heat in search of good grazing. We tried one lane after another, but everywhere the feed was drying up and dying back. Pierce fed the hay he had and scouted for more. It was scarce and high in price. He used the scanty grazing he had held in reserve beyond the barn.

The results of the days of poor feeding began to show up in the lessening milk yield. Pierce loved to point out the golden hue of the milk as he separated or held bottles of whole milk up to the light from the kerosene lamp when we were loading deliveries; but now he was obliged to eke out the failing supply from a dairy in the east end of town that sold its milk wholesale, milk much lower in butterfat than that from the herd. And whether it really happened or not, some customers accused him of watering the milk.

We were still stopping at the hamburger stand after the night deliveries, but Pierce plainly took less pleasure in it. He told fewer stories, they were less pleasant, and there were few jokes. More and more he talked at the hamburger stand and out on the route of the old family ranch of the Elmendorfs on Clear Fork, above Crawford. His parents had retired and moved to Paonia, and the old place was slowly dying in the hands of a feckless tenant. Pierce said he could take it over, bring more water "from around the hill" and make it thrive again. He would take his cows over there, build up the herd, and be the talk of the whole country.

Besides, he said, and this to me only, he needed to do it to save his marriage. He never explained beyond that, but I did notice that although the arguments Shana and Pierce had when he came back from deliveries were less frequent, they were also more heated, her tone more accusatory, his more emphatic, less conciliatory. And on Sundays before evening milking, as I lay upstairs reading, I could hear them going at it.

Towards the end of August, when the herd was often pastured at home, I saw more of Shana. Pierce would be out after breakfast scouting for hay or running water onto the lower pasture—he was trying to leach out the alkali—and Shana began talking to me. Only one subject interested her; a Paonia businessman, a Syrian familiarly known as Connie. All that was required of me in these conversations was an occasional nod of understanding or, on some point she felt needed particular stress, an affirmative word or two, and when I complied, she would set her jaw and nod quietly to herself, as if she had wrung a concession from me, and go on with the ironing or whatever it was she was engaged in.

And I could bring myself to agree that although some thought Connie was homely, he was not that homely, that he was a neat dresser, that he was witty and amusing, and much smarter than he was often given credit for, though the truth was that whatever else was said about Connie, it was generally agreed that he was the craftiest individual in town. It was strange; I participated in this catechism, but never tried to understand what was behind it. To me, it was just grownup talk.

I never mentioned these conversations to Pierce.

When I was with Pierce now he yearned constantly toward the haven of the old place on Clear Fork, sure that the move would resolve all his problems. And gradually the plans crystallized. The tenant on the ranch was willing to give up his lease, Pierce found a buyer for the farm, and now the problem of transporting the herd arose. He was not in a position to have them trucked, so that meant they would have to be driven. Between the farm and the ranch lay twenty miles of weary travel, a dozen or more of them across the Dobies, barren for the most part, with but one stream running through them.

Shana appeared resigned to the move. She made no objections in my presence. But she did insist that she be allowed to go on a weekend excursion with a woman's club she had attended that summer. It was a sort of end-of-summer event; the members would be taken by car to a mountain resort where they would stay two nights, with meetings one day and church services and Bible study the next. She pleaded and complained, and finally Pierce gave in. We took her up to town the last Friday we delivered milk and let her off near the church, where the club members were assembling. There in the dark Shana gave her husband a tender and loving kiss, as if she were making amends for a transgression that had not yet taken place, and it somehow fed in me the conviction that Connie, that amusing and clever man, would play some part in the weekend festivities.

The drive took place the following week. Pierce had enlisted the help of a bluff young fellow, Frank Carver. He was temporarily down on his luck and Pierce and he had struck up a friendship when he stopped in at the hamburger stand to listen to Pierce's stories. Pierce had invited him down to the dairy occasionally to Sunday dinner, and he had officiated at some of the bull's amatory liaisons, and helped with the calving. It was just after Brownie calved that Pierce and he tried to convince me that human mothers, like cow mothers, are obliged to eat the afterbirth. But a boy around men gets used to that sort of ragging, and I liked Frank well enough.

Pierce called me at three o'clock on the fateful morning, the earliest I was ever called that summer and the only time I ever promptly responded. He milked by lantern light, and the cows were headed out the river road for the last time, with Lady in the lead as usual, but Cripple was gone, sold to a neighbor, and instead, behind Dummy came Frank, leading the bull by means of a length of broomstick attached to the ring in his tender nose.

Brownie paused at the railroad crossing for a look down the right-of-way but I urged her on. And, although the bull seemed bent on contesting every step, we moved up the Stewart Mesa grade and out over Bone Mesa making reasonably good time, and emerged into the Dobies with the midmorning sun warm on our backs. Around a low gray hill we looked down a long stretch of dirt road that cut through a gray purgatory splotched with greasewood and sagebrush. The dust rose with the heat. The calves bawled, with Dummy joining in. She seemed convinced that the whole thing was a mistake, and kept trying to evade me and turn back, while the calves took off up every draw and wandered down into every gulch. Frank and I spelled each other at leading the bull and driving the herd.

Pierce came by in the Star. The back seat had been replaced, and was loaded with kitchen utensils. Frank told him that the bull was not cooperating.

"It'll do him good," Pierce said. "He'll find out there's more to life than just pussy."

Pierce was in a fine mood. He was wearing his good gray hat, a white shirt, and freshly laundered overalls and was rolling a toothpick between his teeth. He promised us "a surprise" for lunch, put the Star in gear, and drove on.

The plan was that we would stop at the only ranch in the Dobies around noon, where Pierce had made arrangements for the herd to be fed and watered. By the time he came bumping back along the road from the west, we had arrived at the ranch, consulted with the owner, and forked down hay for the cows. We were sitting in the cool weeds alongside an old shed awaiting lunch and the promised surprise. It turned out to be a half-gallon fruit jar of red wine from a batch that Pierce had set up in a barrel in the barn a month before. It was an unattractive mess then, and the wine that came from it was sour and strong. Even Frank, who tried to show a little enthusiasm for Pierce's sake, could manage only a thin smile. As for me, I had taken medicine that tasted better, and said so. I hoped for ice cream, or at least pie. But Pierce's good humor was not diminished. It was just, he said, that I didn't have enough experience to appreciate it.

The afternoon was difficult. The cows were used to the daily homeward trek after pasturing and moved along slowly but steadily, but the bull's "ass was dragging his tracks out," as Frank put it, and lagged further and further in the rear. The calves had tired, but still managed to wander off at every opportunity. We dragged into another ranch, the Halloran place on the edge of the Crawford country, well after dark, where we would spend the night, with seven miles still between us and our final destination.

On the road again the following morning the sun was taking possession of the little town of Crawford street by street as we limped through. Surprisingly, the bull was in fine fettle, moving along strongly, head high. I was in charge of him as he pushed ahead. I kept up as well as I could, giving him his head, hoping it would last.

And it did, until we turned off on the Clear Fork road. He made the turn, still moving strongly, but on the uphill grade past the Vandenberg place he began to flag. It seemed to me he thought that he would be reasonable and give whatever he was called upon to give, and that if he faced up to it and gave it all he had, no one could ask for more. But as it so often happens in life, even our best is not enough, and that is the way it turned out for the bull that day. I tugged at the nose ring, but he extended his neck as far as he could to alleviate the pain and remained where he was. I jabbed him with a stick, but he did not stir. The cows approached and moved on by. Pierce and Frank and I conferred, and I was left to bring the bull along when I could. It took most of the rest of the day to cover the three remaining miles to the ranch.

Shana had fixed a meal and after milking I went down to commiserate for the last time with the bull. He was standing, but not proudly, and submitted to my scratching his poll without a single toss of his mighty head. I could not help but feel that our relationship had entered a new and tender phase, but Pierce said,

"Try that a couple of days from now and he'll knock you ass-over-apple-cart."

Pierce had to deliver me back in Paonia late that same evening; school had begun. As we started down the road with Pierce and Frank in the front seat and I in the back I could look over to the corral where lay the exhausted bull and the cows, with only Lady, Dummy, and the Holstein standing. Dull-eyed, they watched me go.

That was the last I ever saw of them. I heard that the summer of uneven feed and the journey over the Dobies caused the herd's milk production to slump badly and that indeed they never quite recovered. Pierce's dream of building a herd of purebred Guernseys that would be the wonder and envy of the Crawford country (and maybe even make the pages of *Hoard's Dairyman*) faded away. Though here and there, perhaps still, one may see that warm titian coat and the queenly inverted triangle on the foreheads of milk cows in that country, vestigial reminders of Pierce's vanished herd.

And he didn't save his marriage. There was no second child, and that next summer Shana took her daughter and disappeared into California. Pierce sold the herd and turned over the ranch to a new tenant, and wandered up into the San Juan mining camps, gambling, then running a restaurant briefly. He finally ended up as the lessee of a gambling operation in a Utah coal camp where he amassed a considerable stake, enough to permit him to settle down in Hotchkiss, below Paonia, and live out his days comfortably enough.

I saw him off and on over the years. Frank Carver told me that before Pierce started his wanderings he came over to Paonia one night and called Connie the Syrian out behind the hamburger stand and worked him over. I never talked to Pierce about anything having to do with that summer, though it was one of the most memorable, and in ways I have yet to fully understand, one of the most important in my life.

Maybe that is why I never asked Pierce for the nine dollars he still owed me as wages for the final month of that summer with the cows.

Bright Mufflers for the Holidays

"Sweet Auburn, loveliest village of the plain—" so Oliver Goldsmith's sad poem, "The Deserted Village," begins. And I felt the same sadness about Somerset, when, in the fifties, U.S. Steel bought the mine and closed it down, forcing many of the Somerset miners to move with their families to other company mines in Utah.

Other than their sad fates (and the fact that they both bear English names) I don't suppose Auburn and Somerset have much in common. Somerset, though lovely in its own right, with its narrow streets lined with cottonwoods winding between rows of neat, small houses, does not sit on a plain—far from it. It sits in the gateway to the Ragged Range and the vastnesses of the West Elks with high hills on either side, so that the sun comes up there after ten in the morning, and disappears in midafternoon.

The men and women who packed up their earthly goods and departed Auburn were of English stock; many of those who left Somerset had come there from all over Europe; from the southeast, from Scandinavia, from the British Isles. In the beginning, in the early days of this century, Somerset was a town of tents. Some of the earliest arrivals were Italian, and they kept the streets between their tents well packed down, and played boccie ball there, according to Shorty Hunten, who is generally accepted nowadays as the Somerset scop or bard. Even then it was a lively place and quickly demonstrated its community spirit by organizing a band.

Many of the miners brought their families or sent for wives from the old country. One such new arrival was most eager to make the acquaintance of other wives. She hit upon the plan of giving a luncheon and inviting wives of her husband's fellow miners. She prepared for her little party very carefully. Houses had been erected in Somerset by then, and she put up curtains, scrubbed, cleaned and painted. She even persuaded her husband to teach her some phrases of greeting in the strange new language. He did so, with some apparent reluctance, and when the great day arrived and a group of guests appeared at the door, his wife swung it open and invited them courteously in with:

"Come in, all you whores. Your sons of bitches all working at the mine?"

The good ladies of Somerset knew at once what was wrong and gently straightened her out, and the affair went off well enough, but that afternoon when the hostess's husband returned from work, she straightened him out in turn, beating him soundly with a broom.

Another ethnic segment of the Somerset community, perhaps the largest, was the Austrian. In the towns down the valley, nearly all those from southeast Europe then, not plainly identifiable as Italian or Greek, were known as Austrians because most of them had lived within the boundaries of the dying Austro-Hungarian empire—Czechs, Slovaks, Hungarians, Serbs, Croats. But all of them, and the Greeks and Italians too, fresh from the rocky hills of their ancient homelands, soon felt at home in the hills west of the Rockies.

They brought their dances and their music; their celebrations, such as their elaborate and protracted weddings; they made their sausages, their sweets rich with nuts and honey; they fermented their wines. Sometimes they dynamited a stream or a small, isolated lake for fish to be salted down for the winter. In the old country they had lived pinched lives, and to them hunting and fishing were matters for survival, ways of assuring food, not matters of sport to be controlled by law. Of course, they had been subject to laws, and harsh ones, in the old country; but those laws were for protecting the game for the aristocrats, and in this new, free country they at first thought everyone could behave as he wished and do as he chose.

People came from north Europe too. Finns came, and the Swedes and Norwegians, bringing echoes of ancient, bloody rivalries—

> Ten thousand Swedes
> Rushed through the weeds
> To lick one sick Norwegian—

but in the American West there was room for everyone, and the Scandinavians could laugh at the old feuds.

Germans came. Four strapping uncles of an aunt of mine boarded an Eastern train to come to the North Fork. They had never ridden on a train before, and they did not know a word of English. They were afraid to get off the train lest they be left behind, and they were not aware that there were sanitary facilities on board, so they suffered through four days of the trip without relieving themselves.

Some Germans went to work in the mines, but many became ranchers, as did some of the Italians, or they combined work and lived on small farms near the mine. The Greeks for the most part worked as section hands or raised sheep—they were part of a larger Greek community that extended over into Utah.

Many emigrants came from the British Isles; Welshmen, Cornish-

Somerset Band

men, Scots, Irish. Arthur Brown, a Welsh miner, delved in Cornwall mines that ran beneath the sea—and came to America to work at the Peanut, above timberline in Crested Butte. Among the English who settled in Somerset were the Palmers and the Morgans. One of the jolly, slender little Palmer men told me how confused he was by the way Americans spoke. When he first went down in the Somerset mine he was told to "Go ahead."

"I didn't know what to do," he laughed, slapping his palms alongside his temples, "I had never heard that before. I didn't know what it meant to 'go ahead.'"

Farmers and merchants in the towns in the lower valley then did not altogether approve of, or understand the miners. For one thing, those from southeast Europe were predominantly Catholic, and most of the people in the lower valley followed Protestant faiths, many evangelical, and had grown up listening to dark, bloody tales of popery.

And then, there was the natural antipathy of the farmer for the miner. The old story of the ant and the grasshopper. The farmer worked long hours the year around, but there was little ready money until in the fall after the fruit harvest was in—and if the prices were poor in a given year, there was no money even then. But the miner was paid every week, and the happy-go-lucky ones and their families could go to the movies nearly every time the bill changed; they even ate in restaurants, an unheard-of extravagance among even prosperous farmers then. The farmer, after his work in the fields was done, had to set the water in the orchard rows and milk the cows and slop the pigs—even on Saturday and Sunday. Everyone, farmer and miner alike, went to town on Saturday night. The farmer and his brood, with the chores done and everyone finally presentable, would be driving along Grand Avenue around seven in the evening. But the miner down from the mines with his family would have his late-model car parked in a choice spot on Grand Avenue before the street lights came on.

So the farmers envied and resented the miners, but the merchants knew on which side their bread was buttered. Without the payrolls of the upper valley, commercial prospects in Paonia ranged from bleak to nonexistent. Certainly it was the miners, particularly the young miners, who made things interesting and profitable in my father's barbershop back in the twenties.

Salesmen from the Paonia Hotel next door stopped in for a shave and a shine when they were in town, businessmen came in for shaves and haircuts on weekdays, and farmers and day-workers made it maybe once every few weeks for a haircut. But the miners came in every Saturday night for a trim and a shine and to kill a little time before the movie, or until the gambling games in the pool hall warmed up, or before picking up a date to go to a dance.

There were always stories circulating around the barbershop of the mighty deeds at work of some of the miners. Swede Axelson for one, working under contract, meaning that he was paid not by the hour but by the amount of coal he dug and loaded, was making as much or more in a month than some farmers made in a year; and he, and others of the young miners, lived in a style befitting their incomes.

They dressed well. They wore suits tailored to measure at Norval Bruce's Toggery, or at John Davis's in Delta. Sometimes they had one or two or more such suits on order before the first one even wore out. The bankers and the professional men in Paonia might have two or three suits, but even the schoolteachers, who were considered to be grossly overpaid then, at least by the farmers, usually had no more than two—one for Sunday and one for every day. And as a general rule, male teachers wore the same suit to school day in and day out, sturdy suits, probably mail order, gray wool, two pants and a vest, bought in the fall and shed the following June. A bored scholar, as I was, could count the passing of the weary winter months by the degree of sheen on the forearms and seats of those suits.

The young miners bought not only suits but cars, always new, often sport models in bright shiny maroon and tan. They drove them fast and hard, up and down the narrow rutted road along the Fire Mountain Canal, and replaced them every year.

Naturally, well-dressed, free-spending young miners with snappy cars were looked upon with favor by many girls in the lower valley, both in the towns and on the ranches. Some parents were reluctant to let their daughters go out with them, these carefree young men, sons of "foreigners," who curiously slurred the language and had different ways and religion. But they were presentable, pleasant and mannerly, and brought their dates home at the specified hours, and the prejudices faded. There were some who drank too much, fought too often, and tended to require that a date "come across;" these were of course avoided. And, they were no more common with the miners than the same sort of Lotharios among the rest of the population. I heard tales through a cousin of mine who was a flaming flapper at the time. Or, rather, I overheard her comparing notes with pals about those unreliables who "really went after you;" "wouldn't take no for an answer;" or "tore the clothes right off your back." And even these pariahs did not suffer total shame. I noted they were often able to find attractive feminine companionship despite their reputations.

But though there was some reluctance to accept the miners socially at first in the lower valley communities, the reverse was never true. Somerset was the friendliest town in the valley. The very diversity of nationalities in the mining camp seemed to foster a good-humored tolerance of all the customs and traits of its own citizens, of those living around them, or of visitors or passersby. Unless, that is, you were a boy of twelve or so and came up to visit entirely on your own. In such a case it was assumed you were looking for trouble, and there would be a boy of approximately your size and age deputized to meet you somewhere around the wide flight of wooden stairs leading up to the company store, and uphold the honor of the community.

A fine large community center was erected in Somerset, containing an auditorium and a dance floor. The dances held there on Saturday nights and on holiday evenings were among the most successful, best-attended in the valley, and this was largely due, I think, to the attitude of the people of Somerset. For a time, parents were reluctant for their daughters, and even their sons, to go to the Somerset dances. But it was soon evident that young people from the lower valley, if they behaved, were as safe or safer there than at any dance anywhere. They were treated as if they were children of the community.

There were incidents, but they were rare. One night a miner a bit far in his cups, shoved a fist through a side window; Tony Majnik, local Samson and jokester, once went out during a dance intermission to a row of little apartments called the Terrace, removed all the front doors from their hinges and carried them off. But if one came simply to dance and enjoy oneself, and have a good time, that one could do and welcome. And if one came to make a nuisance of himself, he would be taken promptly in hand, not necessarily by the law, but by any Somerset male or males within his vicinity.

Christmas holiday dances were the best of all. It was exciting to load into a car with friends and racket up through the narrowing valley, with the steep, winter-white hills enclosing you on either side. At Somerset all would pile out in the dark, in the piercingly cold pure air, and run inside to the wide dance floor. Everyone would be there, and especially everyone from Somerset, girls and women, boys and men. Girls would be wearing holiday dresses and presents of jewelry. Some boys would be wearing new overcoats, new suits, new wristwatches, but even the poorest had received bright mufflers for the holidays and strutted self-consciously around, hands in pockets. Sometimes a young Austrian, perhaps only nine or so, would wander in, giggly and unsteady, having helped himself on the sly from the family wassail bowl. At midnight, at intermission, all repaired to the dining room and were served cake and coffee by the Somerset Ladies Club. At two in the morning the orchestra played "Show me the Way to go Home," the hall was cleared, and the cold cars of the visitors, their motors coaxed back to life, rumbled down the narrow icy road.

Somerset is a ghost town now. There have been good and bad times since the twenties, but in the eighties the portal of the mine was sealed, and the vein will be entered somewhere else at some time in the future when fuel needs require it. Many of the people who came to the mines early in this century, and their children, have scattered out of the hills to the mesas and towns down the valley, to Utah, and beyond. The Slavs, the Italians, the Swedes—their names are on mailboxes all over the North Fork country.

In these days of mistrust, suspicion, and the ever-hovering threat of violence; when, in spite of (or more probably because of) the wonders of the electronic revolution, our lives seem to grow narrower, more lonely, more meager, it is especially good to look back on life as it was lived in the old Somerset. People there liked and trusted each other; neighbors overlooked each other's faults and tolerated and even enjoyed each other's eccentricities. Certainly those who lived there, or visited there, will always remember how it was.

Mountain Music

I like music, but I never felt that it liked me. At Paonia High School the band was organized in my sophomore year with Al Graham, a local druggist, as bandmaster. I was in on the ground floor you might say. But that was as high up as I ever got.

My first big break came when another boy gave up the notion of playing the alto horn, and for a small consideration the instrument was passed on to me. The alto horn took a lot of lip, and a lot of wind. And I soon found out there was another drawback—you didn't start right out making music—what the alto horn played was just a succession of notes. Still, I gave it a try. Nothing came of it, partly because it was wintertime, and cold, and the only place where I was free to practice was in the coal shed. It was the winter my mother was looking after Mrs. Jess Bell, a woman confined to a wheelchair with rheumatism, and it turned out that my practicing in the house was more than the poor lady could bear. And, I have wondered since if even my mother didn't have a little ear trouble where alto horn rehearsals were concerned.

But then a few months later, when Mrs. Bell had moved back up to their ranch in the Muddy country, opportunity knocked again for me. My Uncle Doc took in a B-flat clarinet on a medical bill, and passed the clarinet on to me. It was an indication of how desperate Mr. Graham was about getting the band started, that he was willing to consider me again. The clarinet was an Albert system, which even then had been generally replaced by the Boehm system, so Mr. Graham located a valve and numbering chart for the Albert system, and I was once again launched on a musical career.

But the clarinet, I soon found, really didn't come any closer to playing real music—the melody, that is—than the alto horn. Where the alto horn bumped and huffed and burped along below the melody, the clarinet buzzed and screeched along way above. In fact, the clarinet parts absolutely bewildered me, and it wasn't until my senior year that it came to me in one dazzling moment, what the true function of a clarinet in a band really was. Where the alto horn had something to do with rhythm and with the color in the lower strands of the melody, the clarinet supplied all rococo embroidery stuff. And I could never play those endless trills: with me, music had to be made one note at a time.

So temperamentally I was a soloist from the very first. I leaned toward those tunes and melodies, like "Abide with Me" ("fast falls the eventide—") made up of big, fat notes which moved along in a stately way with each note comfortably close on the scale to its fellows. I could even tell I was making music when I played "Abide with Me" on the alto horn. Another early favorite of mine was "The World is Waiting for the Sunrise," which so fulfilled my requirements that the next winter when I was staying temporarily with my Aunt Ina, after she and Uncle Henry moved into Paonia from the ranch, I sat in the front room playing "The World is Waiting for the Sunrise" over and over. In fact I played it so many times one morning that my dear aunt, who never said a cross word to me in her life, came in and requested that I please play something else for a while.

Since my clarinet was a B-flat, all the jazz piano music of the day, and there was a great deal of it, was in the key of C and had to be transcribed for my instrument. But I didn't mind. In fact, I began to feel that I was really getting into the intricacies of the art by doing so. And, I learned more about the clarinet. It was not in good condition and soon needed new pads. I bought a set and painstakingly installed them, and cut and fitted new cork lining for the joints. I attended band practice and sat in the reeds section with several other clarinetists, including George Chermak, several years my junior, who seemed to know what he was doing. So I sat there with my hands in the prescribed position on the keys and stared at all those thickets of little black notes high above the staff, trying to look skilled and conscientious. I've no doubt that lessons would have helped, although Mr. Graham was a cornetist, and knew very little, I think, about the woodwinds. But in any event lessons couldn't possibly be afforded.

There was a real stir in music in Paonia in the middle twenties. Girls all over town in the houses of the modestly well-to-do were flipping through the pages of sheet music at the family piano, playing "The Sheik of Araby," "My Blue Heaven," "Valencia," "Shine on, Harvest Moon," and the innumerable other hits that came tumbling out of Tin Pan Alley like corn out of a popper. And, on records down at the Book Store (where no books were sold) these same hits could be heard on the Brunswick and Okeh labels, or up at the drugstore on the corner which carried the dignified Victor line. Young people were listening to the stars of the day, tiptoeing through the tulips with Nick Lucas, or soaring into a blue heaven on the swooning falsetto of Gene Austin.

The guitar even then was beginning its conquest of the popular field; Wendell Hall, who archly described himself as "The Red-headed

Musicmaker," was a favorite, and Frank Crumit, another guitar-playing vocalist, had a great success on Victor, "Ivan Abulbul Amir." The popular music stars and their photographs were not nearly as familiar to their public as they are today. Goldy Woods, who clerked for years at the Book Store, was disillusioned upon being confronted with a photograph of Nick Lucas and learning that he was "a skinny little runt," as she put it. Goldy was very substantial in size and had evidently been daydreaming of a tenor soul mate at least six feet tall with a good pair of shoulders.

I am sure to the adults of that day the jazz that was inundating Grand Avenues and spilling over into parlors everywhere was nearly as nauseating as many oldsters find rock and roll to be today. A Gene Austin classic, "I Wish I had Died in my Cradle," for instance, could set the teeth on edge of any parent who grew up listening to "On a Bicycle Built for Two," or "Just a Song at Twilight."

As lacking in funds as our household always was, my mother did help to scrape together the eighteen-odd dollars that it required to buy a portable phonograph, sending away for it to Sears, Roebuck, and on it my brother and I played the hits of Johnny Marvin—"You're the Cream in my Coffee" and "There's Something Nice About Everyone" —each piece ending with his signature, some hot licks on the kazoo.

Before he rose into prominence Johnny had toured with a band which played the Paonia Opera House, and he set the local flappers agog by whiling away the early evening hours strolling down Lund's Lane with a bevy of them. Like many another entertainer, he was no longer young by the time his work came into vogue. His hair was growing thin, and he must have wondered whether he was ever going to make it at all.

The fox-trot was the rage then, along with the perdurable waltz. Other fad dances came along, like the frenetic Charleston, which gave a preview of what was yet to be. At the dances at the Odd Fellows Hall in the upstairs of the Opera House one could see an occasional polka or even a schottishe, though the shrine of the old country dances was Maikka Hall above the grocery in the mining town of Bowie. At kitchen sweats, or at the dances in the Crawford dance hall over in the cattle country, played for by the two Christian brothers and one Christian sister, redheads all of them, you saw squares and reels.

But the town kids of that day would have been astonished to learn that there would ever come a time when country music would have any sort of general appeal. Once at the Book Store I put on a record featuring a guitar trio playing "My Little Mohee," with one of their number singing the homely old folk song through his nose in the style later so widely copied and admired. I winced and got it off the spindle as fast as I could.

The big bands mostly came later, but Duke Ellington was appreciated and smaller combos like Red Nichols and his Five Pennies were in vogue. Bands were showing up at the Opera House to play for dances. Dance pavilions were nailed together at Read near the county seat and outside Grand Junction the Mileaway had a classy, multi-mirrored, revolving chandelier. College bands, such as the one from Colorado Aggies came through, and local girls flirted with the band members, and had little debates among themselves as to which was the "cutest," the saxophonist or the trombone player. In Delta, the county seat, the Doyle family orchestra featured a soloist who blew hot licks or "hokum" as it was referred to then, and I was caught up in wonder at these flights of jazz fancy, finding such a musical gift little short of miraculous.

In Paonia there was a rather conservative band called the Bluebirds, which included the cashier at the First National on trombone, and a member from Somerset playing trumpet but only in the lower registers because the aluminum plate in his skull, acquired in World War II, resonated in the upper registers. They played for the more formal affairs.

Once there was a popular band contest which the Bluebirds chose to "sponsor," some said, because they were afraid to compete against such bands as the lively little combo, The Rowdies, which featured our old friend Dutch the shoeshine boy at the barbershop on fiddle, harmonica, and saw, and my cousin James, now known as "Slick" for his athletic skill, on clarinet. The Rowdies won, hands down.

Meanwhile my own musical career was languishing, although I still, by default, occupied third or fourth chair in the high school band and played the olios or "open-season" melodies in the simpler musical numbers. But the band was coming along. There had been a town marching band for years, and so the tradition carried easily over into the high school. It was even planned that the new high school band should attend the spring band tournament then becoming established on the Western Slope in Grand Junction, and the town got solidly behind them, and through benefit suppers helped come up with band uniforms in the school colors of red and black. Marching practice was held every morning behind the grade school.

In due time the competition music arrived, a complicated piece with treacherous alterations in key and tempo, a composition no one in town had ever heard played. Mr. Graham consulted with his lead instrumentalists with indifferent results. Rehearsals were tedious, gingerly affairs. I had the good sense to stay completely out of it.

The great day finally came when we all were herded into cars and were on our way down to Grand Junction. Not only were we going to the tournament, but we were to stay in the homes of Grand Junction people, as honored guests. My bed partner was Harry Woods, who had actually learned to play the French horn. We were dropped off before a pleasant home, hospitably received, and shown to a room at the side of the house with its own private entrance.

Meals we ate in a little short order cafe where breakfast set us back twenty-five cents, and usually we had a hamburger and an ice cream cone and nickel candy bars later in the day. I had at least nine dollars for the three or four days we would be at the tournament. Another marvelous privilege accorded us was entree to the Elks' Club with its comfortable game rooms filled with leather-covered easy chairs. There were card tables and billiard tables and a phonograph in a den where the older and more sophisticated band members danced. It all seemed one long whirl of games and fun.

On the first night, before the tournament was fully under way, we drove around town in the cars in which we had come down as passengers. I had come down in El Schmidt's old Gardner sedan, its sides enclosed in curtains of lacquered black canvas with isinglass inserts. Mr. Schmidt lived in Paonia but worked in the Somerset mine, and he had permitted his son, Johnny, to take the family chariot, sharing the responsibility for its care with two other half-grown boys, Alvin Axelson and Coley Johnstone, members of whose families also were miners.

On that first night of our arrival, as if attracted by a giant magnet, a number of these cars from Paonia and other towns ended up parking before the row of little gray cottages across from the city waterworks. No female band members had been invited along for this nefarious and illicit excursion. Most of us were without sexual experience, certainly without any familiarity with houses of prostitution; indeed, before that night many, myself among them, had doubted whether any such establishments actually existed. But there were older boys among us who knew, or claimed to know about such mysteries. A few swaggered in through the open cottage doors, accompanied by taunts and catcalls from the waiting cars—and came out again in what seemed a remarkably short time. At last one member of our crowd, a high school alumnus and known to be remarkably endowed anatomically, emerged from a house and was escorted off the prim little porch and down the rose-bordered walk to the white picket gate by an older woman, carefully coiffed and elaborately dressed, with an abundance of gaudy jewelry on her arms and at her neck. She kept a friendly hand on the young man's arm, and in a moment of awed silence called out a hospitable welcome to us all, in a high, feline voice, before being drowned out by a chorus of moans, abuse, and nervous laughter from the waiting cars.

The next morning the tournament began in earnest, with soloists on various instruments appearing before judges in classrooms at the high school. These competitions were often static, lame affairs, depending upon the ability of the performers, but the excitement of just being there with all those young people from other schools was enough, and, besides, afterward there was always the Elks' Club.

The third day was the climactic one. The bands paraded in full uniform down the main streets of the city. It was an unusually warm spring day, we were all in woolen uniforms, and our shoes made marks in the asphalt of the street as we waited for our turn to pass by the judge's stand. But it was a great spectacle, to see all those bands in colorful, rich uniforms, with the band marshals in shakos and gold braid, twirling glittering batons. (Our own marshal, Tex Miller, had waited and practiced long for this day, marching on the ditch-bank of his father's farm.) And this was before it was customary for high school bands to be preceded by shapely girls behaving like performers in a Roman orgy. Our two banner carriers that year were modestly uniformed, and wore not a single bauble.

I don't remember how we fared in the judging so we must not have distinguished ourselves. But I was on my best behavior, concentrating as I never had before, determined to do well. And that accounts for the fact, as a photograph verifies, that as we passed the judge's stand I was the only marcher in our band who was in step!

And then, at last, we arrived at the rear stairs of the Avalon Theatre, and slowly, in a funereal silence, filed in and took our places on the stage to play the contest composition. I was still as strongly motivated as I had been during the marching, and was sufficiently involved so that I joined in on one pianissimo passage, achieving a squawk on my clarinet that surely must have set us back a few percentage points.

In the evening the awards were made. Some of us went down to the Elks' Club afterward, but it was closed. It was time to go home. Johnny Schmidt had had such a good time that he had not slept for three successive nights and behaved as if he were under the influence of a drug. It was up to Alvin Axelson to herd the Gardner home.

Alvin himself was a little used-up and not that alert, and we sideswiped the Buick of a local businessman on the way out of town. There was a conference on the dark street to assess damages: the old Gardner was intact, but its bumper had dented the side of the Buick. The driver of the Buick said that the proper thing to do was to drive down to the police station, Alvin agreed, and the Buick took off in advance to show us the way.

That was a tactical error on the driver's part, for at the next corner Alvin swung left into a cross street and we pounded south and east, Alvin driving erratically and frantically, looking for the way out of town leading up-country towards Paonia, while we in the back seat kept a watch through the rear panel to see if we were being followed. Out over the Colorado Bridge we roared, and up the mesa grade. On we went, only confident of our escape when we had passed the White-water turnoff.

The rest of the trip was a nightmare of misfortune. We had flats on all four wheels before we reached the county line. Each flat had to be repaired by flashlight once the spare was in service, and we blundered on, arriving at last in the streets of Delta, where the road turns north and east up the North Fork. At that point, squarely in the intersection of the main street, the Gardner limped to a stop. The tires on both rear wheels were flat, we were out of patching equipment, and out of gas. It was on the dark side of early morning; no garages or filling stations were open. We all collapsed, like the Gardner, and slept.

Hours later we awoke, pooled our resources to buy two gallons of gas at a nearby filling station, a few doughnuts—fortunately Coley Johnstone was better off than the rest of us, since he worked at the Somerset mine—patched the tires yet again, and rolled slowly homeward.

We had not gone far before a head count revealed that Johnny Schmidt was no longer with us. We drove back to Delta and looked up and down the quiet streets for him, but he was nowhere to be found. We could only conclude he had walked on up the North Fork road. We were still twenty-five miles from home, and if we were wrong, we would have to deliver the old Gardner to Mr. and Mrs. Schmidt minus their son and heir.

We saw no sign of him along the road. We pulled up in front of Schmidt's on a flat left rear tire, and debated as to who was to deliver the unsettling news about Johnny. Coley was the oldest, his family and the Schmidts were friends, so he went in.

He learned that Johnny was there, in bed, asleep. He had fallen asleep in the Gardner in Delta with the rest of us, and dreamed a vivid dream. He was the band marshal, leading the band along the parade route, and he awoke well up the North Fork road, marching along, keeping time with his imaginary baton, when a farmer in a pickup stopped and asked him if he wanted a ride. Still confused, he accepted. By the time he realized who and where he was, he was nearly home. Several years later, as a senior in high school, Johnny fulfilled his dream, leading the Paonia High School band at the spring tournament.

The other notable experience of my active musical career came about after a group of us formed a jazz band in direct, defiant competition with the Paonia High School jazz band. We had Ida Lou Mortensen, a good pianist, Leland Wiley, the town's best drummer, and Carroll Wade, playing adequate trumpet. I was along as clarinetist, but I think I was tolerated as comic relief. We called ourselves, disparagingly, the "Cuckoo Canaries."

And we had at least one paying date. It was on a weekend, a Saturday night dance up in the Raggeds, at the Spring Street School. Certainly no small part of the excitement was in getting there, up the twisting, treacherous mountain road, past the coal camps of Bowie and Somerset, with the deep Fire Mountain Canal flowing ominously alongside, and then out the East Muddy road.

The people of the West and East Muddy communities were always hospitable, even to musicmakers of dubious ability, and that evening stands out in memory. I had a date, a pretty girl who liked me—most girls found me a little strange and were further put off by my small size—and I was playing the clarinet, for pay. I had so good a time that I more than once left the bandstand to dance with my date, and one rancher-sponsor admonished me, stating that I was needed up on the bandstand. And even this added to the pleasure of the evening. Not only was I playing with an orchestra, but my absence from the group had been noted and lamented by a paying customer!

Even the fact that the radiator of our car ran dry on the way home failed to put a damper on the occasion for me. Much of the romance of motoring is gone, now that cars are more reliable. Another boy and I, leaving the other members of the party asleep, went after water. As we made our way down through the rocks and brush in the early light of the day, we came upon a pleasant, welcoming sight—a sheepherder's tent, full of the clear, flickering yellow glow of a lantern. Two dark-skinned men greeted us pleasantly as we looked in through the front flap of the tent, and insisted on our sharing breakfast.

It is sad to report that after such a checkered, arduous apprenticeship my musical career faded completely away. Decades later I thought about taking up the clarinet again. I rented a Boehm system B-flat clarinet and although I could fumble through the fingering I found the demands on my lungs to be taxing and I realized that it would be a difficult and tedious process to become even modestly proficient.

Still, if I could find an old Albert system, C-melody, so I wouldn't have to transpose sheet music . . . Woody Allen plays one, so they must still be around . . . who knows? I might give it another try. I even have some reeds laid away, just in case.

Show Time

A substantial portion of the entertainment presented in the Paonia community throughout the twenties consisted of carnivals, circuses, and Toby shows which raised their tents in the old ball park down by the river. In the Toby shows nearly all of the action in the week-long succession of plays revolved around a red-wigged, gallus-snapping character. In one of these dramas, he has come to the city to try to save the old homestead from crooked lawyers. This gives him plenty of chances to show how sneaky, mean, and foolish these city people were, to the great delight of the audience. In between the acts performers would come out to dance and sing, accompanied by Toby on the banjo or guitar. Glenn Taylor, who rose to become governor of Idaho, began his public career singing and strumming guitar in the family's Toby Taylor show.

Another stage company, a little more sophisticated than the Toby Taylor players, were the Brunk's Comedians. Like the Toby's, Brunk's cast members entertained between the acts, and hawked saltwater taffy up and down the aisles in packages that contained loudly trumpeted prizes of negligible value. But instead of a country music soloist or trio like the Toby shows featured, a jazz orchestra was seated below the stage, and soloists sang selections of more or less current waltzes and fox-trots. Anyone who could possibly afford it bought "reserved" seats for the Brunk's shows. This was because if you bought "general admission" you found yourself exiled to the plank tiers cordoned off at the remote rear; the entire remainder of the tent seating space was reserved.

Some entertainments of a superior nature did come through town in the twenties. Foremost among these was the Chautauqua, which raised its broad tent on the grade school grounds for several summers. On magical mornings the children of the community filed in and seated themselves before the stage, their eyes dazzled by the cool amber light sifting down through the canvas from the row of tall cottonwoods along the school yard fence, their noses filled with the perfume of the fresh pine planking used in building the benches and the stage. Then, bright and dedicated young Chautauqua staffers unveiled the mysteries of classic dance, or the intricacies of classic

196

music to the restless but awestruck audience, aided by the artists who would be appearing at the afternoon and evening performances. Sounds arose, sounds seldom if ever heard before in the community— the dulcet whinny of the oboe, the mellow bray of the French horn— sounds that aroused dogs and roosters clear to the far end of town.

The children listened raptly for the most part at these affairs, although some of the less attentive youths engaged in horseplay— more than one youngster, my brother among them, coming home after an early Chautauqua session with chewing gum in their hair.

And all this was prelude. Later in the day came the performances; perhaps an inspirational lecture by a famous speaker of the day on the celebrated theme of "Acres of Diamonds," which had to do with uncovering the hidden potentialities in everyday life. Or perhaps a magic show, or a comic opera, or a talk by a noted explorer, with the rude stage converted into an exotic drawing room, the canvas wall decorated with a collection of icons, rugs, and hangings from the far reaches of the world.

It grew cooler in the evenings but in the afternoon performances the air in the tent could be oppressive, and the audience would give off a faint sibilance and present a wavering appearance, as ladies and young girls cooled themselves with bright-colored cardboard fans provided by downtown merchants.

For a few years Paonia was the smallest town anywhere to support the attractions of Chautauqua's celebrated Ridpath Circuit, but it was a heavy burden on the community. The promoters with the Chautauqua resorted to pleas, and even solicited the help of the young—the very young—calling them to the stage to make solemn testimonials as to the cultural advantages Chautauqua provided, but it was all in vain. The Chautauqua disappeared forever from the school grounds.

By the early thirties tent shows of any description were rarely seen in the upper valley. The Toby shows came less and less often, and Brunk's Comedians no longer found it profitable to come to Paonia, but paused instead in Hotchkiss ten miles down the road. Later they came only to the county seat. Circuses and carnivals followed the same pattern. The motion picture had won.

Tent show prices were beyond the reach of many in the upper valley, and such plebian entertainments were scorned by the more cultivated citizenry. But nearly everyone—town dwellers, farmers, miners—went to the movies whenever they could in those good years of the twenties. This was at the Gayety Theatre on Grand Avenue.

197

Every advertised feature was eagerly awaited, especially by the young, everything from westerns to steamy dramas about "vamps" and "sheiks." Then there were the epics, Griffith's *Intolerance* and *The Covered Wagon,* the latter such a success that the town held a pageant in which everyone dressed in costumes inspired by the film.

And of course the general favorite among motion picture types was the western, certainly among the boys I grew up with. William S. Hart was admired, but others who followed were loved, players like the Farnums, William and Dustin, Tom Mix and Buck Jones, and, later, Richard Dix. The camera liked to dwell on the great stone face of Dix in the midst of coming to a decision during a crisis (he always came to the most difficult but morally right decision) while his cool eyes swept their whole horizontal reach, indicating deep processes of thought.

On a given night, many young western movie aficionados didn't have the price of a ticket for the Gayety, which ranged anywhere from 15 cents to a quarter, but before every performance, around six-thirty in the evening as the lights went up on the marquee, Harold Hammond, the lanky proprietor, would stride out front where a crowd of young boys would be gathered—and occasionally a clutch of brash young flappers—and he would regally choose two or more to earn tickets by dusting seats.

One night as a duster I enjoyed a special privilege. Harold was trying out an automatic pianola that had just arrived to provide accompaniment for the films. It was housed in a tall black mahogany cabinet. The upper door panels were set in stained glass, and behind them a dim bulb revealed a piano roll, a cymbal, a drum, and an upright violin with a bow suspended over its strings in ghostly readiness.

On this special night, whether by accident or invitation, a woman we all called Old Lady Tinkler, a very fat lady living in the east end of town, a woman some claimed had a shady past, was present, and when the pianola clamored out a tune with a ragtime beat she rose, threw off her shawl, raised her skirts to midcalf, and performed a surprisingly nimble and seductive dance.

On nights when I was not one of the fortunate ones chosen to do the dusting, there was nothing for it but to go glumly home. But there was one night when I was so bewitched by the promise of a film that I stood on tiptoe outside on the sidewalk and watched what was going on on the screen through the ticket-booth window. I had to continually keep one eye peeled for the approach of Marshall Hanks, who was as usual conscientiously enforcing the eight-o'clock curfew. Twice he returned to warn me, and twice I retreated to the corner of First Street and waited until he continued his rounds, and then returned to my post. But then I became so engrossed that I suddenly looked around to discover him within a half-dozen steps of me. That was enough. I took off, rounding the corner of the Fruit Exchange Bank under full steam, and by the time he had me in sight again, I was a block away. In his exasperation he called after me a name reflecting unpleasantly on my parentage.

Another time, when Lon Chaney was appearing in *The Hunchback of Notre Dame,* the charge was five times the usual, and I was driven to the desperate length of appropriating the shine profits that I had made at the barbershop that Saturday night. I lied to my mother afterward, providing her with some transparent and shoddy tale, claiming that I had been hit by a motor car when I crossed the street and lost all my change in the dust of the road. I was fairly certain I would be whipped, but I was not, although my mother's niece, who was staying with us that winter attending high school, glared at me indignantly as I stumbled through my unconvincing and shoddy tale. But my mother was suffering from one of her frequent headaches, and she only said wearily and sadly that it was too bad, that we needed the money for I don't know now what important use, and it all ended with my creeping up to bed feeling more ashamed of myself than if my

The Gayety on opening night

mother had resorted to a whipping.

My brother was braver than I was. When a new Buck Jones film came to the Gayety and he and I had exhausted every possibility of gaining admission money, he pleaded with our mother so persistently that she cried,

"If you don't stop I'm going to have to whip you."

"Whip me then," he wailed, "whip me and let me go."

And she was so impressed with the novelty of this approach that she yielded and we were both permitted to go. This was an extreme measure; I don't remember that he ever resorted to it again.

When the Harold Lloyd comedies were at the height of their popularity, a booking agent came through on a rainy spring day wearing face makeup and a costume closely resembling that of the comedian—the dark, skimpy suit with white shirt and perky black bow tie, the horn-rimmed glasses and straw boater. And on request he would turn his back, adjust the boater, snap his fingers and turn again, revealing the brilliant, broad, long-toothed grin, eyes nearly closed behind the empty frames of the spectacles. I followed him and Harold Hammond around most of the day, watching the visitor do this solitary act in his repertoire along Grand Avenue. He was only a pleasant enough man, an ordinary man between performances, but when he snapped his fingers, adjusted his hat and revealed the brilliant grin, it was as if, for one gleaming moment, you were in the enchanted presence of the star.

One spring in the mid-twenties Hammond resorted to a contest to build interest in a new serial he was about to present. The serial was called "Within the Net," and it portrayed the adventures of dashing Jack Mulhall as a government agent pursuing evildoers. Little cards showing exciting scenes in the serial episodes were given out at the door; a complete set of 32 cards would entitle a contestant to attend the Gayety for all eight episodes of the serial, and I bent every effort to fill out my collection.

The days wore down; on the day before the contest was to end, I still lacked two cards. I spoke to Harold of it, and he asked me which cards I still needed.

"Eight and twenty-two," I told him, but added that I had the promise of both. He shook his head and I knew that he thought my cause a lost one. I suppose such contests to this day are run in the same fashion as that one: the truth, as I learned from Harold later, was that in the hundreds of cards of every number given out, only a paltry two or three bore the number eight.

And I did have the promise of an eight; Dave Meeker, a classmate of mine who had quit school in the eighth grade but with whom I was still friends, had one, he said, and I walked out across the river that afternoon to where he lived with his mother and his father Ike, a hardy old coal miner in his seventies, still shoveling coal on weekdays—and shoveling another freight down his gullet on Saturday nights. Dave had gone to work by the time I arrived at his home, but his mother gave me the card he had laid aside for me. He did not know of the value of it to me, but if he had I think he would have given it to me just the same. I obtained a No. 22 that same afternoon, and thus became one of the highly select few to have a complete set, and luxuriously strolled into the Gayety just before the house lights went down for a couple of months, snubbing the dusting crowd.

Late in the twenties the movies underwent a sea change. The talkies arrived. I remember looking through a copy of *Photoplay* in 1928 in the horde of movie magazines treasured by my cousin Mary; at its center was a page-size glossy portrait of John Gilbert, and beneath it in large letters ran the worshipful caption:

JOHN GILBERT. THE MAN OF THE HOUR.

That handsome man, beloved even in his arrogance—dashing soldier of "The Big Parade," lover of the divine Garbo, hero of "St. Elmo"—who would have believed it? Before the silent camera a god, under the merciless microphone a clod. In months his career was swept away in the great wash of the oncoming tide of the talkies.

Harold Hammond at first refused to invest in the equipment to show the new films at the Gayety. He appeared before the Rotary Club to explain why the whole idea of talking pictures was impractical and that it was just a fad like the 3-D films that you watched through tinted glasses. But the talkies came to a movie house in Hotchkiss, and I saw those that I could, once through the help of Paul Hanson, a classmate and friend of mine who had a car. He was willing to go if I could pay for the tickets. I was thinning peaches at the time, and had a little money, so we had a deal.

He was working part time in a garage to defray expenses on his car, a Durant coupe, and our first stop was the alley in back of the garage, where Paul dipped up several gallons of waste oil to take along—the Durant was well into its dotage, and used more oil than gas.

That night Paul and I saw a young Edward G. Robinson in a feature rather more successful than most, "The Hole in the Wall." Most of the early films were murky in subject and treatment. Sound effects were introduced clumsily and ineptly. One early shocker concerned a maniacal idiot tethered in a cellar who escaped periodically to terrorize a neighborhood. And when on the screen the penned monster opened his mouth to emit his fearful cry, the sound that came forth was that of a fire siren.

In the early talkies I saw, an aging character actor, H.B. Warner, appeared in many roles, often even as a virile young hero. He was a rather wispy man, almost cadaverous in appearance, but he was the possessor of a fine voice and spoke with the elegant diction he had learned on the English stage. Later he appeared in Frank Capra's production of "Shangri La," as an aged courtier in the palace of the five-hundred-year-old ruler, a role that fitted him very well.

When Al Jolson came along in "Sonny Boy" the era of the silents was over. Tom Poulos opened a theatre in his new dance hall and theatre next to the Book Store, and the talkies were shown there. With them came the Sons of the Pioneers and the singing cowboys. Soon the Gayety closed down, and Harold Hammond turned his attention to the family farm. I saw him many times afterward, but it was as if he didn't remember who I was. Perhaps it was just that he had put all his days at the Gayety behind him and didn't want to be reminded.

A hundred years ago opera houses were being built all over the American West. In Colorado, H.A.W. Tabor the silver king erected opera houses in Denver, in Leadville, and in Central City. Paonia's Opera House came a little later; in 1906 the Odd Fellows dedicated a two-story brick structure on Second Street, not as grand as the Tabor Grand in Denver but grand by local standards.

As far as the Odd Fellows were concerned, the most important part of the building was the second, or top floor. You entered from the street and walked up the double flight of broad, echoing stairs to the upper floor landing and then turned to the right, past the door to the kitchen, and through the double doors entered into the main hall, a large, airy room floored in tongue-and-groove hardwood like the auditorium below. Rows of windows on the east and west looked out over the town to the foothills of the West Elks. At each end of the hall a dais accommodated the thrones of the chaired officers, with narrow platforms along the side walls on which captain's chairs were positioned where other worthies could be seated.

My Uncle Henry Elmendorf was a member of the Odd Fellows, first in the Crawford Club and finally in Paonia where Aunt Ina and he established their last home. The years rolled on, his beloved wife died, and there was nothing that he yearned for more than to garner the diamond-encrusted pin representing fifty years of faithful attendance with the lodge. The forty-eighth year came; the forty-ninth crept slowly by; only a few months remained, but it was not to be.

On the nights when the public was invited to attend a lodge or club dance, the long tables in the kitchen to the rear would be laden with salads, sandwiches and desserts (high on one wall was a cryptic

The pristine opera house

placard: IF YOU SPIT ON THE FLOOR AT HOME, GO HOME 2
SPIT).

The opera house proper, on the floor below, is still in frequent use
by the community. It consists of an auditorium with a stage that was

well equipped at the time of its construction, with flied scenery and a bank of light switches off stage right. The scenery is no longer there, but the rest of the equipment is much the same. Below the stage are dressing rooms, left and right, and a "green room" in between, which in my day was crowded with leftover props from community or high school dramatic productions. Beyond this room, under the auditorium, is the dirt-floored basement. It contains the furnace. On the east wall windowed recesses extend out into the sidewalk on Poplar Street so the coal supply can be shoveled in. Each recess is covered with planking. On nights when I had attended a horror film at the Gayety down on Grand Avenue, like "Murders in the Wax Museum" with Lionel Atwill or "Dr. Jekyll and Mr. Hyde" with John Barrymore, I had to negotiate this lonely stretch of sidewalk to get to our home directly beyond, and I leaped swiftly over these plank inserts, averting my eyes from the half-concealed windows behind them for fear of seeing some fiend glaring out at me.

I remember lurking in the opera house basement one night when a high school dance was in progress above, listening to the feet of the dancers slipping across the polished floor. There was the rhythmical thump of the talented feet of Dance King Willard Hall, and the sustained scrape and creak caused by the enormous swoops and glides of Paul Hofer, the biggest of the school's athletes and a dedicated and flamboyant dancer.

On the auditorium level, rows of folding chairs in oak veneer provide the seating and could be shoved aside for dances. The balcony is shallow and a railing, gracefully curved, encloses it. On dance nights the balcony was the particular retreat of half-grown boys too shy or young to participate in the activities below. One could lean back and plant one's feet on the sturdy iron railing in solid comfort, or lean forward when one's attention was especially drawn to the circling couples and rest one's upper lip against its cool surface.

On one such night my friend Tippy and I sat on one side of the balcony and could look across to where strange boys were sitting, with one of them absently leaning forward, his upper lip pressed against the railing. Without any premeditated design, Tippy and I each raised a foot and planted it on the railing. We were thrilled and delighted to see the boy across from us jerk backward, startled, and rub his lip with a pained expression on his face. The shock wave caused by our feet had travelled around the curve of the railing.

All that we had to do then was to wait until he had dismissed the incident, which he did, shortly, from his mind, and relax and lean forward again. Again we raised our feet in unison and planted them smartly back on the railing, fetching him a solid whack on the lip. This time his annoyance was considerably increased. He had conceived the notion that someone, with malice aforethought, was inflicting pain upon him, but it never occurred to him that the vibration travelled around the curve in the railing. He looked carefully both ways along the railing on his side of the balcony and finally his suspicions focussed on some boys not far removed from his group, towards the stage from where he was sitting. He kept a baleful eye on them and slowly and very carefully leaned once more into the railing. We obliged by giving him another rap, and he leaped up, rubbing his lip, and looked around in both directions. Then he enlisted the help of his friends in watching for suspicious movements by nearby spectators, and we spent an enjoyable half hour or so obliging him with raps on the lip while his anger and bafflement increased. At last he and his friends arose and left.

It was as well that he never thought to look across the balcony during that time, because the faces of my friend and I and a couple other companions were red and contorted in the effort to maintain our composure.

So far as I know, Grand Opera never graced the stage of the Paonia Opera House, though musical comedy was often seen there in the twenties and thirties, usually presented by local talent. But the house curtain was in the great operatic tradition, its painted surface depicting a view of the Grand Canal of Venice, with what appeared to me then to be an ornate barber pole leaning out of the waters at the right front, and off in the distance the spires of St. Mark's, golden in the sunset.

The original stage scenery consisted of at least three sets of flats and backdrops, existing now only in the memories of those once young who saw them there: a forest scene, a drawing-room interior, and an incredibly clean and orderly small-town main street.

Touring stage companies who played the Opera House did not present much entertainment calculated to appeal to elevated tastes. Sometimes the whole evening would be devoted to vaudeville turns before the main street backdrop. In one such turn two boobies connive against a third, luring him to a stool near the footlights, on the pretext of curing him of a headache. They come and go, bringing materials to set a bonfire under the stool and singing a ditty that went something like,

"O-h-h-h, from Tinkletown to Trickletown is fifteen miles
And, from Trickletown to Tinkletown is fifteen miles ... "

until all preparations are made and the bonfire is set alight. Then the victim jumps up with his coattails smoking and gallops madly offstage while the other two follow him, dousing him with buckets of water. Hilarious.

Some such troupes featured a standup comedian who would take the trouble beforehand to go down to Grand Avenue and learn the names and occupations of business and professional men, and then he would incorporate outrageous aspersions concerning them into his monolog. This delighted one and all. Occasionally a travelling show would arrive practically unheralded, but this did not really matter; the town was so hungry for entertainment that word-of-mouth would bring a good-sized crowd to the theatre that same evening.

I was an eager herald for such events. From our kitchen window my brother and I could look across the narrow alleyway to the double doors opening into the lower two floors at the rear of the Opera House. It was a great thrill to see the livery stable dray pull up in the alley with the trunks of costumes and props for a show. One morning around eleven a dog show arrived and we watched the cages of the stars being shoved into the rear of the dark stage. I don't know how much other publicity that show had, but from the time the baggage arrived at the rear of the theatre until the whistle on the power plant announced noon, every shop and store along Grand Avenue had heard the news.

During these years the citizens of the town did not have to depend entirely on imported talent for live theatrical entertainment. Throughout the two decades, the twenties and thirties, the stage of the Opera House in the late fall and winter would be occasionally occupied by

The Follies

local productions, plays presented by the town's drama society, the high school drama club and in the spring the senior play. These productions were usually three-act comedies or mysteries rented from Samuel French, Broadway successes like *Dulcie, Come Out of the Kitchen, Polly With a Past, Seven Keys to Baldpate,* and *The Cat and the Canary.* Most of them would soon be translated to the silver screen, forerunners of the great Hollywood comedies of the forties.

A play produced by a local club that really gripped me was *The Thirteenth Chair.* In it Mrs. Burke, a dainty little lady, played the medium who conducted a series of seances during which a murder occurred. Opposite her, representing the cynical official world, was the police detective, played by tall, gangling M.H. Crissman, a man with real theatrical gifts which were commonly on display at the First National Bank, where he held forth as chief stockholder and president. I never forgot those scenes in which the two, so ill-assorted physically, faced each other off, each aware of being matched against a keen intelligence.

The most successful of all local productions in the early twenties, however, was staged by the Rotary Club, an extravaganza in which all the many dancing girls and actresses who appeared were impersonated by members of the club in drag. It was directed by a travelling crew who provided the skits, the direction, the elaborate costumes, and supervised makeup.

The Opera House was sold out for the performance and the evening was an uproarious success. Mr. Leicester, the lanky town electrician, attired in a fetching green taffeta evening gown, green stockings and high-heeled slippers, sang Irving Berlin's "All Alone by the Telephone," in a dulcet tenor. "Doc" Mitchell, always plump and bewattled, wore a high-piled wig crowned with a diamond tiara, and in his poisonously red evening gown and smoking his usual cigar, looked like the corrupt Messalina descending the stairs in Toulouse Lautrec's famous painting.

Leo Cady, a local grocery clerk dressed as a Jewish street peddler, bobbed up and down the aisles during intermission selling taffy, while Rowe Taylor, an undertaker from Hotchkiss—intercity rivalries being suspended for the occasion—sang rowdy old songs in a clear tenor, accompanying himself on the guitar.

Another star of the evening was Floyd Hammond, cashier of the Fruit Exchange Bank. He was a tall, wide-hipped man and a graceful ballroom dancer, and when he swirled onto the darkened stage in Spanish costume, flicking castanets and twirling a fan with a subdued spot picking up the spangles on the costume and the rhinestones on the fan and headband, the audience was amazed and enchanted. In those days in remote small towns in the West the terms "fairy" and "queen" evoked only childhood tales like those from the Brothers Grimm, and a "faggot" only referred to the wood consumed in medieval bonfires, so a public-spirited male could accept a role as a belle of the theatre without fear of censure.

One of my early appearances before the public was at the Opera House. This was in a kermess staged for the benefit of the community churches, produced by a matronly and authoritative retired school teacher, Mrs. Huff. I doubt if anyone in Paonia had ever heard of a kermess before Mrs. Huff proposed doing one, and what she had in mind did not in the least resemble the sort of mad, drunken revel that Bruegel portrayed in his paintings. Our kermess was staged in the winter, within doors, and all I remember of it was the dance in which I appeared, performed by eight seventh-grade couples. We were dressed in green, in costumes made by our mothers, the boys with white collars and the girls with white aprons. On the great night we circled the stage, tripping along at a one-two-three-hop pace, arms akimbo, and each boy carrying, of all things, a handkerchief. It speaks volumes for the mesmerizing influence of Mrs. Huff that boys could be enlisted in such a spectacle, but she had the solid support of the leading citizens of the town and considerable pressure was brought to bear, I am sure.

At the end of the dance, after much circling and weaving in and about, we all emerged at stage front, each boy on one knee with his partner leaning amorously over him from behind. Mrs. Huff had instructed the boys at this point to slowly lift their heads and stare up and backward into their partners' eyes. I did this, aware as I did that the rest of the male members of the company were staring stuporously forward into the dark gulf of the auditorium. Touched by what they thought to be a spontaneous and sentimental action on my part, a number of ladies in the audience emitted little whinnies of approval. As we held for the curtain, I noticed that even my partner, Vivian, was moved. Still, in the end, it operated against me. From that time forward Vivian never seemed to have much of an opinion of me. I think that gesture of mine convinced her, indelibly, that I was a nerd.

The kermess was declared a success, and the mothers of members of our dance company, many of them from the upper reaches of Paonia society, felt that the group should not be disbanded, but should remain a social entity, and so all that winter the Kermess Dancers were feted at first one leading citizen's house and then at another. At each home we first sat down to a fine dinner, and afterward there were games and dancing. It was the only social season I ever experienced and it was a bit overwhelming for us all.

At the home of the postmaster, Earl Thaxton introduced the Bunny Hug, and Robert Rockwell, Jr. spilled the mashed potatoes in his lap. We were invited in turn into the home of the head of the First

National Bank, and into that of the mayor, and then that of the district representative to the state legislature. But despite the best efforts of the sponsoring ladies, as the round of parties continued, many of the boys, myself among them, grew sated and cloddish; we ate with wolfish appetites, but dancing and parlor games began to cloy and at last the Kermess Dancers, as a social entity, were permitted to fade into the minor social annals of the town.

Many a noted public building acquires over the years a familiar spirit, like the hunchback of the cathedral of Notre Dame, or the phantom of the opera. At the Paonia Opera House that spirit was Humphrey Dutton. Old Humphrey did not live in the Opera House, it was true, but he very nearly did. He was the factotum who swept it out with the assistance of his wife and other members of his family, ran the lights and the curtain during performances, and rearranged auditorium seating for special events.

If you were performing in a comedy, you could hear Humphrey's deep rolling cackle of a laugh above everyone else's, and if you made an exit down stage right, there he would be, a heavy, bullet-headed man, iron-gray hair clipped short, smiling his pleasure and approval, revealing the lone stubborn yellow tooth remaining in his upper jaw.

Perhaps Humphrey picked up the custom of wearing his hair short during the years he had spent as an able seaman in the British Marine. He had tales to tell; of the time, for instance, aboard ship outside Bombay during a cholera epidemic, when he saw numberless bodies of the diseased dead floating far out to sea. I do not know how he happened to come to our village in the Rockies, but he married there, the daughter of a cowman, though not, I think, a very prosperous one. He fathered a considerable family by this amiable, faithful wife. The Duttons lived just south of old Sid Elmendorf's blacksmith shop, in a small cottage that seemed often in an uproar. Humphrey's rich, commanding voice could be heard at mealtimes summoning his two active sons home from the far corners of the town, in accents that plainly betrayed his English upbringing.

Humphrey did what he could to support his family as janitor of the Opera House, and also of the Masonic Hall upstairs in the old Kennedy Building on Grand Avenue, but that couldn't have brought in much money. Mrs. Dutton and the girls worked wherever and whenever they could, but Mrs. Dutton's duties at Humphrey's side restricted her availability for other tasks. He never appeared in public, especially in his later years, without her. He used a cane, carrying it in his right hand, and held firmly on to his wife's hand with his left. This touched many who saw it, it seemed so affectionate, and to a degree it may have been, but the whole truth was that Humphrey was subject to epileptic fits, which could come upon him unexpectedly. I once saw

The truncated opera house

Humphrey at an event at the Masonic Hall when a fit came over him. His smile froze on his face and he pitched straight forward. Fortunately there were boys and men around him to prevent his injuring himself.

Some criticized Humphrey because despite his limited means whenever a medicine show came to town—they usually set up shop beside the bandstand next to the Book Store on Grand Avenue—he would be the first to buy the Tiger Salve offered at a ruinous dollar a bottle. Still, though this may not have evinced sound judgment on his part, I always felt that it was not so much that he was careless of money as it was that he simply had to show his approval as a patron of the dramatic arts.

I appeared often in dramatic productions at the Opera House up through my high school years. My voice was thin and poorly controlled, but it was loud and I was willing. For several years a minstrel show was presented by high school boys' clubs. Boys wearing rented wigs and with their faces blackened with burnt cork would sing and clog and tell quaint jokes provided in Denison's rented entertainments. I officiated in most of these in a tuxedo borrowed from a young man who had belonged to a fraternity when he went to college. I was Mr. Interlocutor, charged with the duty of introducing the various acts ("Mr. Bones, you don't look at all well this evening.

Pray, what is the matter?").

The Opera House was dark more and more often in the twenties. For a time it was owned by the local real estate tycoon, C.C. Hawkins, and he began showing films in competition with the Gayety. He was booking quality features at higher rentals than his competition which of course turned out to be a mistake. But one in particular was hungrily anticipated: "The Adventures of Huckleberry Finn."

The Opera House was packed that first night. It proved a strange evening. The time for the film to be shown came and passed and still the theatre did not darken. Mr. Hawkins came out to apologize; the reels in their metal containers were not available; they were on the up-valley train and the train was late. Still, the crowd was compliant, there were groans and sighs, but all waited patiently. At last, dimly through the walls of the Opera House could be heard the wail of the approaching train. A cheer went up. More time passed. The film had to be picked up by the dray as part of the mail delivery, taken to the post office, and then redelivered to the theatre. The audience, restive but good-humored, dreamed on of sharing Huck's trip down the broad river with his black friend Jim; his adventures with the scalawag actors, the Duke and the Dauphin; but then out came Mr. Hawkins to announce that the reels were not on the train after all.

A roar of disappointment and annoyance went up, but there was nothing for it but to wait until the film could be shown, and that would not be until the same day the following week, since as he explained, this time he wanted to be certain that the film had actually arrived and that the waiting ordeal would not be repeated. We left, disappointed but reassured. And, somehow, the evening had not been wasted; we had all endured the evening together, in true communal spirit.

In the thirties the auditorium of the Opera House was nearly always dark. Vaudeville was dying. Once in a great while some attraction might play the Opera House. A couple once appeared there with a slide show. The woman, wearing a leotard and shapely but generously proportioned like beauties of an earlier day, positioned herself on stage before a moving picture screen and her companion in the projectionist's booth at the rear of the balcony flashed a succession of colored slides on the screen, so that she appeared, altering her pose to conform to the subject, to be wearing the flowing robes of Queen Cleopatra, or those of an Aztec goddess, and finally, right hand high, grasping the torch of the Statue of Liberty. The audience was friendly, but subdued. It did not fill more than two rows of seats.

The last out-of-town production that I remember consisted of but one human performer, a Professor Andretti, a hypnotist who doubled as a dog trainer. He parked his old bus by the side entrance on Poplar and his two charges and himself slept and ate in it during the run, which was attended by pitifully small audiences. It was a sign of the times, indicative of the depths to which theatre had sunk on the North Fork, that the professor's departure was expedited when some pool-hall hooligans turned the bus over one midnight, tumbling the three performers into the street, like field mice in the mower's wake.

Meanwhile, as with Poe's "House of Usher," an ominous crack had appeared on the blank western face of the Opera House. A steel cable was installed from wall to wall between the floors in a vain effort to contain the damage. The upper floor of the building was condemned, and the Opera House suffered the same fate as the splendid old La Veta Hotel in Gunnison; the top floor was shorn off and a new roof installed.

And then, as a final indignity, the side flats from the stage, built professionally in St. Louis, were trucked down to the high school and wedged under the low ceiling of the stage at one end of the new gymnasium, to help decorate high school operettas and plays.

Now there is the new high school across the river, and nothing remains to whisper of the old days in the Opera House; even the cellar ports through which fiends glared out at me on dark nights have been bricked over. The auditorium, though, is still an important community resource. After the Townsend furor Social Security flowered, and the Senior Citizens and their affairs became prominent, and lunches are served in the auditorium and on election days voters' booths are set up there.

The drama, such as it is, lives on through the school and on the screens of the drive-in across the river and the theatre down on Grand Avenue, although the Gayety has long since disappeared, but mainly it survives in the flicker boxes that dominate the living rooms all over the valley.

Churches, Churches, Churches

In the years I lived in Paonia, man and boy, there were never more than a thousand inhabitants, and for much of that time considerably fewer, but there were always at least a dozen churches, or church congregations, subsisting in the community. Subsisting rather than flourishing, since many residents never or infrequently attended church services anywhere. Some churches were better attended than others, but for all it was a struggle. Many of the ministers in my time were thin, hungry-looking individuals, and with good reason. Lonely, too, because, like the schoolteachers, they and their families were required to set a higher standard of morality.

Third Street runs through the town in a vaguely west to east direction, beginning where the county road crosses the old river bridge. Actually east of there, beyond the junkyard on the north, and the placid reach of Lake Wade on the south, the sewage treatment facility which came into existence during the mayoral tenure of Carroll Wade, one of Paonia's most dedicated and forward-looking public servants, and named for him, facetiously but affectionately. From there, up a little grade, Third intersects Grand Avenue and runs on up over the D&RG tracks, through several pleasant residential blocks, to look out at last on Elephant Butte and the hay fields that stretch away up Minnesota Creek.

Many of the leading churches of the community are still clustered in the central blocks on Third from below the railroad tracks on the east to a block above Grand Avenue on the west. On the eastern end, the Catholics and the Episcopalians formed a little enclave of religious conservatism, removed from the prevailing Protestant factions further down the street. Episcopal St. Michael's, a little wren of a church, slumped at the corner of North Fork Avenue. The Catholic chapel, also an unimposing wooden structure, sat across the street facing north toward the coal towns up the valley, where its support lay, among the aging wives of the old-country miners.

In the twenties the Catholics barely clung to life; they managed to have a priest in for occasional services and sometimes maintained one in the modest rectory next door, but in a community where popery was still feared—a Catholic church was burned in the town of

Hotchkiss ten miles south in those years—a priest's life was bleak and lonely if his faith was not strong. One priest marooned in Paonia disappeared along with a neighbor's wife.

The Episcopalians were in a much better position, since some of the leading citizens of the community provided support. A minister came up from Grand Junction to conduct Sunday services at least monthly even in the leanest times, and during the prosperous years a vicar was in residence at St. Michael's. The one remembered best and with the longest tenure was a small, friendly man with a speech impediment, known affectionately by many of his flock as "our little minister." One of his parish families was headed by Mrs. A.V.S. Smith, who lived next to us on Poplar Street, in the finest house in town, and during his stay in the community he married the Smiths' live-in servant, a quiet widow with a half-grown daughter. He was often accorded the privilege of driving the Smiths' big Nash sedan around town, and finally acquired a small car of his own, an unusual distinction for a small-town cleric then.

Other of the town's leading citizens, a number living above the tracks on Third, were members of his congregation. There was an easy conviviality evident in the relationship of these first families to their little church which appealed to me. Once a visiting minister there put together a program and paid a number of youths around the community to sing in the choir for the less than princely sum of twenty cents a head. Still, it was better than mowing lawns and when word of the offering got around a sizeable group of candidates showed up, myself among them. For a minister to hire singers to appear in church was unheard of—he didn't care a rap, it seemed, for our immortal souls; all he wanted was a decent show. At the one rehearsal he threatened us, in a sly, mocking way, if any of us sang outrageously off key. All very unministerly, in our experience. The actual performance was orderly enough, but didn't hit any musical peaks.

A block below on Third the Christian Church still rears its granite castellated tower, a true fortress of Protestant faith, with stained glass windows on two levels and an interior finished in polished oak. There are meeting rooms, offices and a kitchen belowstairs. Two blocks further down the street is the Methodist Episcopal, built of brick and also of good size and with good appointments, including a bell tower over the entrance once surmounted by a shingled steeple. Unfortunately over the years the steeple fell prey to woodpeckers, and has never been successfully replaced, giving the church an uncompleted air—like a bishop who has misplaced his mitre.

Over the years these two substantial establishments have vied for the patronage of the solid middle class of the town and that of the

The Methodist church

fruit ranchers along the lanes and up on the mesas roundabout. For years an added fillip of excitement at Sunday morning Methodist services was provided by old Mr. Eikenberry, who had a fine farm at the lower end of Lund's Lane. He often came late and had trouble parking. Parishioners who had driven cars listened uneasily to the sermon with one ear, and kept the other cocked for the crunch of metal on metal in the street outside.

Both churches were active in youth work, the Christian with the

Christian Endeavor, and the Methodist Episcopal with its rival Epworth League. Meetings of these worthy societies on early Sunday evenings were even attended sporadically by my brother and me—particularly when a membership drive was on, and cocoa and cookies were served to all comers.

Between these two solid edifices the red brick church of the Friends' sits on the corner of Third and Poplar, a model of churchly architecture with a broad sweep of shingled roof and a procession of stained glass windows that give it an old-world ambiance. Other churches fan out along other streets and byways—the Christian Science chapel on Grand between Third and Fourth, and the Pentecostal, raised by the hands of the faithful up on Second, near the depot and packinghouses.

The Pentecostals were certainly the liveliest congregation. There, particularly during the frequent revivals, the plain little building rocked with the sounds of fervent witnessing and "speaking in tongues." A fruit farmer of German extraction who attended these services devoutly, was paired with a Lutheran wife who not only did not attend but disparaged her husband's faith, as did his burly son. Once, after the wife and son had waited impatiently as an evening service lengthened, the son appeared at the open front door and his father spying him, cried,

"Come in, son! Come in and be saved!"

"Saved, hell," the son grumped. "Ma says for you to come on home."

Sometimes during a rousing revival at this church a group of unwanted visitors, the young pool-hall crowd, would skulk and jeer around outside, like coyotes attracted to a campfire. One such meeting was made memorable by Bill Webb. Bill's father was reputed to be a Harvard professor who had given over intellectual pursuits and chosen the life of a hermit in a remote cave on Hubbard Creek. There, he had taught his son from the scriptures and Bill grew into a handsome, broad-shouldered young man with a full brown beard and flowing hair who stalked around town in his bare feet.

He chose to spend his time in careless company, knockabout lads, seasonal hands on ranches or in the packing sheds, and he was with them this night outside the Pentecostal mission, listening to the hymns and the evangelist's sermon, which ended with an impassioned plea for sinners in the audience to "come to Christ." A thin line of penitents did come forward, and among them, from the outer darkness, came Bill Webb. He dropped to his knees, removed his tattered old Stetson, and called for deliverance from his sinful state, and even seemed to arrive early at that pinnacle of religious elation which the Pentecostals favor, the "speaking in tongues," or prayer language. At last he subsided but remained kneeling, and for a time the audience within and without were in suspense as to what was the true state of Bill's emotions. But all doubts were soon resolved; little wisps of smoke sifted up through Bill's side whiskers. He was smoking a cigarette.

Such a callous act of effrontery did not really discourage the Pentecostals. It was only another proof to them that the devil was hard at work all around them. Besides, there were other occasions when men and women had answered the call and had gone on to turn their lives around. A hard-living miner about that same time, a true pillar of the poker and whiskey set, had been dragged to a meeting by his wife and been saved. He had fallen to his knees and wept and arose a different man. The hard lines in his face softened. His eyes cleared. He smiled and looked out, along with his radiant young wife, on a brighter world.

All the Protestants except the Episcopalians supported revivals, usually led by a minister or ministers from outside. One of these forays into the community to lift it from its state of darkness came to the Methodist Church one summer. The revivalist was a lanky gray-haired man in a dark swallow-tailed coat who paced the small dais like a condemned prisoner, inveighing against sin, threatening fierce punishment for transgressors and binding it all up in fiery strands of testamental prophecy. Attendance grew. Even my mother, who always intended to go to church but seldom did, was lured along with other widows, like my Aunt Addie Rose, and even the young.

The sermon before the last one was a real stem-winder. It was delivered on a Friday evening, and the final sermon of the campaign would be presented that Sunday. The evangelist shook out his shock of gray hair and raised his bony fists toward the ceiling. He adjusted his steel-rimmed spectacles with grim emphasis and promised revelations, startling revelations, in that climactic sermon.

Paonia was steeped in sin, he said, and in the final sermon he would reveal all; he would name names. There was that man, he said, a well-respected man of business, with a fine family, who had another home in which a poor woman whom he had subverted to his evil passions lived a shadow life. There was that woman, a wife, widely respected, who was carrying on an affair behind her husband's back, with one of his best friends. There were others, many others, performing acts of evil; illegal, sinful practices. They would all, all be exposed.

In the intervening day before the great night of reckoning the community buzzed with gossip, with attempts to identify candidates, those souls who must be writhing in torment, awaiting exposure.

"You know who you are," the evangelist had roared, "and soon your secrets will be known to everyone."

When Sunday night came, the Methodist Church was crowded to the rafters. There was not a seat to be had even in the balcony, which as a usual thing was only used for Sunday School classes. The evangelist appeared, dressed not in his black swallow-tailed coat, but in a fine suit of gray silk and wool, and a white ruffled shirt with a black string tie. This night his manner was sad and dignified; he did not pace fiercely or gesture broadly. It was as if he were disappointed to have so many come; disappointed, perhaps, not only in the community but also, obscurely, in himself, for having stooped to the measures he had to bring in such a crowd.

The sermon was thoughtful, its main burden that of faith in God's redemptive powers, and he ended with the plea that neighbors should be tolerant of each other, be careful not to condemn; to forgive, and try to understand. The audience filed out that night avoiding each other's eyes. They had been had, no doubt of that; still, they deserved it, and they knew it.

Another religious campaign, and one which closely affected my family, took place about this time. It was conducted by a Reverend Yates, a member of an offshoot of the Mormon faith, the Reorganized Church of Latter Day Saints, with headquarters in Independence, Missouri. According to Reverend Yates, this sect followed Mormon teaching but differed in some important respects. Reverend Yates was a somewhat portly man who dressed in neat dark suits, white shirts and white cotton ties. These ties immediately prejudiced me in his favor because they were just the sort of ties my father had worn and that my uncle still did.

He was a persuasive speaker. He told the gripping tale of Joseph Smith, of how a simple, unschooled man was divinely led to discover the sacred golden plates on which were inscribed the books of Mormon, and was given a way of translating them, by means of a pair of unique spectacles, out of a forgotten language. A group of converts had gathered around him, but this sect—witnesses, as they were convinced they were, to a latter-day miracle—were scorned and reviled, and their leader like Christ himself was hounded into martyrdom.

This revival came at a time after my father's death when my mother was lonely and confused; she needed something solid in her life—something to hang on to and believe in. Hers was not a particularly religious family, but the life of her father, Elisha Perry, had been spared in the Civil War when a metal plate covering a small Bible had prevented Yankee bullets from reaching his heart. And her sister's husband, my Uncle Henry, was strongly influenced by the teachings of Judge Rutherford. Then there was Aunt Florence, the widow of my mother's brother. She and her daughter had found great comfort among the Seventh-day Adventists.

So my mother listened to the preaching of Reverend Yates and was powerfully affected. The highlight of his campaign came one Sunday evening when we arrived at the meeting hall above Goodenow's grocery to see, spread clear across the far end of the hall behind the speaker's platform, a vividly painted panorama on muslin entitled "The Way of All Life." It represented the way that all mankind, every human soul, had to travel, "from the cradle to the grave."

Reverend Yates took his pointer and began near the cornice at the upper left on the wall and at first he told us The Way led across green, pleasant fields and through villages where children romped, with sunny days and days of rain. Then the path turned left again; thorns now and then tugged at the clothing of the growing boy, and he was attacked by beasts and suffered thirst and hunger.

At last, on a trip back across the map, he came to a fork in the path. Before each of the new ways stood a being, both well-favored, but one more imposing than the other in a robe all woven in purple and gold.

"Take my path," said this being, "and you will taste of all the joys of the world and live happily all your life."

Behind him the path he favored could be seen, leading gently downward, free of any obstruction, with beautiful trees and flowers growing on all sides.

Then there was another path, leading to the right, and the being who stood before it was thin and dressed in homespun gray.

"My path is not easy, but hard," this being said, "and you will suffer want and know sorrow. But the path leads up, not down, and at the end is salvation and your soul will live in paradise forever."

Reverend Yates then had the man choose the wide, down-sloping path. I could have done with a little more elaboration by him regarding the delights to be savored on this path, but it did look attractive—until, down near the lower left-hand corner of the chart, the path suddenly ended at a high cliff over which the traveller fell into a fiery pit, where we were told he would burn in torment forever.

We now followed the traveller along the other path, recommended by the personage in solemn gray. It was rocky and narrow in places and led across quicksands and over deserts and through canyons and thick forests where ravening beasts lay in wait and poisonous snakes struck out at the unwary, and at last the traveller came to a great mountain, steeper and more difficult than any of the obstacles he had encountered before. The traveller had prayed before along the hard way, but this time he prayed even more, and overcame his fears and doubts and climbed steadily on. At last he came out on a windswept summit and saw before him a great gate of gold set with pearls, that opened to reveal a radiance that filled the skies—the white radiance of paradise and everlasting life.

I was entertained and moved, but my mother was overwhelmed. She wanted to join the church, but still she held back. All her life it was difficult for her to make decisions. She was sickly as a girl and when

At Sunday School, Mother on right

her older sister married and moved away, she had stayed on to keep house for her father, a dominating and self-centered Southern male. She had not expected to marry and have a family, and when she was widowed and faced with the need of looking after two active young boys with the few resources available to her, she was ill prepared. It was no wonder that she was confused and lacked confidence. No doubt she talked to her relatives about this decision she was pondering, and it is not likely that they were very supportive. It was true that it was the reorganized church she intended to join, but still they were Mormons. And Mormonism, among the evangelical Christian Protestants who dominated religious thought throughout the West then, was in poor repute. Popular novelists even, like Zane Grey and Sir Arthur Conan Doyle, had painted it as a dark kingdom.

Still seeking support, and this showed how desperately, she turned to her sons, talking to us separately, in her elliptical way, hoping to win our approval. We were frail reeds, both of us. The night when my turn came for the talk was after church services, and she and I were sitting on the bench on the front porch in the dark. I fended off her questions. I was selfishly afraid that if she joined it would make for difficulties, that restrictions would be imposed, and I raised objections until suddenly she lowered her head into her hands and began to weep. This alarmed me; it was the first time I had seen her cry since my father died. For one of the few times in our lives together, I felt close to her, and touched; I dimly recognized her predicament, and I put out an arm and swayed her toward me. But she had asked, and been refused, and she pulled away and rushed into the house.

In the end she joined. I remember a confirmation ceremony held at the home of some other converts, where I sat in a throne-like chair and listened as she made responses she had memorized. The chair quivered under me. I closed my eyes and the chair seemed to move sideways, the same sensation I had had when standing on the town bridge and looking down at the water moving swiftly underneath.

For the baptismal ceremonies the Christian Church generously lent the use of their auditorium and some days later the Reverend Yates, his dark suit-coat removed, waded into the baptismal font and baptized a respectable group of converts, my mother among them. He cradled her in his arm, covered her face with his spotless handkerchief and laid her back into the glittering, dark water.

The revival had ended but for a year or so afterward we three attended Sunday School services in this or that household, and occasionally were taken to services in the county seat. Strangely, my brother and I did not find these services as arduous as we had expected. We liked all the people involved, and felt for a time like members of an enlarged family. But gradually the little congregation disintegrated; some members moved, others fell away. Still the memory of those friendships remain, like the glow of a lighted candle in a darkened room.

My mother never really returned to her church, though she attended other churches quite regularly in her later life. But that pleasant little excursion into the meadow of the Reorganized Latter Day Saints was the only sustained experience in organized religion I ever made.

Seeds of skepticism were planted early in my mind when I had prayed for a camera which God saw fit not to deliver; and there were all the difficulties and complications I envisioned in making the orthodox dream of a hereafter come true. Once I overheard a lady baptized with my mother talking about what she expected to find on "the other side." Her beloved first husband had died, and she had remarried, but she was confident that the three of the them would be together over there, and inseparable, but I heard another woman speak later to my mother about that, and she said,

"Her first husband knew this fellow she's married to now, and take it from me, they'll never get along."

So, there were going to be problems. Of course it's all a question of faith. In the novel *Jurgen,* by James Branch Cabell, whose reputation has fallen into eclipse, he told how the soul of a little old lady imbued with faith wandered out into the universe and somehow ended up in the presence of the supreme being Koschei, the God of Things as They Are. She told him she was seeking a heaven behind pearly gates, where the streets were paved with gold and everyone wore white and sang before the throne, and he was so amused by this quaint concept of this little being from a remote speck of a planet, and so impressed with her confidence, that he created such a heaven just for her.

I had always thought that the Episcopalians, who seemed to me a sophisticated lot, would have a concept of heaven that would impress me. Once in Gunnison where I was in college the wife of a rector invited me to dinner, assuring me that she could overcome the doubts I had expressed to her husband, and after dinner she read to us from *The Ladies Home Journal,* a tale of an afterlife. What it amounted to was that everyone would be free to wander over an earth restored to pristine beauty, through green valleys and along the shores of lovely lakes—places that he or she hoped to visit in life, but now there would be no impediments; one could be whisked wherever he or she chose, and meet there with whom he would. She read all this to me, and I searched her husband's face for some sign of amusement, some flicker of skepticism, but there was none.

No heaven I have ever heard of impressed me much, although the one described in *The Green Pastures* struck me as the most pleasant, but the drawback there was that that particular heaven was off limits, apparently, to whites.

Paonia is still a churchy town. Cars still park in goodly numbers along Third Street on Sunday mornings. Episcopalian St. Michael's is no more, but across the street the resurgent Catholics have built a fine new church, and further east on Third, beyond the homes of the city leaders of the twenties, houses now grown shabby with neglect, the Bible Center has its chapel and parsonage. North beyond the city park the Mormons have a handsome meeting complex and the splendid Baptist Church sits over the river beside the county road. Nazarenes and Seventh-day Adventists meet in the community, and the Jehovah's Witnesses have become a force to be reckoned with.

Out on the mesas certain sects have their adherents, some of these groups survivals from the adventurous East-looking sixties, and below Hotchkiss on Rogers Mesa members of the Church Without a

Harold—up to his usual tricks

223

Name flock to a summer revival every year.

All this in a community where times are not so good again, but everyone hopes they will somehow be better. And certainly in this world which now seems so full of threat and danger, one cannot help but know that exercising the right freely to believe, as the churchgoers in Paonia have always done, may be the last great hope of Man.

Gambling in High Places

Gambling goes on everywhere. In the twenties and thirties up on the North Fork, in Paonia, you could even find it on the school playgrounds in the spring, but that was only among the big boys and only for marbles. The men played "Pig" in the pool hall, a primitive poker for penny stakes. But that was at the table at the back. At the big table up by the cash register a game was played for higher stakes, including well-heeled players like Matthew Colt, who ran the hardware store, and George Epirus, who ran a store and had other interesting investments. Colt was a pudgy man with a voice couched high and squeaky, a mannerism he seemed to cultivate for comic effect, and George clowned around too, speaking in the accents of his native Greece, but both of them were uncommonly shrewd, at business and at poker. Whenever a pot showed promise, Colt would cease to roll his cigar from side to side in his bejowled face, and the pupils of his little blue eyes would contract, like those of a hawk hovering over a baby rabbit.

It was well known that both men were regulars at the poker games that really counted, those that were played on the big table in Frank Shields' little shack below the ditch on Main Avenue, across the alley from the barbershop on Grand Avenue where Frank worked. On a good night eight to a dozen or more players would sit in there, shoulder to shoulder: local businessmen of a sporting turn; a couple of travelling salesmen; a young rancher from the Crawford or Gunnison country; a couple of local fruit ranchers; a contingent of up-valley coal miners; a sprinkling of small-time gamblers, men who prided themselves on being professionals; and a day-laborer or so. These were the mainstays of the game. The miners played recklessly, there was always next week's paycheck to fall back on; the laborers played desperately, often risking rent and board money.

The small-time gamblers, who liked to delude themselves that they were living off their winnings, were cagy and calculating, often pairing up as partners, setting up a set of signals for moving strategically in and out of important pots, a practice that even gamblers like Epirus and Colt resorted to as well, for although they could afford to lose, they did not expect to and seldom did.

Many of the small-time gamblers had an ace or so in the hole when luck went sour: relatives they could sponge on until they could put together another stake. Most of them were drifters, loners, but some had families of their own. In the barbershop one fall a story was told about the Baddeley brothers, Charlie and John. They were overheard making plans for the coming winter. Both had good-sized families, a wife and small children. John did not gamble; he was a laborer and teamster; he figured that it would take $35.00 to see his family through the snow months. But Charlie did gamble, so his professional needs had to be looked after; he had to put together a good stake; he figured $25.00 was all he could spare for his brood.

When the sheriff began to show too much interest in the games at Frank Shields' cabin, the action moved up to Mr. Nagy's big old frame house on the hill near the Union Fruit packing shed. One day when he was in an expansive mood, Mr. Nagy, a prim Hungarian who liked playing his flute on Sunday afternoons in summer, gave me and another teenage boy a tour of the facility.

The gambling room was in the basement, down a long passageway behind a series of locked doors. It was a capacious room with a large round table in the center. High, narrow, horizontal windows gave out on the yard, but wooden blinds on pulleys could be dropped over them in an emergency, and the table was cleverly designed with panels in the playing surface through which chips or money or cards could be dumped out of sight. The walls, too, were lined with storage drawers behind innocent-looking wooden panels. Still, all that ingenuity in the end was not enough. Mr. Nagy confided in us that running a game was too risky a proposition. Six months in the cooler in the county seat with paid board and room, though not so bad a prospect in itself, meant that his house would go unprotected, and the extensive garden he planted every spring would be forfeit as well.

Over the next years, though, as the North Fork moved into the motor age and roads improved around the valley, the game moved to an outlying ranch. Fences, locked gates, space, made for greater security, and enabled a good host to supply not only his guests' gambling needs but liquid refreshments of the illegal sort.

When I taught school in Paonia one winter in the late thirties and my mother was in California, I had the good fortune to board with Mrs Alvina Dwayne, whose husband Dave worked at the Somerset mine. Alvina was a florid, hearty woman who doted on Dave and on a ten-year-old niece of theirs whom they had adopted.

The evening meal was a particular pleasure. Around five-thirty in the growing gloom of a winter night we would gather around the table in the bright kitchen and listen for Dave's footsteps as he plodded along the side of the house, his boots crunching in the snowy path, the empty glass jar in his dinner pail clanking as he whistled a nameless tune. Soon he would be stamping at the back door, to be heartily embraced and tugged inside by his "two women," as he called them, and pulled over to be seated at the table. The meals were always good: meat and gravy, potatoes, beets or home-canned green beans, and pie or home-canned peaches and cake for dessert.

There was but one evening meal I ate at Mrs. Dwayne's that was below standard. I arrived shortly after five to see only a platter of fried potatoes and a bowl of canned peaches on a table that was usually so heavily laden; nothing was cooking on the stove, the oven cold, and Mrs. Dwayne in a restrained, melancholy mood. I had the poor taste to offer to go to town and make a couple of purchases; cookies, say, or lunch meat; but Alvina sadly and firmly declined my offer.

Dave was not whistling as he came around the corner of the house this night; his niece ran to greet him at the back door, but Alvina busied herself around the table, her eyes down, and accepted, resignedly, a rough kiss on her cheek from her husband. We sat down to our scanty, funereal meal, and only later in the week did I learn from Alvina that Dave had gone to Shorty McKorkingdale's ranch on the south river road the previous weekend, had got drunk, and lost his entire weekly paycheck at the poker table.

"I had to teach him a lesson," she said. "I was sorry you had to be in on it."

I was sorry too.

I never witnessed any of the games. The nearest I came was through listening to my cousin Sid Elmendorf, who was in a category by himself as a gambler. In the days before the miracles of surgery were commonplace, he had grown up with club feet on a ranch and his parents, sisters and brothers had all spoiled him. His parents had hoped that he would become an accountant because he was good at ciphering and he did finish the eleventh grade while his brothers dropped out earlier to work on the ranch, but only one calling attracted him—gambling. He spent all his adult years—he died in his early fifties—at tables all over the West, from Deadwood to Butte, to Denver, Salt Lake, Ely, Reno, and Las Vegas. How he fared in the bigger towns I never knew, but he spent much of his time on the Western Slope, so I think it fair to conclude that he found the pickings better there.

Inevitably there were lean times and then he fell back on relatives for support. This often meant that he came to our house—to the home of his aunt—to sleep upstairs with my brother and me and occasionally put his twisted feet under our mother's table, though his appetite was always small and his hours unpredictable.

I still remember late at night—or, rather, early in the morning—

hearing the downstairs screen slam, and then the slow clumping up the stairs, his leg braces creaking. The light would go on, even when the morning light was creeping through the blinds, and Sid would sag down on the bed, strip to his winter underwear, roll a cigarette, and have a last smoke while he painstakingly examined and rubbed his feet and fumbled through his toes.

Sometimes he whiled away an afternoon or an early evening by laying out cards on our kitchen table, staring down at them with his head cocked up to keep the cigarette smoke out of his eyes. His fingers and thumbs were so supple that they seemed to bend backward. He could lay out half a dozen poker hands and then slowly pick them up and riffle them into the deck, accept your cut, and then snap the cards out again and tell you every card you were holding, or coax you into betting matches against him and then beat you by having one card higher in his otherwise worthless hand than you did in yours.

But he stated as a general rule that he didn't require trickery. He knew the game, the odds, watched the play and the players, and most of the young bravos, the plungers—miners, ranchers, cowboys—were more than willing to be fleeced. But even so, he liked a little insurance. I spent an afternoon with him once, as he visited shops downtown— and eventually the city dump—trying to put together a ring with a large glass setting in it, under which he intended to insert a small mirror, so that he could turn the setting toward his palm and watch cards through it as he dealt them out.

I don't think he himself took such devices seriously. It was the challenge of getting away with something that appealed to him. And maybe he was infected with the spirit of the times, when mechanical devices fascinated the public. But it was a dangerous flaw in a gambler. Once in a game in Grand Junction he was caught wearing a device under his shirt which on the summons of a deep breath would deliver a card down his arm. I heard that the ripple of movement of the extension under his shirt was observed—poker players are always watching for behavior clues in other players—and he was lucky to get out of the game with his life or at least without a good beating.

He must have been, even in the normal run of things, many times in danger. His parents, especially his mother, sorrowed over him and worried that he would be found dead sometime in an alley in a strange town. And once he shot and killed a drunken man in self defense. That happened in Crawford and although he was acquitted there were men around who said they hoped he would be hung—men who owed him money.

That was another drawback to Sid's profession; gambling debts are hard to collect. I gave him a ride in my car out to the West Coast once, and he tried to persuade me to go by a remote route through Ely,

Nevada, telling me how scenic it was, but as I suspected and learned later my suspicions were true, people there owed him money. He occasionally made a gesture to earn a little good will, as he did one night when he cleaned out a young man, recently married, of money and ranch, and then returned it all to him, extracting his promise never to gamble again. And he needed good will; he was very unpopular in Grand Junction, especially after the incident with the down-the-sleeve device, not only with poker players but also with the law; the sheriff was continually rousting him as a vagrant, without any visible, legitimate means of support, or "for no reason at all," to hear Sid tell it. It was in the days when his skills were not as sharp as they had been and he resented bitterly any interference in his livelihood; he did a lot of thinking and planning, trying to come up with some scheme to make the sheriff look bad, but without any success.

He had a low opinion of women, with the exception of his mother and other female relatives. Although that isn't quite correct; it was not that his opinion of them was so low; it was more that he felt that most of them didn't properly take advantage of their capabilities. After all, he said, the easiest way in the world to make a good living was as a prostitute, and he didn't understand why more women didn't take it up—if he were a woman, he said, he certainly would.

Once he brought home to his parents a wife, a pleasant, shapely little creature. The family had a pretty shrewd notion of what she may have been doing to make a living before the marriage and were all prepared to find her wanting, but she was so open-hearted and friendly, so respectful of everyone, that she quite won them over, and they agreed that she could surely only be good for Sid and would perhaps give him some kind of home, make his life less lonely. She stayed with him a year or so, had a daughter by him but finally left him; it was said because of his treatment of her. Once, according to his own report, he came home after gambling and found the kitchen in disorder:

"Dirty dishes in the sink, dirty dishes all over the table," he said, in his slow, thin drawl. "I decided to give her a little lesson. I took the ashes out of the stove and I really decorated that kitchen."

He truly enjoyed encouraging young people—nephews, nieces— to lie, cheat, malinger, giving them reasons for taking the recommended course of action: "You hadn't ought to have to take that kind of thing—I wouldn't if I was you. If I was you this is what I would do—". Everywhere he went his influence could be felt; he was the most malicious man I ever knew. The only time I ever felt genuinely sorry for him was the night when his mother died, and he cried like a little boy.

The truth is that Sid was an atavism, a throwback to those times in the West when if the law existed at all it was a very elastic thing, and often the sheriff or marshal in a boom town would be on the take in the gambling halls, and vicious characters like Doc Holliday could be looked upon as heroes. Gambling as a way of life in Western boom towns lost most of its viability when the big payrolls at the mines dried up, but the old ways die hard, especially in the old mining towns like those in the San Juans. There were always games going in places like Ouray, Silverton, Telluride, and there probably still are.

There was a time when I was teaching in Paonia and early in the summer vacation Ned Busby, a fruit farmer, invited me to go along with him in his pickup while he peddled fruit and vegetables up back of the beyond—over the Uncompahgre Plateau, out through the Paradox Valley, and at various points in between. He loaded up with produce from his mesa farm, we stopped in Montrose to pick up bunches of bananas and other staples of the trade, and by evening we had canvassed the town of Ouray and were looking for a place to spend the night.

It was then I made the ill-starred suggestion that we look up another cousin of mine, Pierce Elmendorf, a brother to Sid who had given up ranching and gone back to mining. We made inquiries, and we found Pierce in the little shack he rented behind a liquor store, and we all repaired to a short-order joint where we had Salisbury steaks and then went to a pool hall down near the wash, where the unruly Uncompahgre, a year or so before, had nearly wiped out the town.

It was a slow night. A few players were at the pool tables in the front, and a poker game was going at the back. Pierce had a bottle and passed it generously, both before and after dinner; I declined after the first fiery mouthful, but Ned, a strict observer of the laws of hospitality, began to shake off the cares of the day. Still, he was in sufficient possession of his faculties to wish to take out a little insurance. He came to me and doled out fifty dollars in bills from his billfold.

"Take this and put it away," he told me. "And no matter what I say, don't give it to me." Then he gravitated to the poker table where Pierce was already in residence.

I wandered around the place, shot a few practice games of pool at a vacant table, dropped some nickels in the slot machine by the front door and then I discovered Ned at my elbow. I always liked Ned's sense of humor. He was a slender, reticent man with a little quirk of irony in most things he said, and with a raised eyebrow and skittery smile. I never knew when to take him seriously. Now he sidled up to me and after a moment said quietly,

"Give me my money."

"What do you want it for?"

230

"None of your damned business." The raised eyebrow and the skittery smile again.

I took this as just another example of his waggishness and a test of my reliability.

"No," I said.

"Give me my money," he said, the smile flickering a couple more times. "It's mine and I want it."

"I can't do that, Ned," I told him, "you made me promise not to give it to you."

The smile totally disappeared. His voice rose. "I don't give a damn what I said. It's my money and I want it."

"Look, Ned—" I began.

"Look, hell," he shouted.

By this time the poker players in the back and everybody else in the room had turned to listen.

Ned lowered his voice. "You got my money," he hissed, "and I want it. Now give it to me."

I gave him his money.

The poker game went on for a couple more hours. The stacks of chips grew in front of my cousin Pierce, who shoved in a tall stack or so at every opportunity and hauled in most of the pots. The stack in front of Ned diminished to a precious few and the game broke up. By now a cold rain was falling and we stumbled and floundered our way up to the liquor store. On the raised plank sidewalk before it a half-breed Indian was doing a dance. We went on back to Pierce's room and piled into bed.

There was only the one bed and I was in the middle. I lay sleepless most of the time. There was a drip over my head, and an hour or so after we retired the bed slats broke. My bedmates snored on. The thunder trundled around the peaks, the drip dripped steadily, but my companions never stirred. It was a long night.

A chastened Ned shook me around daybreak. Pierce called out a good-bye, felt around under the broken bed and came up with a half-full pint which he tossed off and pulled the covers back over his shoulders.

Neither of us made any mention of the Ouray poker game the rest of the trip, or at any time afterward. We peddled our way through Telluride and then out over the Uncompahgre Plateau into the Paradox Valley through Norwood, Naturita and Nucla. On a canyon wall outside Uravan we saw the remains of a half-completed flume. It was supported by logs inserted in holes drilled in the solid rock—the work of an audacious and desperate gambler of an earlier day.

When we arrived back at the Busby ranch early one afternoon, Mrs. Busby, a trim little lady, began to question her husband about the results of the foray. She asked; he answered cautiously. She asked further; he answered evasively. It was plain I was in the way, and I felt a little guilty. I thanked Ned for the trip, and headed home.

It seemed that any trip I took through western Colorado towns in the twenties and thirties included a visit to the local pool hall to see a poker game. On a Sunday night in Westcliffe, up in the Wet Mountains south of Salida—I was with another trucker this time, moving a family from a town near Walsenburg to the North Fork Valley—we stopped in the pool hall and observed a game going on. The town was much shrunken from boom days but the poker game, though small, was a robust one with pots regularly running into the hundreds of dollars. The players did not look rich, or even prosperous, and the owner of the pool hall who was also the game banker wore bib overalls. I asked him about the big pots we were seeing.

"Oh," he said, "these fellas just play by theirselves, no outsiders allowed, and over a winter they all just about break even."

But the game I saw in a pool hall in Alamosa in the San Luis Valley one Christmas vacation when I travelled with the Western State College basketball team was not only rich but appeared to be wide open, with a dozen or so players. As we watched, a big pot developed, several hundred dollars, and one by one players dropped out until there remained but two, a heavy man in a tan suit with a stub of unlighted cigar in his mouth that looked as if it had grown there, and a rangy man, hunched over in his chair, elbows on the table, with a style of talk and manner that labeled him a cowboy in town for the winter. His thin, black straight hair, parted carefully down the middle so that locks sprouted on either side like horns over his forehead, looked as if it were freshly cut, since the neck line was razor sharp along the back exposing a little rind of white skin above the deep tan. His blue denim shirt was clean, the sleeves rolled up halfway to his elbow, and his long, lean hands and forearms were reddened as if he were spending his time around a different range, perhaps washing dishes in the adjoining short-order joint.

He had been cheerful and cracking jokes until this hand came up, but now the man in the tan suit shoved in a ninety-dollar raise. The cowboy studied his cards, studied the pot, and studied his opponent. The man in the tan suit only looked at his cards, sitting as solid as a gob of mud, his dust-red face still under the tan hat, dead cigar stub in the corner of his mouth, his little eyes behind the gold-rimmed glasses unwaveringly on his cards, the big stubby fingers gripping them steadily.

The cowboy crossed and recrossed his long legs, studied the cards, studied the ceiling, studied the pot and studied the man across the table. At last he laid his cards carefully on the table, face down, and addressed the ceiling.

"I don't know, Doc," he said. "It's my turn to make a pot, that's for a fact, and you've made plenty, God knows." He then conducted a seminar on the hand.

"You drew two and I drew one, and the chances are you was drawin' to threes, which means you either filled on the threes or come up with a pair to make a full house. Of course, you could be drawin' to a straight or a flush, but that ain't your style. You don't take that kinda chance, drawin' to a straight or a flush with just three good ones. You don't hafta."

A hamburger arrived for the cowboy. He ate half of it carefully, delicately, and all this while "Doc" never changed position or looked up. At last the cowboy said,

"It ain't fair, Doc, by God it ain't, you know. I scrabble around for any little piecea change I can get, do anything I can lay my hand to, just to keep my head above water, while you have that fine house and little ranch layout on the road below town, and your fancy office, and a new Buick that you buy every year . . . why, that last raise of yours, it don't mean Shinola to you, just another paira tonsils, maybe not even that. But that could practically break me, if I was to call and you was to have a full house, which I don't think you do. It ain't fair, by God, and that's a fact." He finished with the hamburger and tidied up with a paper napkin.

"Let's get on with the game, George," another player finally grunted, and there were other murmurs.

The cowboy straightened up in his chair and slapped his cards down, one by one, face up. He had a small straight. Doc, still expressionless, tucked his hand into the deck and raked in the pot.

In college in Gunnison I sometimes witnessed games in the men's dormitory but we were all poor together, and stakes were never high. The same was true in the two pool halls downtown. I played occasionally in the old Elkhorn pool hall, once a famous saloon, but there I played not poker, but a game called Sluff. Tip, a ponderous man with a formidable jaw, wore a greasy stockman's hat and dominated the game with his big voice and positive ways. He decided that I was sufficiently skilled at the game to be taken in as a sort of a junior partner, and he began bumping my knee under the table when he sat out as dealer and had a chance to size up the kitty—the three cards to be claimed by the highest bidder. I discouraged this by promptly passing each time he nudged me, and he gave me up as a poor candidate for his favors.

Then there was Henry, a lank Hungarian, and Morris Columbine, a burly little Swiss prospector. Both of them were wary of college boys, considered them uppity and enjoyed seeing them in trouble in a game.

When a hand did not go well for a college boy, Henry would gloat.

"You sure hockeyed in your own nest that time, didn't you."

And if Morris engineered what he considered a coup against a young player he would chuckle patronizingly through his droopy mustache—"Theesea damma keeds!"

Poker was played at the Elkhorn, but not big games. A laborer, Clyde, was a dedicated poker player both at the Elkhorn and at the "real" game, which during this fall and winter was taking place up the Crested Butte road at the summer resort of Almont. Clyde always concentrated fiercely on the game but never did well. If he bluffed he was invariably caught; if he had a good hand, everybody dropped out of the pot. And then, one night when he had had a particularly disastrous session, a friend acquainted him with a disturbing intelligence. Clyde was being regularly betrayed by one near and dear. He had a loyal little black dog, a border collie, which sat worshipfully by during the games, and when Clyde picked up a hand that promised well, his dog's ears perked up and his tail thumped the floor; when his master picked up a dismal hand or failed to improve on the draw, the faithful companion would lower his head and lie down. All that the other players had to do, to learn how Clyde was faring, was to keep an eye on the dog.

Throughout my life, as long as I observed the rule that *Games of chance are spectator sports* I was safe. But there were those times when I forgot the rule. Sluff at the Elkhorn wasn't so bad; I even won occasionally. But the nearest I ever came to being absolutely destitute when I was in college in Gunnison was that afternoon when Rex Bondurant and I tried to overwhelm the dime slot machine in Bratton's Sweet Shoppe.

We each had five dollars and watched as dime after dime rattled down the metal gullet, while colorful, mismatched melanges of cherries, oranges, plums and the dreaded lemons waltzed tauntingly across the display. And then, one dime away from a week of starvation, the machine dispensed a ten-dollar strike. Or Providence did—I gave it the credit; the true road once again had been pointed out to me.

My most serious lapse since was in the stock market, but that is too painful to go into. And, occasionally, I have dropped a nickel, a dime or so at Las Vegas. I even entertained the notion that I could learn to shoot craps, and I read a book about it—I still don't really understand how the game should be played—and I later approached a table in the Babylon-on-the-Colorado one afternoon with five dollars clutched in my warm, perspiring hand. I lost it promptly, and ignominiously; when I was passed the dice I was so lacking in confidence in my luck that I bet against myself. And lost. As I slunk away, the croupier raked in my wager with disgust written large on her face.

And even yet, sometimes, I dream of making it big at the slots or at craps at Las Vegas. Like many another, I have plans as to how I would spend the half million or so. Charities, relatives, a Mercedes or a Porsche, a few trips, but mainly good, solid investments.

In Nevada chicken ranches, say—an investment which even my gambling cousin Sid would have favored.

Shine on, Harvest Moon

Done laid around, done stayed around,
This old town too long.
Summer's almost gone,
Winter's comin' on—
And I feel like I want to travel on.
                                        —Folk song

On a cold day in early November three of us sat around the forge in Old Sid Hetzinger's blacksmith shop. We were watching Little Sid shape a length of white-hot iron, and listening to the young fruit bum tell about his mixed feelings.

"Work's over here, ain't nothing else doing at the packinghouse, and to tell the truth I'd have been gone weeks ago if it hadn't of been for her." Here he couldn't conceal a conceited smile—"that woman just can't bear to see me go and I do hate to leave her." He was a skinny little boy-man, languidly graceful, tight black curls close to his head, a face prematurely old, probably from malnutrition in childhood. And the girl he was speaking of, the one so enamored with him, was the daughter of an indigent family, an awkward girl to whom no boy around town would give a second glance. But this out-of-town boy saw her with fresh eyes.

The boy with the tight black curls is gone now, long ago, a few days after he talked to us in the shop, but he was not forgotten. The girl was bearing his child, and had to bestir herself and find a man, and get him in the marriage mood.

The fruit harvests still come to the North Fork, but they are not as big as they were in former days, when the heat of summer softened into fall, the peaches swelled and blushed and thumped into the packing sacks and rattled into the boxes to be stacked on flat-bed wagons and tugged into town by patient teams, to the packing sheds where men with hand trucks brought them to the packers, women slap-slap-slapping peach into tissue, peach into tissue, cull into cull box, hour after hour.

The tightly packed boxes than went to the nailers, those aristocrats of the craft, tap-tap-tapping away, up one side of the lid and down the other, with their clever hammers. Back to the truckers went the finished freight, stacked high, bright labels gleaming, and were trundled across the echoing platforms into the refrigerator cars; set in, ceiling high, in the cool dead silence. Into the night went the cars, out east to Denver and Kansas City, west to Salt Lake, south to Santa Fe, hooted along by the restless locomotives that chuffed and whistled around the clock in Paonia in harvest time.

Workers came from everywhere that time of year—drifters who followed the fruit and vegetable harvests up and down the western and southern states, and bevies of girls from nearby towns, to stay with respectable widows like my mother and "work in the fruit" to lay a little something by for school or a trousseau or to help the family. And local young men, and men not so young from everywhere, up from Palisade, another fruit center, some of them fruit farmers themselves needing money to tide them over until their crop money came in. In the evening as the dust of the day's harvest traffic settled back down along the mesa roads, the streets of the town were lined with out-of-town jalopies and trucks, and men sat hip-to-hip on the sidewalk curb in front of the pool hall, suit coats or denim jumpers over their knees, hunched forward, waiting for transportation to an orchard job, or just waiting, strangers in town, not knowing which way to turn, or where they might spend the night.

One evening, in a spurt of inspiration and enterprise, I invited five of them to come up to our place, because I knew that the little house we rented on the alley was vacant, and my mother passed out blankets to them, and they bedded gratefully down there, each shelling out a dollar the next morning for the night's lodging. Dignified, well-intentioned men, temporarily down on their luck.

The well-to-do citizens of Paonia often looked down their noses at these autumnal visitors, but over the years many who came in poverty stayed on and did well, especially in the thirties when the Great Depression reigned, landing on small farms roundabout, with their families and their flivvers piled high with frazzles of household goods. They stayed over the winter in bunkhouses or in packing sheds, found work, enough to live on, scrimped together payments and ended up with ranches of their own.

Even some of the young rovers who worked in the packing houses, unlike the slender Lothario with the tight black curls, stayed on into the winter months and prospered. There was Brent, for instance. The thing about Brent was that everyone recognized at once superior qualities in him. He was bright, waggish, amusing, handsome, with coal-black hair and eyes and amber complexion, a black Irishman he called himself, probably with ancestry running back to the time when the great galleys of the Spanish Armada foundered on

The depot in harvest time

the Irish coast and half-drowned soldiers crept ashore to find new lives among Hibernian bogs and meadows. And here was this case occurring again, for Brent was a refugee, not from the sea but from the road, where he had sunk down among the lowest of the low, a beggar and perhaps a part-time thief, who if he stole a loaf of bread the chances were that he was going to use it to filter a can of Sterno for a cheap drunk.

But the town took him to its heart and weaned him from his wretched life. He was allowed to sleep in the back of a grocery store, and help in the daytime moving stock from drays to stockroom shelves; he drank, but not so often. What clothes he had were laundered, and he bought white shirts and new striped overalls, and a neat hat, sold on credit by Norval Bruce's Toggery, to replace the tattered one which he had worn into town. He rented a room in a rooming house and his bumming buddies went south on the freights and stopped coming around looking for help from him. His eyes cleared, his cheeks were no longer gaunt, and no longer covered with black stubble. Ben the Barber gave him free haircuts at first, but soon he was paying for them of his own election.

By apple-packing time he was far enough along the road to recovery that he was given a job at a packinghouse. He worked hard, and was part-time shift boss on the loading platform after a week. The girls, the packers, shouted remarks at him, and he shouted back. At lunchtime he told stories of the road to the other men. A businessman took him to Rotary Club as a guest, dressed respectably in a blue windbreaker and striped overalls, and wearing the little polka-dotted blue bow tie and one of the white shirts that he favored.

And involved in this change that everyone applauded and marveled at was Bonnie, the beauty operator. She was a straight-backed, shapely woman of perhaps thirty, with hair as bright and black as Brent's, not a beautiful woman, but a striking one. She wore her hair short, in a bob, the style of the day, though she kept it straight, never permed, and it was a delight to see the two of them on the dance floor—there were dances nearly every night during apple harvest—and by this time he was the owner of black oxfords, and a dark blue double-breasted suit, along with the usual white shirt and blue polka-dot bow tie. Each dance they danced together was a courtship in miniature; she leaning back straight and supple against his arm, and he pursuing her, gently and steadily, until, at the turns, their dark heads swayed together.

I was in my teens then, but as a member of the town family, as deeply engrossed and pleased with Brent's rise as anyone, and I can still see him, standing near the front door of the Opera House at intermission, enjoying his cigar—and a good cigar he himself had bought—his head back, hands in his trouser pockets, puffing away, at ease with himself in this new world of his.

After harvest he was given work in a grocery store in Montrose and moved there, he and Bonnie, after a lively wedding, and she opened a new beauty parlor.

Who knows what happened then? One can well imagine it would be difficult for a man who had lived as checkered a life as Brent had, to settle down completely. And he was very attractive to other women. Perhaps it was only one other woman, one affair, but for Bonnie it was too much. She loved him passionately, and she could not accept it. On a warm afternoon in summer, as Brent sat in an automobile in a street in downtown Montrose, the other woman beside him, Bonnie walked up, reached in her purse for a revolver, and shot her black Irishman dead.

There was work for everyone during peach and apple harvests, and for my family, my mother, my brother and myself, a total commitment. On the floor below the main floor in the Union Fruit, we set up shop as labellers of peach- and apple-box ends not yet assembled into boxes. My mother, who always had trouble with her feet, padded around in carpet slippers with a housecoat over her dress to keep away the chill, for here on this floor packed boxes of apples were stored, sometimes for months, awaiting a favorable market, and it was always cold.

At the south end of the floor a dusty light bulb illuminated the nailer's stand and his tapping went on throughout the day, as others bore away the finished boxes into storage. At the north end we were under our own lights, flecked with paste as everything about us was, but near the big metal door which slid back along the concrete wall to reveal a view of the town.

We made a science of it, taking turns at the various operations. The bundles of box-ends were cut loose from the wire building and dealt by one worker along the narrow table. A second worker came along behind and brushed the box-ends clean, and a third behind him, slapping the paste on the upturned ends. Next, fished from the tub of cold water where they had been at soak came the labels; we riffled them out and slipped them across the shining boards, and brushed water over them before pushing them into a mechanical stacker at the end of the table to be lifted off and set aside to dry.

It was drudgery, but light drudgery, and had the advantage of employing all three of us equally and completely, and the days went swiftly by. We could look out through the big door and see the quiet town below, and hear the trucks and drays rattling by on the road that sloped alongside the packinghouse. Our family was not a cohesive one and often a quarrelsome one with my brother and me often at odds with each other, but uniting against our mother whenever questions of attending movies or other entertainments arose, attempting scornfully to convince her that she was out of touch with school and community affairs and just "didn't understand" our many needs of a cultural and social nature. But here, at the labelling table, we were a team.

By the time I graduated from high school, my brother had joined the Navy and my mother was occupied with other pursuits than the labelling venture. With a succession of pursuits, actually; she cooked in restaurants, ran a beauty parlor in her home, and sold a line of ladies' hats at various times. So in the fall after my graduation, I was on my own. I found employment at another packinghouse, run that fall by a man named Lee, around thirty then, a man who dressed well and drove a Buick station wagon.

The fruit crop was light that year and the fruit came in an unsteady flow. I did whatever job came to hand, along with several other employees, off-loading boxes of apples or trucking freshly packed boxes of fruit out to the waiting railroad cars. At noon or at the odd moments when we were not fully occupied we listened to the tales of Bud Davis, fresh from a year in Southern California. He had gone to dances at the big ballrooms where bands of fabled names were playing, at the Pasadena Civic, the Aragon down by the beach, the Avalon out on Catalina Island. We had heard of men, called variously queens, fags and fairies, who walked the streets out there, and of strange crimes and glittering sights. We had heard and read of such things but had assumed that the stories had little truth in them, but Bud said that they were true. And he had known the pleasures of the flesh as well, had worked at an ice plant and declared that a man had never really lived who had not had relations with a colored girl on a block of ice—a claim none of us were competent to refute.

One day, in the week when our work was drawing to its close, Lee discovered he was growing short of labelled box-ends and inquired if any of us had ever labelled "shook." I responded, and he took me upstairs and showed me bundles of box-ends, the usual work table, and cartons of paste and labels. Since this was the last week of work he told me, I could choose to do the labelling as piecework rather than by the hour, and he quoted a figure of perhaps a penny a labeled box-end which he would engage to pay when the work was done. I agreed and he said,

"Now you're sure that's what you want, the way you want to work. Because if it isn't, you can just finish out the four days of the week on the hourly rate."

I assured him that the piecework agreement was to my liking and he went away.

Ah, I knew every move to make. I mixed the paste and put the labels to soak, cut the wires holding the bundles of box-ends together and stacked them at the upper end of the table, and put on an apron, so stiff with paste that it almost stood by itself, and dealt out one bundle of box-ends after the other, slopping on the paste, whipping the labels into place, brushing them off and running them into the stacking box at the lower end of the table, and then stacking them in finished piles nearby.

The day went smoothly by, as smoothly as days had done at the same work years before. There was even a sliding door at the far end of the floor where I could look out at the poplars and cottonwoods along the streets of the town, their leaves bright with fall color, and, far in the distance I could hear the faint, musical clamor of the school bell, and feel a clutch of nostalgia, glad that it was no longer clamoring for me, but missing, too, the prospect of running up the worn granite steps of the high school, where the rooms waited along the quiet dark hall for their human freight of which I was no longer a part. I was free to go out into that strange, fascinating but also threatening world that Bud Davis told about.

In less than two days I had gone through the hundreds of box-ends I had engaged to label, and went downstairs to the front office to so inform Mr. Lee. He was sitting at his desk fiddling with his dark glasses lying on a paper before him and turning over something—probably figures—in his head in this last, for him, uncertain year. He hardly seemed to hear what I said until I repeated it.

"Not all of them," he said, "you haven't finished them all."

Yes, I said, and he followed me upstairs and walked along the table and looked at the stacks of box-ends, picking up one here and there, and occasionally lifting up one in the middle of a stack, not, as he assured me, that he didn't trust me, but just in the way of business. After he had counted them he put on his dark glasses, then took them off again and counted them again. At last he admitted the count was correct, and, to his credit, did not attempt to bully me into accepting less than was promised, or try to convince me that I still owed him a day and a half of work, but went down to the office with me and made out a final check.

Oh yes, I learned to label peach and apple shook. I learned it the right way and I learned it well. I can close my eyes and hear the whisper of my mother's carpet slippers along the paste-wattled floor behind the pasting table, and the rattle of the box-ends as they drop into the receptacle at the far end. I remember it all in my hands, my fingers aching again as I fish the labels from the cold water and riffle them out and lay them glistening down. I could do it in my sleep, and I have.

I remember it so well, and that is a shame, because the big fruit crops have dwindled in the valley; the peach and apple trees that seamed the mesas and slopes around town have many of them fallen to the developers' saws and axes, or have been pushed ignobly over by the grunting power shovels. There is not much demand, any more, for labelling—just not that much demand any more.

Mama and the Motor Car

My mother saw the first motor car that came up the North Fork Valley to Hotchkiss from the county seat. She was a girl then, clerking in a store across the street when the car rolled in from Delta and pulled grandly to a stop in front of the hotel, making nearly as much dust as the stagecoach did, she said. Everybody in town came by to have a look. I am sure my mother must have stood there on the wooden sidewalk in front of the store where she worked, staring down at the weird vehicle, her arms folded as they always were when she was confronted with something she wasn't all that sure about.

She never did actually learn to drive a car. I tried to teach her once, all one long afternoon as she and I motored up through Utah, more than a quarter century after she had seen that first motor car in Hotchkiss. She willingly got behind the wheel—it was her idea—and listened to my instructions, or appeared to, responding every now and then with a pleasant little "Um-hm-hm," a mannerism of hers. I purposely tried to keep the instructions simple. I didn't trouble her at all telling her how to start the car, or how you got it into gear, or even how you fed it the gas. All I wanted her to do at first was to get used to guiding it.

She sat there, both hands gripping the wheel, her chin tucked in, looking rather dreamily out through the windshield, while I kept one foot on the accelerator, and every quarter of a mile or so, the car would begin to sidle over to the shoulder.

"Mama! You got to keep adjusting the wheel. Just a little bit... No! Not that much. Here... just a little ... see?"

"Oh yes. Um-hm-hm."

But I wasn't getting through to her. No wonder, really. She simply did not have the concept of guiding a mechanical device. She'd never even had the advantage of learning to ride a bicycle. And driving a horse to a buggy, as she had done occasionally in her life, didn't really help because in that situation the horse is a sort of inferior partner. The only time a horse-drawn buggy sidles is when the horse has his eye on a patch of sweet clover or other delicacy over by a fence post. And when that happens you only have to rap him smartly on the rump with a whip or the end of a rein, and he jerks his head up and gets back on the road.

Mother never felt all that much need for a car in our earlier years as a family. There was always someone around to help. Even when she joined the church, other members of the small congregation always saw to it that we had transportation if the church meeting was any distance away. Then there were uncles on both sides of the family who looked after other travel needs for the three of us.

And she carried on her manifold enterprises as a widow quite well enough without one. To make a living in those times, she ran beauty parlors out of her home, importing a trained beauty operator several different times and later going to Denver to take training in a beauty school, leaving my brother and me in the care of Aunt Connie and Uncle Doc. Then there were the rentals in our home, in the house at the rear, and in the two little houses which old Steve Morgan built under her direction out of the lumber culled from the demolition of the blacksmith shop and livery stable across from the Opera House.

After Harold joined the Navy and I went to school in Gunnison, she cooked in restaurants, once coming up to Gunnison and running two small restaurants there to help support me. And then, after I began to teach, first at Clear Fork and then in a private school in Pasadena, she began to look farther afield. She sold the home place, and visited with friends in Pasadena; our whole family from that time forward looked west. Harold often came ashore on the Coast, at Long Beach or Seattle, where the big battlewagons berthed, so to see him as often as she could, she had to be out there. After both her sons were married she continued to live independently and turned her attention to the real estate field, managing to earn a real estate license, which entitled her to work actively out of real estate offices selling properties and "sitting" on houses—the quaint phrase the trade used for describing the duty of a realtor who was looking after a house that was on the market. This task was often assigned to middle-aged women, and always evoked for me a picture of a large sitting hen with the face of a pleasant woman such as my mother sitting on this vacant nest, with the purpose of hatching, not a family, but a share in the commission on a sale.

And now, approaching her seventieth birthday, for the first time she keenly felt the need of a car. She spoke of it, both to my brother on his occasional shore leaves, and to me, in her elliptical way, about this need of hers and received no encouragement. Both my brother and I had had our share of trouble in learning to drive: my brother was involved in a serious accident in a rental car on a trip to Paonia on one of his leaves from the Navy—it may have been through no fault of his own, but the fact remained that neither of us had had the opportunity to acquire the skills and the confidence to drive well during adolescence.

Mama's bungalows

Besides, I had already suffered through that one enlightening experience in trying to teach her to drive, with no success at all. Of course, there was Aunt Plum, the bright little widow of my mother's only brother, who had come out to the Coast with her daughter years before; she worked in rich people's houses, and needed, as every Southern Californian does, to get around from place to place in the course of her work. She had taken driving lessons, and on a solo drive had stalled in one of the busiest intersections in Los Angeles. She told of that occurrence in a hushed voice, and only survived, she said, through the help of a traffic officer. But, she was able to drive in less busy streets, and this encouraged my mother.

She never told us about it, but we did learn, probably from her grandson, Robbie, that she had suffered just the same sort of crisis as had Aunt Plum, but where Aunt Plum did manage to earn a drivers' license, Mama didn't. Driving schools are notoriously patient with student drivers, but some driving teacher put it plainly to my mother—perhaps more than one driving teacher—that there was no hope that she could ever qualify for a license.

Still, my mother did not give up. And, there was one other possibility; an electric car. One could pilot one of those small cars around without a formal driving permit. My mother set her heart on acquiring one of those vehicles. The price of a new one was prohibitive, but there were plenty of ads for second-hand ones, and my mother worked her way through them, journeying here and there by bus to investigate promising buys, and at last her choice alighted on one owned by a lady living near my mother's apartment in east Hollywood.

I was dragooned into taking my mother in my car to pick up the purchase. The plan was that the owner, a Mrs. Shelton, a rather large lady who had taken the car over after her mother had passed on, and my mother, would ride back to my mother's apartment in the new car, and then I would convey Mrs. Shelton back to her home. The car, which we will call Rosebud, was dark red in color, an open-air coupe with a black fabric top and it seemed in good repair. The owner took over at the wheel, and with my mother beside her, Rosebud was herded along the street toward its new home in the garage of a neighbor lady, a Mrs. Shaw, which my mother had been able to rent.

In a way, I had even more reservations about my mother being able to drive Rosebud than if it had been a conventional gas-driven vehicle. It was true that there were no gears to worry about, but instead of a steering wheel, Rosebud sported a tiller, and my mother was even less familiar with that means of vehicle guidance, if that was possible, than with a steering wheel.

But there was nothing for it but to follow along behind the little red car as it bumped slowly through the streets, hugging the right-hand curb. Halfway there, the new owner took over at the tiller, and Rosebud assumed a balky uncertain demeanor; still, with the seller's help—I could see her reaching across every few minutes and adjusting the tiller—our little procession moved slowly toward our destination.

Once before the apartment house, I pulled up behind Rosebud, and watched as Mrs. Shelton provided some last-minute advice. After a little conference she prepared to step out, and perhaps to show her satisfaction that everything was in good order and that my mother was showing promise as a driver, she stepped nimbly from the passenger seat to the curb. Rosebud sagged over in that direction, in deference to Mrs. Shelton's considerable weight, and then sprang smartly back in the opposite direction and on over on its side. Mrs. Shelton emitted a little muffled scream, but there was no such response from my mother who kept her inner equanimity at least, and the car was quickly righted.

We delivered Mrs. Shelton back to her home, and returned to drive Rosebud to the small garage in the rear of Mrs. Shaw's residence. Mrs. Shaw, a maiden lady of English extraction and a good friend of my mother, came out as we drove up—I was at the tiller, and in no mood that day to continue with my mother's instruction—and stood with her hands folded together, staring at my mother's new purchase.

"What do you think of it?" my mother called out.

Mrs. Shaw shook her head. "What next," she said.

I did not look forward to the coming Saturday, when I was scheduled once again to wrestle with my mother's inhibitions regarding mechanical devices. That night I lay in bed thinking of my mother out in the middle of an intersection, say at Hollywood and Vine, attempting a left-hand turn in Rosebud.

The next morning I arrived at her apartment and we walked over and backed the car out of the garage. I made her promise that she would not attempt, ever, to take Rosebud into heavily travelled streets, and she agreed readily enough. We repaired to a vacant lot nearby, and I drove slowly around in a circle showing her how to manage the tiller. She nodded often and dreamily added her pleasant "Oh yes. Um-hm-hm-hm."

At last I hopped out—carefully—and added the final, fateful cautionary instructions.

"Foot on the gas, the accelerator I mean, but very gently, and keep adjusting the tiller like I showed you."

"Oh yes."

"Now. Are you all right?"

"Yes. Fine."

I stepped back and Rosebud wavered away. On across the lot it ran, beating up a little whorl of dust.

Mama in Rosebud

"Turn it around and come back, Mama," I called.

I could see my mother through the isinglass rear window as she leaned to the left, and the car came slowly around. I felt encouraged.

"Now straighten it out, Mama, that's the way."

But as the car faced toward me, I saw that Mama was not straightening it out, but was maintaining her grip on the tiller and pushing it even further to the left, and on around the little car spun, and faster and faster, in ever-tightening circles. I think I called out, but I knew it was of no use.

Rosebud flopped heavily over on its side. Dust rose in a column. My mother was nowhere to be seen, and I was certain, as I ran toward the car, that she surely must have sustained some injury, perhaps a serious one. But as I came nearer, from the interior of the car my mother's head slowly came into view, her hat canted over on one eyebrow, and a reassuring smile on her face.

There are other memories of escapades I shared with my mother in the years we spent in Southern California, most of them having to do in one way or another with real estate ventures of hers, but none of them gave me more concern than did the one with the car. But I must say that in the end, her decision to purchase Rosebud was the right one. I sometimes awoke late at night and constructed a nightmare of my mother inadvertently trundling the little car into freeway traffic— and I heard, roundabout, from my nephew Robbie, my brother's son, that something of the sort did indeed happen—and there was the time she created a traffic snarl at the intersection of Riverside Drive and Los Feliz, though mercifully I was not along to see it, but the little car did give her a measure of independence. She drove it for years, often accompanied by her nephew, who was at the time of its purchase five or six years old.

And in the perverse wisdom of childhood he found more pleasure riding with her in Rosebud than in the Lincoln his father drove. As well as I could understand, it seemed that it provided a contact with the passing world that he missed inside his father's big car. I even verified this for myself, and I had to agree that you certainly had more road sense, as car buffs say, and were more aware of your surroundings in her little car than in the conventional gas-powered machines of that day or this. But, for one reason or another, I was never very comfortable in Rosebud, with my mother at the tiller.

A Rocky Mountain Education

I early began to have trouble in school. I was not a discipline problem, not having the courage for that. I was a sort of undiscipline problem. Almost no one could reach me. In Lamborn Mesa School where I spent the end of my second year and all of the third, Miss Lundine was like a loving older sister, praising me for volunteering answers in seventh grade geography—which I monitored from a nearby seat—and forgiving me my shortcomings in second- and third-grade arithmetic.

In Paonia in the grades I was haunted always by my failure to master the multiplication tables, and by the time I arrived at the sixth grade I was a continual source of annoyance and bafflement to my teachers, a situation which pleased me on the whole, but which resulted in certain inconveniences and crises. One of these occurred in the sixth grade over my problems with decimals and with long division. A strong-willed teacher decided to straighten me out, to shame me into compliance by sending me to the blackboard (interrupting my reading of a juvenile novel) and forcing me through the steps of a long-division problem.

When I failed utterly to carry the steps forward she sent another boy to the board to finish it and left me up there as she put my case before the class, soliciting opinions about my performance in other studies and my general level of intelligence. The consensus was that my performance in other studies was as unsatisfactory as it was in arithmetic, though my intelligence was adequate, but no one had any helpful advice as to what could be done to bring me out of my lethargy. This ploy of hers only confirmed for me that I was an outsider and would remain one.

The principal of the grade school, Mr. Johnson, had me the following year and he, too, was determined to straighten me out. Once I showed up in his arithmetic class carrying a couple volumes of the Little Leather Library, *The Rubaiyat of Omar Khayyam* in the Fitzgerald translation, and Oscar Wilde's *Ballad of Reading Gaol* which I displayed ostentatiously on my desk. Mr. Johnson picked these up gingerly, one at a time, leading me to believe he was about to congratulate me on my precociously developed taste in literature. I was disabused of this notion when he said, with a sharkish smile,

"Glen, have you ever heard how farmers feed chickens they are getting ready for market?" Mr. Johnson spoke in a musical Southern drawl.

I indicated that I hadn't.

"Well," he went on with his false air of joviality, "I'll tell you. When a chicken eats until it won't eat any more, he picks that chicken up by the neck," and he crooked a hand to pantomime the act, "and he takes a kernel of corn and he stuffs the corn down the chicken's throat, one kernel at a time. And Glen, that's just exactly the way I'm goin' to teach you arithmetic."

He leaned back, pleased with himself, and grinned at me again. Mr. Johnson's skin must have been tender; his hands were too white and his face too red, probably from exposure to our high-country sun during recesses. He wore a sweater often, a shapeless gray job. I never liked Mr. Johnson.

His wife, a thin, intense woman, taught history. She whipped Tippie and me for not turning in a history notebook. I didn't like her either. And of course I learned little history and less arithmetic, despite Mr. Johnson's cunning strategy. Mr. Johnson delighted in history and once came and lectured to our class on early American history, and told us some tricks to fix in our minds the chronology of a period. The one that I remember, and of course it is a tribute to his success that I did remember it all my life, was the acronym WAG which at one clever stroke provided the student with the succession to the British throne during the French and Indian War: King *W*illiam III, Queen *A*nne, and King *G*eorge I.

But that was the trouble with history, or at least as it was taught then. It always came down to a succession of names and dates, which neither the students nor often the teacher could recall the significance of, like the Edict of Nantes or that ever-memorable Diet of Worms which remained with me because of the faint nausea it inspired.

And arithmetic baffled and repelled me utterly. It seemed so dull and useless. What was the advantage to me of learning how to measure a field? Would it have helped if I had been told how the Egyptians or perhaps even the Sumerians developed it in the beginning for just that purpose? Perhaps. No one who attempted to teach me arithmetic ever demonstrated with any conviction the romantic aspects of the subject; its beauty, its symmetries, its application to voyages which men made on unknown seas and oceans and those they would one day undertake in space. Only once did I know of a teacher who inspired his charges with a curiosity in and an avidity for the subject, and that was years later when I was a teacher myself, and walked by his classroom on the way to my own, and caught the feeling of elation and pleasure it was possible for that subject to evoke.

Penmanship was deadliest of all. In the seventh grade we came to it directly after lunch. The Palmer method was in vogue then. "Get your arm into it, children! A nice, free and easy motion!" Marching stick men and endless O's.

And civics. Civics came alive for me once, when little Miss Ritchie, a frail crippled lady who walked with a cane, presented our ninth grade class with a case to be tried, with the class acting as jury.

I was appointed by the class as one of the lawyers, and David McKee, a much more diligent student than I, and one who indeed later became a lawyer, was my opponent. I don't remember the proposition upon which the case was based or even whether it was civil or criminal in nature; what I do remember is that I went to the office of Attorney Clements, up in the old Kennedy Building, and sought his advice as to how I should best proceed. I remember his leaning back in his chair before a wall lined with books and grinning, attracted to the challenge. He then instructed me in some useful tricks of the trade. The most attractive to me was his advice to rise whenever my opponent introduced new evidence and object to it as "incompetent, irrelevant, and immaterial."

The day of the trial arrived, the case was presented, and I made the air ring with my objections. Result: I won handily, in the jury's opinion. It was indeed a popular decision, but chiefly I think among class members swayed by my verbal pyrotechnics, and perhaps also because I represented a democratic element in the class—that segment, largely male, which occupied the nether regions of the grade percentile.

But matters were not allowed to rest there. The redoubtable group who inevitably garnered the highest grades in all subjects, the members of the upper percentile, were outraged by this blot on the justiciary escutcheon, and descended on poor Miss Ritchie in a solid phalanx; the daughter of the banker and her bowers, the daughter of the postmaster and the daughter of a coal mine manager, and petitioned for a new trial. I don't know that they had new evidence to present and I do know that I was not allowed to protest. Miss Ritchie agreed, David and his backers set to work with a will, but I had no stomach for it. The case was lost on appeal.

It may well be that the opposition's case was better from the outset, but I have always felt that Miss Ritchie should have allowed my victory to stand, and pointed out that justice is not always even-handed, and that clever if shabby tactics sometimes prevail even in courts outside the ninth grade civics class.

I muddled on, careening off the road in junior high, where I was

The Paonia High School

left back a grade, dropping out of Latin, which I sincerely regret, realizing much later how valuable the study of that language can be to anyone interested in writing. Any study that demanded discipline I escaped or was driven from.

When, after an initial warning that if I didn't learn the postulates and theorems in geometry there would be no point in going on, and when it was clear that I had not learned them, Mr. Virtue frostily exiled me to study hall. In the liberal arts I managed to hang on, since after all I was able and willing to read. I always sat in the back; any boy with self respect would, or so it was thought among the boys I was usually with. And even there I managed to absorb some grammar. Once in a sophomore class I so succeeded in rearranging a sentence in a workbook, substituting vulgar words for innocuous ones that my friend Cecil Tipton cackled so loudly that he was sent from the room. And while the class at the front of the room was plodding through the sonorous periods and weighty Homeric similes of "Sohrab and Rustum," several of we more privileged classmates at the rear of the room were poring over a classic of anonymous parentage entitled "The Tale of the French Stenographer" ("Up my lace-trimmed panties his cunning fingers stole—").

But there was Shakespeare. "As You Like It," "Julius Caesar," and "MacBeth;" even my cynicism and torpor were not proof against them, and in the vacation between my junior and senior years while lounging around town,in full sunlight, and in a book of fine print, I read all of his plays.

The sciences were as impenetrable to me as mathematics. Physics in particular, although chemistry proved a breeze. Our instructor, a strange young man who walked around with his elbows cocked like the wings of a grounded bird, possessor of a doctorate in the subject, early despaired of acquiring any worthwhile laboratory equipment. So, he conducted the class through the manual of experiments by dictating to us the results of each experiment, which we then copied into our workbooks. A remarkably neat and economical way of attacking that often smelly and difficult subject.

I did encounter one teacher who was able to deal with me effectively. On the surface she seemed an unlikely choice; she was not young, not attractive, like Miss Santarelli or Miss Stevens, and the subject she taught, bookkeeping, had no appeal for me at all. Her name was Miss Ellis and she was small, slender, middle-aged, with thin graying hair pulled back in a bun, a thin nose constantly reddened by a cold or a sinus condition, and sharp gray-blue eyes. She came alongside my desk early in the term, her arms full of booklets, and fixed me with a stare.

"Have you done today's assignment?"

"No," I said, selecting an excuse from a long and battle-proven list of types, in this case Type 3-a, The Failure to Comprehend Instructions, but I was interrupted before I could get fully under way.

"Listen," she said, in a low intense voice, "You may think that you're going to get me to send you to study hall for the rest of the term, but you're very much mistaken. You're going to stay in this class, and you're going to do the work."

"I don't know that I—"

"You can do it. And you are not going to just slip by with a D, either. You are going to do at least C-plus work." She was not only intense, but she was indignant. I looked into those cold blue eyes. No mercy there.

It may have been due to the fact that the accounting classes were at a low ebb and Miss Ellis felt that she had to hold on to a certain enrollment level, but be that as it may, it sank into my consciousness that this woman was not to be trifled with, and not to be put off. She continued to stare at me until I felt obliged to meet her eyes again. There was a little red spot burning in both her cheeks. I had hoped at least she would give me the satisfaction of pointing out that I was intelligent enough to do the work, but she did not.

"Just so we understand each other," she said, and moved on.

This proved a very difficult time for me. To this day I cannot understand even a simplified tax form, applying for Medicare has proved daunting, and I don't clearly understand the difference between a "put" and a "call" in the stock market, though it has been explained to me numerous times. But there was no escaping Miss Ellis. I did turn in assignments, and when they were unsatisfactory, she returned them to me as if the smell of them offended her red-tinted nose, and continued to return them until they were done to her satisfaction; and since in bookkeeping a thing is either right or it is not, I spent many a grim hour over my columns of figures, in journals and ledgers; Accounts Receivable, Debits, Credits, all spun around in my head. She did not seem to appreciate my superhuman efforts, but she no longer took that icy tone with me, and often returned rejected work with a pert smile. And I did survive. With a B.

In my last year in high school I was obliged to play football, or felt obliged to, and this required that I pass subjects, which I managed to do, and as president of the senior class it also seemed incumbent on me to graduate, and this I finally managed as well.

I did better at Western State College, even distinguishing myself somewhat in the humanities, and eventually I came back and taught successfully—English and drama—at Paonia High School. The stolid white brick two-story edifice no longer stares out at the community from its upper-story, assembly hall window eyes; the white wooden Ionian columns that framed the entryway are splintered and destroyed, but the old school is enshrined in my memory, and also enshrined in my memory are the faces and characters of many of those teachers who labored there, most of them with commendable zeal. Now that my life has moved into its autumn, I can stir the fires of memory as we used to stir the fires of burning leaves raked from the lawn before the old house on Poplar Street, and watch the sparks fly upward, like the names of those teachers, each glimmering for a precious moment as it mounts toward the skies.

IV. EPILOG

My Town

After I had left Paonia for California in the thirties, I attended a Paonia picnic in north Long Beach. The day proved a strange one. The program was presided over by a well-dressed, buxom white-haired lady, a former Paonia High School teacher she said, but I had never heard of her. And she talked familiarly of community leaders she had known, of Merle Vincent, lawyer and legislator, of the Honorable C.M. Hammond, and of the celebrated horticulturist, W.S. Coburn—and I realized that her Paonia was not my Paonia, but an earlier one. For like so many American towns, particularly in the West, every generation shapes a new community, while the young, the restless, and those least endowed with worldly goods follow the piper toward the setting sun.

Paonia has existed a century. The founders of the upper North Fork communities, the Hotchkisses and the Wades, arrived in the 1880's. They came on the heels of the departing Utes, who were pushed out of their beautiful homeland into the barren reaches of a reservation in northeastern Utah, the territory governed by the Mormons, who had no say in what the federal government might wish off on them.

The Utes were naturally reluctant to leave and troublesome occasionally for a long time afterward, making little sorties back onto the Western Slope in the next years. One pioneer Paonia merchant, A.S. Goodenow, was driving over Black Mesa in a covered wagon, his wife beside him, when they were accosted by a party of renegade Utes led by Buckskin Charley. The Utes were truculent, but Mrs. Goodenow was suddenly inspired to pull out her upper plate and flash it in their astonished gaze, and they swiftly vanished into the brush.

Cattle spreads were soon established in the high hills, and Enos Hotchkiss and his sons ran sheep there. By the turn of the century the lower mesas and the river valley were being cultivated and orchards planted. In the burgeoning town of Hotchkiss, ten miles down the river, *The North Fork Times* brought out an ambitious special edition extolling the glories of the upper valley and the heroic virtues and accomplishments of its leading citizens. Part of this edition consisted of statements in Swedish from ranchers and farmers already settled. The North Fork was heralded as a "paradise" and an "eden" in those

255

days before the peach mosaic and the codling moth had put in an appearance; the virgin land grew tremendous crops and investors and well-to-do farmers were lured from as far away as the East Coast and northern Europe.

In Hotchkiss, many citizens had close ties to the ranching industry, ties that went back to the first beginnings, when some of the pioneers had lived in, and run businesses from, hillside dugouts; and to them and to residents of other upper valley towns, like the mining towns of Bowie and Somerset, Paonians often seemed a rather snooty lot. The fruit from Paonia orchards was acclaimed in Eastern papers. Paonia lawyers represented their districts in the state legislature as did, later, Robert F. Rockwell, who belonged to a prosperous mercantile family in upper New York state and had the distinction of having as a young man flunked out of Princeton. He would eventually run for lieutenant governor, and then represent his district in Washington.

And there were many among this moneyed generation of Paonians who aspired to "Culture." They treasured collections of classical music for piano or phonograph and boasted libraries that usually included a set of the Harvard Classics, Victorian novels, and a variety of high school and college textbooks abandoned by sons or daughters who had attended college or university. Pitkin Mesa, on the heights northwest of the town, was a choice place to live then as now. Orchards of cherries, peaches and apples flourished there.

Two of the best-remembered of these early dwellers on the heights were Omar Wilson and a near neighbor of his, Miss Hayward. Once when a worker in Omar Wilson's orchard suddenly resigned, Omar, who customarily wore a dark suitcoat, white shirt, flowing blue polka-dot tie and striped bib overalls tucked into calf-length boots of soft leather, kneeled down by his team, took up a smooth slab of apple box wood and wrote a check on it, signing his name with the usual flourish. The check was honored downtown by the First National Bank.

Omar held musicales occasionally on winter evenings to which he invited a select group, which included Dorothea Clements, daughter of a local lawyer and an accomplished pianist, and her brother Herbert, also a devotee of the arts. Omar regaled these gatherings with selections from a large collection of 78's, which he played on his phonograph, and was said to become so inspired by the military music in *Il Trovatore* that he would arise and march around the room, shouting "They're coming! They're coming!" and, at the climax, "They're home!" whereupon he would collapse in a chair, whip out his polka-dot handkerchief and wipe his high, narrow brow.

Omar was widowed early, and stayed single many years, raising his son and daughter by himself and sending them off to college; but in his seventies he recalled a childhood sweetheart and went back East to seek her out. His diary referred to that period as "wooing."

His suit was successful, but with the new wife there were complications. She objected strongly to the cottonwood coffin he had long kept in his living room, expecting to use it during his final repose. She had her way: the coffin was relegated to the attic.

Miss Hayward spoke in accents acquired at an Eastern finishing school and superintended work in her orchards personally too, first from a horse-drawn buggy, and then, as late as the 1930's, driving down the orchard rows in her Ford sedan, with the doors open and swinging to permit quick egress and ingress. One problem with this means of conveyance was that she was often damaging or ripping off the doors on the turns at the ends of the rows, and absent-mindedly bumping into stone fences. She had a handsome house, beautifully furnished, and followed the social and cultural events in the community below with aristocratic interest.

When I was growing up in Paonia the population mix in the upper valley was changing. Coal-mining operations had lured a flood of working-class emigrants from Europe: Finns, Swedes, Italians, Yugoslavs. They lived in Bowie and Somerset and many homesteaded in the hills, harvesting hay in the lush mountain meadows, raising truck gardens on the narrow benches. The men worked in the mines in the winter, many of them, to make ends meet. The day of the big cattleman in the high hills was coming to an end.

As the twenties waned, the prosperous generation of Paonians that ran affairs after the first world war, the boosters, the Rotarians, the prototypes of the businessman in the novels of Sinclair Lewis, the generation that had made the Paonia I knew best, faded from view. In 1929 ruined stockbrokers in far-off New York jumped from skyscraper windows; in the early thirties both banks in Paonia failed, the mines cut production, and prices of farm produce plummeted.

And a new generation of settlers began arriving. They did not have as far to come as the ones who had come before. Not from Europe, not from the East Coast, but from eastern Colorado they came, and from Kansas and Oklahoma, where grasslands that should never have tasted the plough gave up their riches to the black winds of the Dust Bowl. These emigrants arrived in jalopies crammed with all their worldly goods, and found temporary refuge in bunkhouses and storage barns on small ranches, taking any work offered, sometimes only for room or board.

People lived on somehow—on a farm you could always eat, and others made out the best they could. You couldn't afford a movie, maybe, but there was radio, and if your family couldn't afford one, some neighbor or relative could, and invited you in of an evening to listen. Those who were better off shelled out good money for the Atwater Kent, seated on a sturdy parlor table with the batteries positioned on the shelf below, the grids immersed in acid like torpid shellfish, with the radio above presenting an array of dials on a bakelite panel, and behind it the glowing tubes, the condenser towers, the combs of rheostats, feeding the horn of pebbled metal reigning on the lid of the box.

Carl Fuller made the two-mile round trip from his house in the east end of town to Grand Avenue of an evening to pick up the mail—and to stop in Brad's Confectionery to listen to Amos n'Andy. On New Year's Eve groups played cards, ate popcorn and taffy and followed the waning of the old year, listening to the music of the big bands, wafted on the airwaves from ballrooms clear across the continent ("from the penthouse high atop the Hotel Wakefield in beautiful downtown Kansas City, Missouri, we bring you the rippling music of Wayne King...").

I know this latter generation well because I taught in Paonia in the thirties, and married a daughter of a family who had drifted to the North Fork after losing everything in New Mexico, in a valley that was hip-high in grass when they arrived there from Oklahoma, and within a couple of years had reverted to its true high-desert character. But although these people are now my people, the Paonia I visit is less and less my town, the town in which I spent my youth. My father's old barbershop has disappeared, the old school buildings are gone, although across from the truncated Opera House the twin bungalows that my mother created out of the old livery stable still stand, neat and occupied, monuments to her determination and travail.

A man I knew who had brought his family West to Paonia from a town in Nebraska went back there long years later to visit.

"Most of the ones I went back to see were up on the hill," he said.

And so it is with me. The ones I was young with have scattered, and the ones who took me in, looked after me as a member of the larger family of the community, are in residence now on Cedar Hill, in the cemetery the cows I herded in country lanes up there desecrated one day. My father's headstone, donated to his nearly destitute widow by the Woodmen of the World lodge, stands in the family plot, with my mother's ashes nearby, under a modest but respectable stone I think she would have approved. My uncle the doctor is there, and his parents.

When I wander out through the cedars I come upon headstones that bring back all sorts of memories. In a central location is a large stone inscribed with many names, the community's testament to the fallen heroes of World War I. The fact that many of them lost their lives in training camps, victims of influenza, does not diminish their sacrifice. And there were those other young men who did see action. There was the man who ran the pool hall, Dutch Paulicheck (later the janitor at the Methodist Church). He left a leg at Chateau Thierry. And there was Walter Heaston, a mild-mannered little man, who participated in the desperate action at Belleau Wood. Another mild-mannered little man, Harry Hayes, a part-time barber in my father's Paonia shop and one of the walking wounded, was once persuaded to bring in his medals and a commendation he had received, and for the only time I ever saw him truly animated, he described the day when, as a battlefield courier, he was set upon by several Germans and single-handedly disposed of all of them.

There is the little stone marking the resting place of Billy Osboldstone, city clerk in the palmy days of the twenties, a slender, reticent man with a club foot who wore neat tweed suits, and like my father-in-law, also resting nearby, was never to be seen out of doors without a hat. Billy lies alone, perhaps brought back at his request when he died in retirement near Denver.

A tastefully ornamented stone marks the resting place of the sisters Lepoltak, two maiden ladies who lived up under the McNutt hill in a well-furnished cottage. They attended church regularly; always, as I remember them, decorously veiled and gloved, in modest cloth coats with gray fur collars, and in little hats decorated with imitation blue cornflowers. They once provided me with a book of Bible stories which I treasured.

I have wondered sometimes how it would have gone with me if my father had not sold his Ridgway barbershop and I had stayed to attend school under the stern eye of little Miss Cusick. Perhaps I would have learned the multiplication tables, and I might not then have made such a shambles of my education both in grade school and high school. This scenario also presumes that my father had not died; I am certain my brother and I would have spent many painful interludes in the kitchen with the razor strop if we had brought home the sort of grades we did later in the Paonia schools when my poor mother was wrestling daily with problems of keeping us in food and clothing.

But as it was we did move to Paonia, my father died, and my education took place less in the school than in the barbershop, the pool hall and the Book Store. I felt as if I had been adopted by the town. But member of a larger family as I was, no one felt responsibility for my future; my mother was a poor widow, and expectations for me were low. Well-dressed men came occasionally to address Paonia High School students in assembly and nearly always their topic was the marvelous possibilities lying before us. "Hitch Your Wagon to a Star," they said. But to me those stars seemed far away.

Much the same can be said for my brother; he wandered aimlessly through adolescence, and finally the best solution for him seemed to be the Navy—a common solution in those times as well as today for footloose lads in small American inland towns. When a hitch would be over he would come back to Paonia and look for other employment, but always end in going back aboard the big battlewagons.

But with World War II, ironically, his prospects improved immeasurably. He moved up swiftly through the ranks and became at last the executive officer on a floating drydock for submarines out in the Pacific; he married a hometown girl who bore him a son and heir. Once the war was over it was decided he would not reenlist, but ashore he was once more adrift. And then, at last, he found his way into real estate and with the warm support of his wife and son, he achieved a notable success.

In memory I walk late at night through the empty streets of that town that no longer exists; but where, nevertheless, I have in a very real way never ceased to live.

And I will come in my time to Cedar Hill to lie there among those near and dear, some more dear than others—one at least will be near whose company in life I sedulously avoided. But there will be all those dear ones, like my Aunt Addie, my father's ill-starred sister, so tender-hearted that she rescued flies from the laundry tub and to whom everyone she met was a "poor soul."

We will all be poor souls together then and just lie there quietly, and enjoy the view.

Harold in the Navy

Grand Avenue today

Paonia of yesterday